STUMBLING BLOCKS

A Second Generation Holocaust Memoir

Jennifer Krebs

Legacy Book Press
LLC

Camanche, Iowa

In memory of my family members no longer walking the earth, with hope for those to come, and with special thanks to those walking alongside me, most especially Amy, my love, who makes every journey magical.

Table of Contents

Stumbling Blocks

My father was born in Berleburg, Germany. Today in that town (now called Bad Berleburg), the only traces of the former Jewish community can be found in its *Stolpersteine*, which can be translated as stumbling blocks, stumbling stones, or stumble stones. Like so many cities and towns across Europe, Bad Berleburg chose to participate in Gunter Demnig's public art project to remember the victims of National Socialism by installing "commemorative brass plaques in the pavement in front of their last address of choice."[1]

My dad's Stumbling Block, 5 Ederstraße, Berleburg.
Courtesy of Rikarde Riedesel

[1]https://www.stolpersteine.eu/en/home

You can step on the stumbling blocks, step over them, or step around them. But their presence causes you to hesitate. When considering a cataclysm as enormous as the Holocaust, who can do anything other than stop for a breath?

Recently, my dad mentioned something about his school days in Berleburg, and his Nazi teacher. I'd heard Dad's stories about having to wear a dunce cap, listening to a barrage of vitriol against Jews in general and him in specific, and having to sit isolated in the last row of the classroom with an empty row of desks between him and his classmates. I knew he'd been miserable. I asked him how often he thought about his old teacher, Brockmeier.

"Every single day."

I paused. Did he see his teacher's face when he napped? Remember the sting of corporal punishment? Or find himself overcome with feelings of humiliation and anxiousness?

Dad didn't elaborate; he valued history over psychology. By his definition of terms, he hadn't been sent to a concentration camp, so he was not a Holocaust survivor. He was a very lucky man.

When Dad, his sisters, and his parents told a story about a relative left behind, a relative sent off to their death, they didn't talk about feeling guilty. They didn't say a word about survivors' guilt.

No one would have entertained the idea that I, my sister, or my cousins would suffer intergenerational trauma by our second-hand exposure to the Holocaust.

These pages describe my trips and falls considering the journey of my relatives from that sparsely populated region of Westphalia (now *Nordrhein-Westfalen*), Germany, to the United States. I have not always known what to make of the stories, why I was being told something, or what exactly I was supposed to do with the knowledge. Perhaps I was being asked to acknowledge how much work my relatives put into their achievement of freedom. Or perhaps they needed to unburden themselves. They couldn't stop the stories from coming no matter how hard some of them tried. Perhaps they wanted me primed to answer my children's questions, to help them understand adversity and perseverance. Such is the weight on my shoulders, all of us children born to parents who survived the Holocaust.

A Note on Names

Certain names recur frequently in the following pages. My grandmother had a brother Fritz who died in the First World War. Two nephews were named after him: Fritz Bachenheimer and Fritz Oppenheimer. Fritz Bachenheimer was called Lange (the tall one). Fritz Oppenheimer was Freddy. Lange and Freddy lived in the metro New York area. I saw them mainly at family parties.

On the other hand, Uncle Fritz was my Grandpa's brother. Every time I visited the farm to see Grandma and Grandpa, he'd pop into the kitchen to say hello. The photo on the front of the book was taken around 1970. I had spent most of a humid August day driving the old tractor during haying. Dad and Uncle Fritz brought sodas for me and the rest of the help. Uncle Fritz was probably delighted that I had not yet ground the tractor's gears to smithereens.

Grandma had a first cousin Alex Katten, whose son was also a Fritz. Fritz Katten spent most of World War II living underground in Berlin. I never met him or learned his story until I moved to San Francisco and met his son Alex Katten, named, of course after his grandfather.

Speaking of Alexes, my sister named her older son Alex, because she liked the name, not as an homage to Alex Katten. Or to Alex Rosenberg, a cousin of Dad's that we never met as he lived near Louisville, Kentucky. Alex Rosenberg survived Bergen-Belsen along with his brother and parents. I heard him describe his time in the camp in a video recording that is among the holdings of the USC Shoah Foundation Library.

My sister's name is Amy, as is my spouse's. Though my spouse Amy Oppenheimer's mother went to high school with my mother, they were several years apart and did not consult each other as to what to name their babies. Amy Oppenheimer's large extended family is unrelated to my Oppenheimer cousins, the descendants of my Aunt Frieda and Uncle Max Oppenheimer.

Another name that appears often in Stumbling Blocks is Julius. My grandmother Lina Bachenheimer married Julius Krebs in December 1922. At the time of this marriage, she already had a brother Julius Bachenheimer (father of Lange). Then her younger sister Anni married Julius Frank, a banker from Frankfurt. My great aunt Anni became Anni Frank, though she was not a world renowned diarist.

In Chapter 28, Children of the Holocaust, I describe one of my first attempts to sort out how I was related to this confusing group of relatives sharing the same few names. As that family tree was not very readable, on the following page, I have provided a cheat sheet so you can place the various Juliuses, Fritzes, Alexes, and Amys in context.

Family Tree

Julius Krebs
(father of Paul,
Lucie, Hilda)
Parents: Levi and
Johanna
Siblings: Fritz, Adele,
Rosa, Mathilda,
Adolf

Paul Krebs
Rosalind Hirsch
(spouse)

Jennifer Krebs
Amy Oppenheimer
(spouse)
Children
Talia, Adin

Lucie
Stanley Weinstein
(spouse)
Child: David

Amy Krebs (sister)
Children:
Alex and Max

Hilda
Samuel Zimmer
(spouse)
Children:
Barbara, Joan, Linda

Lina Bachenheimer
(mother of Paul,
Hilda, Lucie)
Parents: David and
Auguste
Siblings: Herbert,
Julius, Fritz, Leo,
Mathilde, Frieda,
Paula, Martha, Anni,
Albert, Otto

CHAPTER ONE

Demons

Grandma called them the Nazis. Dad called them the Germans. Then he'd correct himself: not just the Germans. The French, the Polish, and most of Europe with their entitled upper classes. They were riddled with antisemites and retired generals itching for the next war. Aunt Lucie remembered a few people with strong moral compasses who acted with *Zivilcourage*. Aunt Hilda remembered the Hitler Youth activities, how betrayed she felt when her friends joined. Tears formed at the outer corners of Grandpa's blue eyes when his children reminisced, but he said nothing.

As I listened to the stories of my family's escape from Germany, the hair on my arms stood up as if each hair follicle held a special antenna. I held my breath, afraid I'd miss something. When I was very young, I thought the endings of the stories might change. That no one would die this time. No one would be left behind. Dad and his sisters would still emigrate to America as they had, but all their cousins, aunts, and uncles would come along too.

But the ending was always the same. They didn't make it. Not smiling Doris or stuck-up Lore. Not sweet Anneliese or little Hilda, who was only five. Not blue-eyed Ruth, nor fusty Aunt Mathilde, nor the two bookkeeper aunts Bettie and Adele. Why them? I'd ask.

No luck was Grandma's answer. Grandpa shrugged, wiping tears from his eyes.

"*Schlaf gut*," Grandma said tucking me in when I spent the night at her house. "Sweet dreams." I'd fall asleep quickly but wake in the middle of the night breathing loudly. I saw barbed wire and industrial looking buildings with smokestacks. I watched guards with masks and horns dancing around a fire. I was sweating and I felt trapped. But I wasn't supposed to wake Grandma until the morning. I practiced holding my breath. I wondered how long I could hold it. I wondered if this skill would bring me good luck.

One day when I was eleven, I stood in front of my Hebrew school class prepared to talk about a trip to Israel my family had just taken. I wanted to tell my classmates about the day Dad and I spent at Yad Vashem, the Holocaust memorial. The teacher had asked me to tell them.

I knew a thing or two about public speaking. I stood up straight. I smiled. I raised my voice. I tried to establish eye contact with my classmates. Two girls towards the back of the room chatted quietly. No one would make eye contact. I said a few sentences about how the Hall of Remembrance reminded me of the chapel at our synagogue and that I had learned a lot.

But I kept to myself my fear about going into the exhibits, seeing the gelatin prints of starving people in striped pajamas, and watching my dad's eyes tear up. Then being left by my dad for what felt like hours while he went into the records office. Yad Vashem was compiling names and statistics of those who had been murdered. It was Dad's duty to fill in those forms. Grandma's too.[2]

It was my duty to remember, to make sure people knew that this should never happen again, how my entire family had almost been killed. I should watch out, pay attention, talk down any antisemites I encountered. I couldn't seem to do this with a Jewish audience in Hebrew school. How would I do it in the wider world? Who would listen to me?

---

[2]https://yvng.yadvashem.org/nameDetails.html?language=en&itemId=11580826&ind=0

YAD VASHEM   DAF·ED   דף·עד

Martyrs' and Heroes'
Remembrance
Authority

A Page of Testimony

P.O.B.84
Jerusalem, Israel

חוק זכרון השואה והגבורה —
יד ושם תשי"ג 1953
קובע בסעיף מס' 2

תפקידו של יד ושם הוא לאסוף אל
המולדת את זכרם של כל אלה מבני
העם היהודי, שנפלו ומסרו את נפשם,
לחמו ומרדו בצייב הנאצי ובעוזריו,
ולהנציח שם וזכר להם, לקהילות, לאר-
גונים ולמוסדות שנחרבו בגלל יהדותם.
(ספר החוקים מס' 132 י"ד אלול תשי"ג)
(26.8.1953)

THE MARTYRS' AND HEROES' REMEMBRANCE LAW, 5713 — 1953

determines in Article No. 2 that

The task of YAD VASHEM is to gather into the homeland material regarding all those members of the Jewish people who laid down their lives, who fought and rebelled against the Nazi enemy and his collaborators, and to perpetuate their memory and that of the communities, organizations, and institutions which were destroyed because they were Jewish.

תמונה
Photo

Family name *Lindheim*		שם המשפחה 1.
First name (maiden name) *Matilde née Bachenheimer*		שם הפרטי 2.
Name of mother שם האם 4. *Auguste Bachenheimer*	Name of father שם האב 3. *David Bachenheimer*	
Place of birth מקום וארץ הלידה 6. *Roeddenau - Hessen*	Date of birth תאריך הלידה 5. *February 14 - 1892*	
Residence before the war *Frankfurt ⁹/Main - Germany*	מקומות המגורים לפני מלחמה	
Residence during the war *Malines Belgium*	מקומות המגורים במלחמה	
Place and date of death *unknown*	מקום המות	
Circumstances of death *unknown*	נסיבות המות	
Name of wife	שם האשה	Maiden name	שם משפחתה לפני הנשואין
Name of husband *Hugo Lindheim*		שם הבעל
Children deceased under the age of 18		שמות הילדים עד גיל 18 שנספו
Lore Lindheim, (Concentration Camp - unknown		

I, the undersigned *Lina Krebs*   אני, החת"מ
residing at *120 Big Ridge Rd., Spencerport, N.Y. 14559* חתו/ה ב (מתובת מלאה)
relationship to deceased *Sister*   קרוב/ה מכר/ת של

hereby declare that this testimony is correct to the best of my knowledge.

מצהיר/ה בזה כי עדות זו נכונה לפי מיטב ידיעותי.

Signature *Lina Krebs*   חתימה
Place and date *Spencerport, N.Y. - April 8 - 1972*   מקום ותאריך
Signature of Registrar   חתימת הפוקד

1972 Testimony by Lina Krebs, for her sister

9

CHAPTER TWO

My Birth / Rosh Hashanah 1957

My parents saw themselves as modern, what today we might call mid-century modern: spare, utilitarian, simple. Religion was for the old country, where you piled one thick European carpet atop another, instead of laying down a homemade rag rug on a wooden floor. I don't think either of my parents prayed or looked to the heavens when Mom's water broke on Rosh Hashanah. Dad simply called Dr. Grainer, who instructed him to bring Mom to Rochester General, and then went about his day. Dr. Grainer would call when there was news.

Restless, Dad drove over to the farm. He knew Grandma and Grandpa were at the synagogue in Rochester, where Mom and Dad had been married four years earlier. Dad had hardly been back since. Dad saw religion a bit the way he saw propaganda, crafted with someone other than him in mind. He only followed traditions when not doing so would have created waves. Today, having volunteered to mind the cows, Dad had a good excuse not to waste a morning in Rochester.

Dad parked his car outside the milking parlor, with its familiar smells of cooling raw milk with underlying notes of manure, urine, and mud from yesterday's rain. Dad breathed in deeply, trying to calm himself as the cats roamed underfoot. They were always hungry. How many were there these days? Too bad the cows didn't multiply like the cats, or he would have been a millionaire already.

Don, the hired man, was sweeping out the central aisle of the barn. He was a tall, gangly man from Ontario, Canada, who looked down at his feet whenever he spoke. "There may be a break in the fence out in the back lot," he told Dad. "I saw a couple of heifers wander over that way earlier. They all came in for dinner and milking, so none got out. But I haven't had time to get back there to look."

Dad didn't really feel like walking to the far end of the property. As he looked out the barn door, he realized that in the few minutes he'd been in there, some of the brilliance had faded from the sky. It was only a few days after the equinox and the days were shortening quickly. Outside the barn's back door, the leaves of the cherry trees in the orchard had begun to brown up around the edges. The old maple behind the farmhouse was turning yellow. The first cold gusts of air foreshadowing winter would come in a week or two. Before Dad walked out of the barn, he slid his shoes into the knee-high rubber boots that were next to the barn door. There was sure to be plenty of mud. Too bad that he forgot his coveralls!

Walking out there, looking for the rupture in the fence, doing a quick repair and heading back shouldn't take too long. Dad didn't want to be far from a telephone, didn't want to learn about the birth of his first child from Don. He wanted to hear what Dr. Grainer had to say directly. Then he remembered that it had been only a couple of hours since he dropped Mom off. It would probably be a while longer. And, if he took care of the fence problem – if there was a fence problem – then he wouldn't get a 2:00 a.m. call from the neighbors about a heifer wandering into their backyard and eating their vegetable garden.

Dad thought about his upcoming four-year wedding anniversary, and the other events of 1953, a banner week during a banner year. On September 30, 1953, he said goodbye to Fort Dix, goodbye to his drab green army uniform, and put on white slacks and a civilian blue shirt. He went back to New York, to my mom's apartment, where they spent a couple of nights behaving like newlyweds and then took the train to Rochester to get married in Rabbi Rosenberg's study. Grandpa and Grandma were the witnesses. Small and discreet was fine. There were plenty of parties in the world; he could have one later. He didn't need to make a speech. He just wanted to get in the car (Grandpa's, that is, as Dad didn't own one) and drive to Niagara Falls for a honeymoon.

At the back end of the back lot, Dad carefully inspected the 100 yards of fence, looking for a broken piece of barbed wire, a downed fencepost, or a fencepost vulnerable to blowing over in the next wind. He looked for places where the cows might spend time, where there was lots of mud and manure. He shoved a few fence posts forcefully into the earth, then tried wiggling them. With all the rain lately, it was a wonder the fence posts hadn't floated up and away from the soupy soil. He retwisted a few nails that bracketed a strand of sagging barbed wire. He pounded in a couple of new nails, too. The post was still going to move around a bit unless he brought back cement. And cementing this hole would send the problem down the line to the next post. They couldn't afford the time and money to cement every post.

Loping back through the field to the barn, Dad spied something out of the corner of his eye. Fox? Raccoon? Opossum? He squinted and then suddenly found himself on the ground, having tripped over a stone. Standing back up, his white slacks were soaked in mud on the right side. Why hadn't he worn coveralls? Mom might get annoyed at him. He couldn't blame her.

In September 1957, Dad was almost 29 years old. The years since his classroom humiliations in Germany, the march through Belgium to France, the sealed boxcar out of Germany were over half his lifetime ago. Yet, Dad's anger and fear sometimes visited him when he least expected it. Driving yesterday, he thought he saw Brockmeier, his evil Nazi teacher, crossing the street out of the corner of his eye. Brockmeier in Spencerport? But no, Brockmeier had been killed by a drunk driver when Dad was still in Belgium. It was another man. He probably looked nothing like Brockmeier. There was just something about the man's posture, or arrogance, or was it a smirk?

Back by the barn, Dad spotted his parents' car. He took off his rubber boots and tried to smooth away the mud still clinging to his pants. As he approached the house, Grandma came outside holding a little piece of paper. In German she said, "Come quick. Dr. Grainer will be at this number for only a few more minutes. He has news."

Dad ran to the small corner office off the kitchen that held all the farm business documents, an ancient and enormous safe (inherited from the farm's past owner), and the telephone. He dialed the number, and Dr. Grainer picked up after the first ring. Dad was told to come back to the hospital. I was born, a small girl with a shock of black hair and dark, dark eyes. Mom was resting. Dad should come and meet me because I will need him. I will want to get to know him. I will love him and he me.

Dad told Grandma and Grandpa the news. For once, Grandma didn't pressure him to sit down and eat a little sandwich. "Fast, fast," she said. "Get back to the hospital!"

I was my grandparents' fourth granddaughter. Still no boy! But it was too soon for anyone to wonder if there would be someone to take over the cattle business. Grandpa and Fritz were strong; Dad and Uncle Irv were young and still learning the ropes. They could be blessed by many more grandchildren.

CHAPTER THREE
The Schlechte *Brockmeier*

When Aunt Hilda called to wish me happy birthday several years back, I was trying to open a jar of apricot jam. I had tried all three kitchen implements we owned that were designed to help people open jars: the plastic grabber, the metal turn-key affair, and the burper thingee. Nothing worked. I wanted that apricot jam. I was going to boil it down and strain it to become a glaze for the *Zwet-schkenkuchen*. I am not the only one in my family who bakes plum cake every fall. It seems to be a German-Jewish thing, or a my-family thing. *Apfelkuchen, Zwetchkenkuchen, Kirschentorte*, summer and fall are one long fruit cake for me.

This year, I told Hilda, I was trying a Joan Nathan recipe for a quintessentially German-Jewish version of a classic *Zwetschken-kuchen*. The dough seemed very similar to Grandma's, though the baker was supposed to slice the fruit just so, and then spend a goodly amount of time arranging plum slices into concentric circles, something Grandma would have considered too time consuming. Grandma typically baked her *Zwetschkenkuchen* on a large cookie sheet where it was simple to form neat lines of plums. The glaze, something else Grandma didn't bother with, was supposed to make the cake gleam under the light. Trying to hold the phone while wrestling with the jar was not going well. "I can't be that weak," I complained. "Maybe they glued the jar shut."

Aunt Hilda laughed. "You know, in Berleburg, I was the strongest in my class. I could climb up the pole in the schoolyard faster than anyone!" In the pictures I'd seen of Hilda, Paul, and Lucie in Berleburg, they were three skinny kids, none of them particularly athletic looking. I myself couldn't have made it to the top of a pole if my life depended upon it. I hadn't viewed anyone in my family as talented in the athletics department. Hilda continued, "I was the champion in my class. I won in climbing every time. One day your father's teacher, the *schlechte* Brockmeier, was our substitute teacher..."

"Who?" I interrupted her.

"Your father's teacher. I called him the schlechte Brockmeier." Hilda giggled, as if she was still talking behind his back.

"Brockmeier?"

"Yes, Heinrich Brockmeier. He had the lowest party number in Berleburg."

I rolled the name around in my mouth. Hein-rich Brock-mei-er. I hadn't heard this name before. Or if I had, what had stuck was my dad's curses or pejorative references, "my awful Nazi teacher," "that damn teacher," or "the SOB." I had a feeling Dad might use even more colorful language when I was not around. That the man had the lowest party number in town indicated that he joined the Nazis before anyone else. He was a super believer, a fanatic, someone probably considered a nuisance or crackpot before 1933. And after Hitler took power, someone to fear.

Hilda went on. "That man was furious that I won the contest. He pointed at me in front of the class and yelled, '*Was tust du hier? Du gehörst in keine deutsche Schule, geh zurück nach Palestina!*' You know what that means? You don't belong here. Go back to Palestine! He was *schlecht*, awful."

"I'm stuck on his name," I said. "I can't believe I never knew it." If Dad had been puny as a child, by the time I was born he had admirable biceps. If he saw me struggle with a jar, he would have taken it, popped it open, and then handed it back, telling me he couldn't do it. I should try again.

After I put the glaze on the Zwetschkenkuchen and sent Hilda a picture of the finished product, I went upstairs to consult the worldwide web. I learned that Heinrich Brockmeier (or Brockmeyer) was born in 1895 near Hannover. He married someone named Lina (same name as Grandma), and he died in a car accident in October 1942 near Berleburg. After his death, the Nazis gave his wife Lina a pension.[3] No mention of children. No clue as to whether there's a Heinrich III or Heinrich IV getting into trouble with the AfD or some other right-wing group in Germany, the U.S., or somewhere in South America. An index of regional teachers during the Nazi period confirmed that Brockmeier was indeed the first active Nazi in Wittgenstein,[4] and was responsible for desecrating the Berleburg synagogue on Kristallnacht.[5] Who knows? Maybe Dad and Aunt Hilda are the only people still walking the earth who remember the schlechte Brockmeier.

[3]REGIONALES PERSONENLEXIKON ZUM NATIONALSOZIALISMUS IN DEN ALTKREISEN SIEGEN UND WITTGENSTEIN (http://akteure-und-taeter-im-ns-in-siegen-und-wittgenstein.de/)

[4]Berleburg, or Bad Berleburg as it's now known, is in the district of Siegen Wittgenstein in the state of Nord Rhein-Westfalen. It is nestled in the thickly wooded Rothaar Mountains.

[5]https://www.siwiarchiv.de/wp-content/uploads/2014/09/Lehrer3345.pdf

CHAPTER FOUR

First Day of School 1934

In pictures of Dad as a young child, like this one, when he was four and his sisters were about six and eight, he looks like a happy little guy.

Hilda, Paul, and Lucie Krebs, undated family photo

The neighbors called him Booby (or little boy), though his real name was Paul, pronounced Pow-ell in German. He was small for his age. His older sisters kept him in line and on his toes. Lucie was sharp and quick, curious, determined, and intrepid. Hilda, too, was quick and opinionated, but she won people over with her charm rather than with arguments. Hilda resembled their father, Julius, with twinkling blue eyes and hair a wee bit darker than auburn. Paul and Lucie resembled their mother, Lina, with hazel eyes, jet-black hair, a high forehead, and a large pointy chin.

Being a boy, Paul was allowed to tag along with his father, encouraged to learn about cows. He was given a kid sheep to raise, which he did very proudly. He and his sisters participated in their first strike when the former pet was served for dinner. I'm sure Grandpa and Grandma taught him to count and handle money long before he started school. He told me he used to love to go to the butcher, Goldschmidt (a Jewish neighbor who ran a non-kosher shop), because when he bought a wurst for Grandma, he was given a slice or two of a wurst to enjoy on the way home.

On Dad's first day of school, Grandma sent him off with his sisters after a good breakfast of an egg, toast, and milk with a bit of coffee. She would have inspected his hair, his teeth, his hands. Gone through his bookbag several times, showing him where to store his pencils and pens so that he could extract them cleanly and efficiently when needed. Perhaps on this special first day of school, Grandpa came home from the barn, or delayed his departure, so he could wish the children well.

Dad and his sisters were at least the second generation of Krebses to attend the Berleburg *Volkschule*. Grandpa and his five siblings had all studied there, education being compulsory through the eighth grade. At the time that Dad was enrolled, Berleburg had about a dozen Jewish families including the Elsoffers, Wolffs, Blumenthals, Gonsenhausers, Sterns, and Goldschmidts. But Dad was the only Jewish student in his grade.

Did Grandpa and Grandma know they were sending their little Paul off to be instructed by the person with the lowest Nazi party number in the region? Family lore held that Grandpa had been assured by his World War I veteran friends that the town was too staid for the Nazis to get a toehold. Hitler was a kook, a fad, a crazy person who'd be gone in a year or two. When Torahs were burned in Berlin, or Jews beaten up and arrested in München, Grandpa was assured that no one would let something like this happen in Berleburg. Even if Grandpa and Grandma knew that Brockmeier would harass, humiliate, and traumatize their five-year-old, education was mandatory. The town had only one school. What else could they do?

I picture Dad and Hilda skipping together in the direction of the *Volkschule*, Lucie having gone her own way by herself or with a friend. Before long, Dad and Hilda would have joined with another pair of children, or perhaps three, four, or eight. After walking her younger brother to his classroom, Hilda would have taken a quick look around, and assuming everything looked like what she expected, given him a little shove if he hesitated to go in on his own. And there, my five-year-old father met the enemy.

"Good morning, students!" said a slightly stooped man in the front of the classroom. "Come in. Take seats, all of you."

Dad knew that the *Hakenkreuz*, or swastika, on his teacher's lapel was a symbol of the Nazi Party. It was not a symbol of bravery in war like his father's Iron Cross. Dad had seen Grandpa and other World War I army veterans wearing their Iron Crosses at funerals. The veterans paraded down Main Street following the hearse as Berleburgers watched the funeral procession quietly from the stoops of their houses.

But what did little Paul really know about antisemitism before this day? He had in mind words of advice from Grandma, "Listen carefully to your teacher. We want to you learn everything. We expect you to do as well as your sisters." Looking at that swastika at the front of his classroom, Paul struggled to calm his racing heart.

The teacher cleared his throat and said, "I am Herr Lehrer Brockmeier. I will instruct you this year. We will work together to build a strong German culture. You will grow physically. You will gain knowledge. You will become strong Aryan children and work to better the Third Reich as it fights against our enemies abroad and at home. We must rid ourselves of this lesser race, the Jews, still living amongst us."

Paul must have felt himself go red in the face. He was not an enemy. He was a child of loyal Germans. His father was a veteran. His grandfather had been born in this town. Should he say something or stay quiet?

Herr Lehrer Brockmeier motioned for the students to stand up. "Raise your right arm straight out from your shoulder," he commanded. He walked around the classroom, inspecting each child. "Just so!" he said brusquely to students whose arms were not stiff enough or were sloping downward instead of maintaining a slight upward cant. Standing again at the front of the classroom, he shouted "Heil Hitler." Only one or two students responded in kind. Brockmeier shouted louder, "Heil Hitler," and he repeated this until he could hear all thirty voices shouting back in unison.

Dad thought his arm would fall off. He was relieved when this activity ended. But his teacher didn't allow anyone to sit down yet. He read from the list in front of him, calling the name of each student. Somehow, Brockmeier already knew that Dad was Jewish. He instructed Paul Krebs to move to the back of the room, and had another child take his place in the third row by the window. As Paul walked to the back, he could barely breathe. He didn't look at any of the other children. He was too embarrassed. As he walked—it seemed to take forever—he heard Brockmeier explain that Jews belonged at the back of the line because they were thieves. Jews had stolen the wealth of the town, the province, and the nation from good people. Jews had made Germany poor.

Paul sneaked a peak out the window as Brockmeier continued talking. The school, like most of the houses, was in the valley. Dad saw the hills above town, the verdant pastureland, and the darker conifer forests. He pictured his father walking with the cows in the pasture that was his favorite color, green. His father never said "Heil Hitler." His father detested Hitler. What would he say when he heard that Paul had learned the Hitler salute?

Was it last weekend, or the weekend before, when he and his sisters had played soldier with Grandpa in the pasture? Grandpa pretended to be their commander and ordered them to sing a silly marching song as they climbed the hill. He handed Paul a stick to hold as a pretend rifle and gave Lucie a stick to hold as a bayonet. Hilda reached the top of the hill first, and he picked her up and tickled her. She slid out of his arms and rolled down the hill. Paul and Lucie followed, rolling and rolling. When Paul stopped rolling, he saw a cow looking at him. Paul looked straight into the brown of the cow's eyes. He watched the cow bat its eyelashes. They studied each other for a moment or two before Paul got back up.

Back at home, Grandma was not happy to hear about the marching, the bayonets, the rifles. "*Schrecklich!*" she shouted, whenever she heard about war games. Grandma didn't believe in war. She believed in words. "Talk about your problems," she said. "Don't hit each other. Hitting solves nothing!"

When Dad told her about his first day at school, he wasn't surprised to hear Grandma say, "*Schrecklich!* How could they teach young children that *schrecklich* Hitler salute?" Grandma's favorite word seemed to be *schrecklich*.

That evening at dinner, Grandpa was angry to learn that Dad's teacher was a Nazi. Hilda said she would tell her friends to be especially nice to her little brother. Lucie said that if anyone was mean to Paul, she would tell them a thing or two. Grandpa said, "*Jude sein heißt Kämpfer sein.*" To be a Jew is to be a fighter. That is the way of the world. Grandpa had been taught this by his grandpa. They were not too young to learn this.

Grandma said the important thing was how you fought. You could fight with words. You could fight with persuasion. You could fight with cunning, with jokes, with tricks. She told Dad, "You must learn to fight with your head. Luckily, you have a good one." Dad thought he might have had a good head, but it was a good Jewish head. He wasn't looking forward to going to school the next day and seeing that terrible man again.

CHAPTER FIVE

First Day of School 1962

If Dad and his sisters were skinny little things in Germany, growing up in the land of large portions, second helpings, and plenty of desserts showed on my frame. I was always one of the largest kids in my class until junior high. I had plenty of friends and the three R's, "reading, writing, and 'rithmatic," as they used to call them, came easily. I also followed Dad's suggestion that I participate in as many extra-curricular activities as my schedule would allow.

We were encouraged to appreciate what we had. I collected rocks and fossils; I observed frogs, turtles, caterpillars, moths, and butterflies. I found the North Star and the constellations around it. I took to maps immediately and was the family navigator by the end of elementary school. If the history textbooks at school were dull and repetitive, the school librarian supplemented these with biographies. I remember a series about accomplished women like Jane Addams, Eleanor Roosevelt, and Clara Barton. When I noticed how cool a friend of mine looked carrying around a thick novel, I started raiding my parents' bookshelves filled with books by Leon Uris, Sylvia Plath, John Fowles, Truman Capote, Vladimir Nabokov, and other popular writers of the 1960s. That these covered themes beyond our schoolbooks, or had bizarre protagonists, made them even more alluring.

If taking tests, making friends, and joining school clubs came easy, I still experienced anxiety when I had to tell the teacher that

I was Jewish. This usually came the first or second week of school. My mom told me that I should tell my teachers in advance that I'd be missing class for Rosh Hashanah. I didn't know my teachers well at that point in the school year. I always feared their reaction. Mom said to smile and be direct. Some teachers said, "Thanks for letting me know."

But many teachers said, "I didn't know you were Jewish." I'd keep smiling even though I thought this was a rude thing to say. It wasn't like Jews had horns.

Worst of all were the teachers who said, "When you come back to class, you can tell everyone about YOUR holiday." Standing in front of the room on week three of school and telling my classmates about the Jewish New Year or the Day of Atonement was about as appealing as sitting in synagogue for a whole morning. No one was interested in MY holiday. Why should they be? It wasn't important enough for them to get a day off from school.

Mom and Dad (mainly Dad) thought I needed a Jewish education. Unlike my friends at school, whose parents seemed concerned about their souls in the afterlife, my parents had no worries beyond the life I was living. But it must have occurred to my parents that I was going to grow up illiterate when it came to Jewish subjects. Starting in fourth grade, Mom picked me up early from school twice a week to schlep me to Hebrew school, which began at 4:00. I had to mind the clock during band practice. At 3:25, I had to quietly stand up and scoot out of the clarinet section without knocking over a music stand or banging into someone's chair.

Come Hanukkah, there I was front and center at an assembly, telling the entire school and their parents about the eight nights when the oil never ran out. The chorus of all Christian kids sang "Dreydl, Dreydl, Dreydl." Why, I wondered as I tried to skirt off the stage as quickly as possible, did we live in a town where we were the only Jewish family? On the way home from school, I asked my parents why there weren't any other Jews in Spencerport, and if I'd always be the only one.

"Is there a problem?" asked Mom.

"What are you complaining about?" asked Dad. "I thought the evening went very well."

I was incapable of expressing my discomfort in a way that sounded like something other than petulance or paranoia. They didn't see what my problem might be, that I didn't like asking for an exemption from making Christmas tree ornaments in art class. They didn't hear my classmates discuss how people who didn't believe in Jesus were going to hell. That was going to be me. I wondered if they hated me for it.

There was the time that boy in the back row tried to trip me when I went to the water fountain. Another boy, when the teacher asked us to write on a secret slip of paper who we did not want to buddy with for a project, wrote my name in capital letters. One girl scowled at me every day. Did they hate me for being a Jew? For being a smarty-pants? Had I slighted them in some way? What was I to make of my peers' mean actions?

Perhaps Dad dismissed my concerns because they did not concern swastikas or Nazi anthems. He did not try to understand what I might be concerned about, how I should navigate the passionate and sometimes disturbing religious (or political) beliefs of my peers. For him, Spencerport was far from his turbulent youth, and I didn't appreciate how good I had it.

But I couldn't let go of the idea that being the only Jew in my class was dangerous. After all, it hadn't gone so well for Dad being the only Jew in his class. And what tools did I have that he hadn't? So I asked again, why Spencerport?

CHAPTER SIX

Safe Deposit

"Why Spencerport?" I asked Grandma. It was so far from New York City, where most of her siblings lived. Surely, they could have bought a farm in closer proximity. We were the only Jews in Spencerport.

Grandma said that though she loved living in New York City, Grandpa was mis-er-A-ble. He hated his work painting apartments. He always felt dirty, didn't like working indoors, couldn't stand the smell of the paint. New York was killing him, Grandpa told Grandma one evening after a very long day at work. Grandpa wanted to farm again. He missed his brothers, the fresh air, the pastures, even the flies and the manure. He missed the cows. He was a *Viehhändler*. He was not a New Yorker. He cried. Grandma couldn't remember the last time he'd cried like that. Grandma said if you loved someone, sometimes you had to compromise.

As Grandma told me this story, I could see her and Grandpa sitting at a kitchen table in New York just like the one where I was sitting with her in Spencerport. It was rectangular with a yellow Formica top. The sun shone through a window, illuminating a diamond shape of bright yellow. Grandma was probably peeling and slicing apples. Her hands were almost always moving, doing some chore. She would have had to look up from her apples to see Grandpa's tears. When she did, maybe her eyes teared up too.

Grandpa piped in now, "We found this farm. A nice town. Good people. Lots of customers." By this, I knew he meant he and his brothers Fritz and Adolf. These three were the original Krebs Brothers, as was written on the signs on their two green cattle trucks. Fritz had arrived in the U.S. before *Kristallnacht*. He found his way to Rochester probably through another family from Berleburg, the Gonsenhausers, who'd immigrated before Fritz.

Adolf hadn't come to the U.S. until after the war. Grandpa had helped Adolf get from a concentration camp to England, where Adolf spent the rest of the war. Adolf was supposed to help get his wife and daughter to safety. But tragically, his wife Betty and daughter Ruth had been killed by Hitler while Adolf was in England. Now he had a new wife, Erna, another refugee from Germany. Adolf and Erna moved to Spencerport for the farm.

"This used to be a fruit farm," Grandma added. I already knew that. The cows wandered into and out of the milking parlor via the orchard, where they chewed their cud under the cherry trees after their evening milking. When Grandma, my sister Amy, and I went to pick cherries, we had to step around the cow manure.

Dad and Uncle Irv joined their fathers in the cattle business after Uncle Adolf left Krebs Brothers to start Albion Cattle. Mom and Dad bought a house about a mile away from the farm. Mom didn't want to live in the farmhouse, though Grandma and Grandpa offered it. Mom wanted to live in a new house. She wasn't like Grandma in that she wouldn't have wanted to serve bowls of beef soup every day at lunch to uncles and customers. She might have taken messages, but she wouldn't run to the barn to give them to anyone. Mom liked privacy.

Jerry Miller, another German-Jewish *Viehhändler*, had a farm not too far from our house. Jerry drove to the farm every day from Rochester, like Uncle Fritz and Uncle Irv. Uncle Irv was a couple of years older than Dad and had two children close in age to me. Along with Jerry Miller's children and the Gonsenhausers' children, they went to a school with lots of other Jewish kids, located close to the synagogue my parents joined when I was eight.

Though I never said this directly to Dad as a child, I had to wonder, hadn't he had enough of being different? Why did Dad want me to go through the same thing as him when there were other options nearby?

I couldn't ask this directly. So instead, I asked, why Spencerport? Did the corn grow better here? Was the land cheaper? Did they like Rochester better than Buffalo, Syracuse, or Albany? Why not Long Island where Aunt Hilda lived? Weren't there farms there, too?

Grandma returned to the story about Grandpa being *mis-er-a-ble*, and her moving to Spencerport because that's what you did in a marriage. "You have a good life here," she said. "What more could you want?" But I wasn't asking *for* things, I was asking *about* things, and how people made decisions.

"You love the farm. I know," said Grandpa, poking a finger into my ribcage to make me laugh. "You love the cats, the cows, and the manure."

"The mud, too," I added, laughing. "I also loved it when you lifted your arms so high that your pants fell down." This had recently happened when Grandpa was trying to help Dad unload cows from the truck.

When I was ten or eleven, I was deemed old enough for farm work. Dad said I could drive the tractor during haying, the busiest time of year on the farm. Haying took place in June and again in August for a week to ten days each time. The hay loft needed to be filled to the top so the cows would have enough to munch on all winter. Dad, Irv, Grandpa, and Uncle Fritz deliberated: Was the grass high enough? What was the weather going to be like over the next ten days: rain, sun, heat, cold front? These factors influenced how good the yield would be. High yield with good nutritional value was the goal.

Haying involved a lot of expensive equipment—a mower, a bailer, hay wagons, and tractors—as well as laborers. Dad hired workers, generally Spencerport high school boys hungry and strong enough to throw 80-pound hay bales up onto the hay wagon. As I climbed on the tractor for the first time, I saw myself as a team leader. I would keep the tractor going at a steady pace. I would smile. Everything would go well. I'd been watching this operation for years. I knew what it was about.

Dad spent five minutes showing me how to operate the tractor. Here was the brake, the clutch, the gears, the gas, and the steering wheel. The brake, steering wheel, and gas were obvious. But what were gears? And what did the clutch have to do with gas and gears? At this point in my life, I'd never even ridden a three-speed bike. I was utterly confused. Dad was too busy to explain it again. He told me to watch what he did, and I'd get the hang of things quick enough. He spoke as he showed me, "Put your left foot on the clutch, your right foot on the brake, and gently apply the gas." We took off at a slow, smooth pace.

"Now you try." Dad got up and let me sit in the driver's seat.

I felt like queen of the farm for about five seconds. Then I couldn't move the gear. "You have to depress the clutch, otherwise the gear won't move."

I tried to do as he said. Eventually, I got the tractor to lurch forward, pop out of gear, and stall. "Release the clutch slowly!" Dad ordered. Pop again. Jump. Jolt.

I could hear snickering from the high school boys. I was not off to a good start. But eventually, between Dad and me, we got the tractor moving down the row. Dad jumped off and wished me well. He watched for several minutes while we went up and down a couple of rows. Things seemed to be going smoothly. Dad waved goodbye, got into his car, and drove off. I was now working. Everything was fine on the straight-aways, but at every curve I panicked. I slowed down, and that darn clutch would pop out. The boys were not happy with me.

Dad and Uncle Fritz came with cans of sodas for a mid-morning break. Mom came, too, with her camera, and took this picture of me on the tractor with Dad and Uncle Fritz.

My maiden voyage on the tractor supervised by Uncle Fritz and Dad, 1968 or so

By the end of the day, my driving skills had not improved much. One of the high school boys had shaken a fist at me when we stalled out while he was sitting atop hay bales four high. He practically fell off and broke his neck, or so he said. But by the end of hay season, Dad asked me to drive the hay wagon to the barn. This involved a trip on actual roads. I was nowhere close to sixteen years old, had never read a brochure about driving, and knew nothing about interactions with other vehicles.

I looked around. Why hadn't Dad selected one of the high schoolers to drive? Surely there was someone else. "Really?" I asked.

"Of course. That's how you'll learn," Dad said.

I gulped, put the tractor in gear, and headed for the road. I slowed down and turned onto the road without popping the clutch, then I headed for the farm. I drove two miles, maybe three, on real roads, my body tensed in high alert. With all those hay bales behind me, it was like driving a semi-trailer or a small building. I was terrified.

As I turned onto the driveway at the farm, Grandma came out of the house. She waved a little handkerchief as I drove by. I stopped the tractor where Uncle Irv motioned. Then someone else backed it up to the hayloft. Success! Had I known the word, I would have said it was the pinnacle of my tractor-driving career. Maybe working on the farm would be in my future. Who said girls couldn't do farm work?

Later that evening Dad gave me my wages, not enough for the camera I wanted. Not even close. He gave me another lecture on how important it was to save money. Grandma and Grandpa were great savers. If they had not been great savers, they could never have moved to Spencerport. First, they had to pay back Aunt Frieda and Uncle Max and the rest of the aunts and uncles who had all pitched in so they could get out of Germany just in the nick of time. Then they had to take in boarders who paid the rent on their apartment in New York. Dad had to work delivering dry cleaning after school. They had to put all their money in the bank. I'd heard this dozens of times before.

When Grandma gave me ten dollars for my birthday, I was always supposed to turn it over to Mom and Dad, who put it in the bank for me. No one taught me about budgeting, or how to balance a bank account. I just knew that you could spend your money, which was what stupid people did, or you could save it, which was what anyone did who was worried about the next cataclysm—not that there was ever going to be a madman like Hitler in the U.S.

It was only when I was in my 60s, and Dad was over 90, that he finally saw it might be a good idea for me to help him manage his finances. (He could no longer get his checking account to balance.) He also thought he would show me his safe deposit box, where he stored the life insurance policy he'd purchased way back when. Eventually, I'd need to know.

I drove Dad to the bank with my cousin Linda, who'd also come to visit Dad. A bank clerk led the three of us to a private area where we could open the box. There were no secret jewels or bundles of cash like there would have been if we were in a movie. Instead, in a neat stack of papers, somewhere between Mom's high school diploma and Dad's army discharge documents, was the deed to the farm. Three typed pages that referenced a mortgage, taxes, and electrical easements. Grandpa and his brothers had acquired the farm on June 8, 1950.

Though Grandpa had only been in the country for nine years, he'd stashed away $9,000, which he sunk into the farm. Uncle Fritz had contributed $7,000. Though Uncle Adolf contributed no assets, he was listed on the deed too. The grand total for the purchase (including taxes) was $27,523.88. This included roughly 118 acres, a farmhouse and barn, and several sheds.

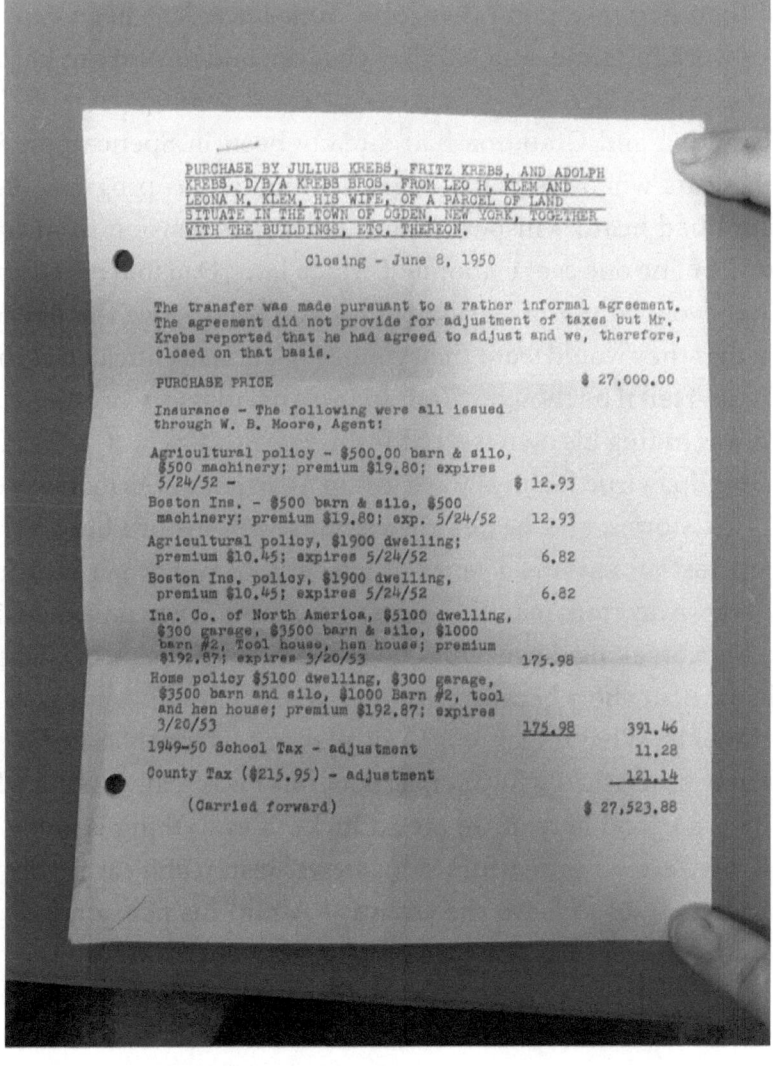

Farm Purchase Closing Agreement, June 18, 1950

Though this document didn't answer the question of why Spencerport, I got a better appreciation of Dad's comment that the only thing Grandpa knew how to do was work. Grandpa had saved $9,000 at a time when the average worker in the U.S. made under $2,000 per year. Of course, everyone else had had to work too: Grandma had cooked and cleaned for tenants. After school, Dad had delivered rugs for a dry cleaner, then had worked as a busboy during summer vacation. Aunt Hilda had started out babysitting and then had taken on other jobs. Aunt Lucie had been expected to work full time, much to her chagrin, and to study in her off hours.

Grandpa and Grandma had already been in Spencerport for three years when Germany began its reparations program. As a child, I had heard whispers about "Grandpa's pension from Germany" but no one ever elaborated. Much later, Dad told me Grandpa had worried that if Germany knew he lived above the poverty line, that they would want their money back. Dad chuckled at this. I couldn't tell if he thought Grandpa was needlessly worrying, or if Dad was hiding his own worry for the same thing.

Grandpa's true feelings were lost in a torrent of German words, phrases, stories, and heated discussions with his brothers. What wasn't lost on me was a sense of concern, of worry, perhaps just one step away from fear. If it wasn't a sick cow, it was an expensive machine breaking down. Our trip to the Canadian side of Niagara Falls was cut short because Grandpa didn't have his immigration documents. What if Customs Control didn't let him back in?

I may have asked why Spencerport, but I was really asking why, if life is so good here, if we are so lucky, if everything is going so well, why are we so fearful? Why do we scrimp and save? Why is Grandpa afraid to leave the country? Afraid his pension will be revoked? Are we okay, are we safe, or not?

CHAPTER SEVEN

Passover 1967

Although I watched parts of the nightly news and tried to understand the reports, I found lots of things confusing. I have a dim early memory of John Kennedy's shooting, which was broadcast over and over on television. Neither Mom nor Dad nor the commentators on television offered an explanation. Mad man. Crazy person. Nut. Dad called bad drivers nuts. Sometimes he called Mom, me, and Amy crazy. I even knew how to say, "You are crazy," in German, because he said it so often, even to Grandma. Wasn't an assassination a few notches crazier than Grandma asking Dad to slow the car down because he was speeding again? After all, he'd gotten a speeding ticket just last month.

Not long after Kennedy's assassination, race riots broke out in Rochester. These were explained as "very angry people who had been mistreated for too long; however, burning down parts of the city was terrible." For several weeks after the riots, we stopped buying Jewish rye bread at the bakery on Joseph Avenue, and Mom stopped shopping downtown.

Events from Germany were often bandied about as if they happened yesterday rather than decades before my birth: *Anschluss, Putch, Kindertransport, Kristallnacht.* Even if I couldn't have placed them on a timeline, I knew each of them caused tremendous changes in the lives of my grandparents, father, and aunts. Would Kennedy's assassination lead to another earth-changing event? How might my life change?

I remember one Passover when Aunt Hilda, Uncle Sam, and my cousins came to Spencerport. Aunt Hilda's daughters were all older than me, and Aunt Hilda didn't baby down a conversation like Grandma sometimes did. In the photo below, I am nine and still sitting on Grandma's lap. My younger sister Amy sits on Grandpa. My cousins are ten, twelve, and fifteen.

Passover 1967. Seated: Me on Grandma's lap, Sister Amy on Grandpa's,
Behind us: my cousins Barbara, Linda, Joan; Dad & Aunt Hilda

Grandpa's English was fractured. He went to school only through the eighth grade, which was the norm for children born in 1893 in Berleburg. Then Grandpa began working for his father, eventually getting his own cattle-dealer's license. Cattle, he knew. Numbers, he knew. And Hebrew, he was an ace at that too. He could chant Hebrew at a level far beyond what I came to learn going three times a week to Hebrew School for four years (plus a summer studying Hebrew in Israel while in high school). As far as I could tell, Grandpa could chant the entire Passover Hagaddah, and would have done so had Grandma not told him to speed it up: we kids were hungry, the *matzashalot* was burning, and it was enough already.

Grandma orchestrated the meal. She had a certain succession of dishes. In her line-up, the *matzashalot*, a sweet kugel made from matza and apples instead of noodles, followed the soup, which was always beef, never chicken. That the *matzashalot* was served with lemon pudding and could have easily been dessert made no sense to Grandma. *Matzashalot* was the second course, period. Then she would emerge from the kitchen with stuffed veal breast with gravy, green beans, cucumbers, and potatoes. Once everyone was full, Grandma cleared the dishes and Grandpa went back to chanting, which sounded a bit like a lullaby after all that food.

I must have dozed or began chatting with a cousin because all of a sudden, Aunt Hilda was speaking in English, loudly. Perhaps she started out talking about seders in Germany. But when I tuned in, she had segued to *Kristallnacht*. That story was not entirely new to me. But I could never tell when it was and wasn't appropriate to discuss. Dad usually didn't want to discuss it.

It was the middle of the night, November 9, 1938. Aunt Hilda, then twelve years old, was fast asleep when a pounding on the door woke her up.

"Julius Krebs? Julius Krebs!" Someone banged on the door and called Grandpa's name. Grandma put on her robe and went downstairs. She told the men that Grandpa wasn't home. He was in the hospital.

"The hospital?" the man shouted.

"Yes, he just had an operation," Grandma said, "for a hernia."

Aunt Hilda didn't recognize the man's voice. But she heard Grandma shut the front door and come back upstairs.

Grandma looked down the table to me and my cousins. "I told the children to go back to bed. They had school the next day. I had no idea why these men had come. We didn't know that they were knocking on all the Jewish houses in town. We had no idea this was going on all over Germany. I thought this was just someone looking for Grandpa."

Dad chimed in. "The Hitler fanatics, the goons, they started it all. They were the SA. They loved making trouble. They threw a rock through our big front window."

"Yes, we heard this huge crash." Aunt Hilda gestured skyward with her arms. "I didn't know what it was."

"Who does such a crazy thing?" Grandma said. "I told the children to hide under their beds. I didn't know what would happen next."

I looked back and forth between Grandpa, Grandma, Aunt Hilda, and Dad. Grandpa said nothing. He was listening like we children, though surely Grandpa must have known the story. He kept looking at the space where his dinner plate had recently been. Dad had both of his index fingers pressed into the table as if the table would levitate if he removed them.

Aunt Hilda, sounding a lot like Grandma with a warbly voice, said, "Why would someone have broken our window? I was terrified."

"After they broke the window, they went away. I heard them walking down the street," Grandma said. "I went downstairs to clean up the mess. I didn't want the children to worry. That was my job."

The rock through the window. If Dad's Nazi teacher had been the first indignity, if the ante had been upped when Grandpa's business license had been revoked, *Kristallnacht* was the third, or maybe thirteenth plague on my family. It seemed just like the Passover story we were reading. Later on, I realized that I was nine years old, the same age as Dad the night of *Kristallnacht*. What would I have done if our living room window was broken? What would Dad have done?

CHAPTER EIGHT

The Morning After Kristallnacht

The morning after *Kristallnacht,* Dad and his sisters said Grandma kept them on their routine as if nothing had happened the previous night. She got them up and went downstairs to make breakfast.

Paul was tired and didn't think about what she said. He got up and saw that his older sisters were already vying for the bathroom. Paul got dressed quickly, and when an opening presented itself, he went to the bathroom to use the toilet, wash his face, and part his hair. When he came downstairs to the living room, he noted that there was no broken glass on the floor, but he felt chilled by the cold gusts of November air blowing in. Paul looked at the curtains flapping in and out of the window casing. His mother called out from the kitchen, "Watch your step. There may still be glass."

When Paul slid quietly into his seat in the back of the classroom about an hour later, he noticed that each of his classmates was twirling a little prism in their hands. Paul noticed he had no prism on his desk. He wondered why the prisms were there. There was a familiar look about them.

Then the *schlechte* Brockmeier entered the classroom. "Jew," he said to Paul, "You are no longer welcome! Get out! Go to the principal!"

Paul walked down the hall to the principal's office wondering what happened. Usually, Brockmeier disciplined Paul in the classroom. Paul already had the entire back row to himself. None of the other children sat near him. What could Paul already have done today that he must go to the principal? He came into the anteroom to the principal's office and saw that Hilda was already there. Paul peered into the office, and the principal waved Paul and Hilda in.

"I'm sorry," the principal said to the two children seated in front of him. "You can no longer attend this school. Jews are not allowed in German *Volksschule*." The principal coughed a bit and looked down at his desk. "*Es tut mir leid.*" Paul wondered if he really was sorry. He doubted it. He was probably as happy as Brockmeier to be rid of him. Paul and Hilda turned to each other, then Paul followed Hilda out of the office. They walked toward home, their rucksacks never even opened, the pens all still in their case, their papers organized. *Good riddance*, thought Paul. None of his classmates spoke to him anymore. Then he wondered if Mother would be angry. He asked Hilda what she thought.

"It's not our fault. Why would she be angry?" Hilda said.

When Paul and Hilda opened the door to the kitchen, Lucie was already there, crying. Her red school cap sat on the kitchen table in front of her, her rucksack on the chair. Lucie yelled at Hilda, "This is so unfair. How can it be legal?" Mother walked toward Lucie to try to comfort her, but Lucie was too agitated to accept any comfort. She glowered at Mother.

Hilda said, "I heard that they arrested all the Jews last night. All the men, that is."

"Father?" the children asked in unison looking at their mother.

Mother said to Paul, "Walk quickly to the hospital and make sure that Father is safe. No stopping. No talking to anyone." She looked at him very seriously, as if this was the most important thing she had ever asked of him. "Can you do that?"

"Of course," Paul said. He was relieved to have something useful to do, to get away from the raw emotions at home. As Paul walked to the hospital, he wondered how he'd spend his days without school. Would Mother give him assignments? Or would he be allowed to read as he saw fit? Maybe he'd be allowed to play outdoors or go for a walk to the duck pond. However Paul looked at it, his life without the *schlechte* Brockmeier, the angry man with the evil sneer, barking voice, and swagger, would be an improvement. Paul skipped a bit thinking that.

But the unpleasant odor at the hospital slowed him down. It smelled like trouble. Something chemical or rotten. Not a welcoming smell like soup on the stove. Not even the familiar smell of manure in the barn, or women perfumed up for Jewish holidays in the synagogue. What was that smell? A disinfectant? Someone who vomited? Someone who had died?

Paul saw a blackboard and looked for the name Krebs. Room 4. Paul poked his head through the door into room 4, which was slightly ajar. Father was lying in the bed, his head propped up with pillows, his eyes partially open and partially closed, the blankets tucked in tight around him. "Hello Paul," Father said. "Aren't you supposed to be at school?"

Paul remembered Mother's words. No stopping. No talking. Just make sure he's safe. Paul waved meekly at Father, and then turned around and left.

Back outside, the sky was gray, but still no snow. Paul wondered when Father would be coming home, and what would happen to him. He remembered Hilda saying that all the Jewish men had been arrested. They had been looking for Father last night. Maybe that was why they broke the window. Father had been at the hospital under Dr. Hammer's care.

"Thank God," said Mother when Paul reported that Father was safe and resting in Room 4 at the hospital. "You did an excellent job checking on Father. Now can you go check on Grandfather? See if his windows were broken and if he or Uncle Adolf were arrested."

"I can do that," Lucie said angrily. "I don't want to sit here all day."

Not wanting an argument in her already full hands, Mother said, "Paul should go to Grandfather, Lucie to Tante Adele. And, both of you, help out if they need it. Don't just walk away." Then with Hilda looking at her questioningly, she added, "Hilda, you can help make dinner. That, too, is important. We have to eat."

Paul walked down the main street of Berleburg. There were only a couple of dozen streets in town, and only the main street covered more than a few blocks. The main street had been called Emil Wolfe Strasse, after a Jewish man who immigrated to the United States in the last century and then sent money back home to build the synagogue and other buildings. But in 1935, the Nazis took down the old street sign and put up a new one, Adolf Hitler Strasse. Paul called it Emil Wolfe Strasse under his breath as he walked by the sign. Adolf Hitler Strasse. Never.

None of the houses between Paul's house and Grandfather's house looked any different from usual. Like all homes in Berleburg, these stately two- or three-story black slate buildings looked well-maintained and buttoned up tightly against winter drafts. Even on an overcast November day like this one, the sun rays cut through the gray clouds and shimmered off the slate.

"No, no, no, no," Paul said, seeing the empty window frame at Grandfather's house. Why it surprised him, he could not say. He should have expected it. Feeling queasy about what he'd find in the house, Paul decided to open the door to Grandfather's barn. Pulling the door open, he was assaulted by the shame of it all. Instead of the dozen or more cows that Grandfather and Uncle Adolf used to have in the barn, there were only two, looking lonely in their stanchions. But at least they were there, chewing on hay, not far off from what was normal. In his head, Paul heard his father's bass voice saying, "What a shame!" Paul almost said it out loud. His sadness over the broken windows gave way to anger.

Paul was angry. It wasn't just Brockmeier, the broken windows, and getting expelled from school. There had been parades with songs about Jewish blood flowing in the street. There were new regulations and laws. Jews could no longer sell cattle. Jews had to sell off property and business. How was the family to keep going?

Paul shut the barn door, realizing that eventually he would have to open the door to the house. Would he or wouldn't he find his uncle and grandfather there?

Paul knocked on the front door. He heard two sets of footsteps inside, walking towards him. Aunt Betty opened the door a crack. When she saw it was Paul, she opened the door and quickly pulled him inside. Cousin Ruth grabbed Paul and squeezed him in a big hug. "I am so happy to see you," Ruth said, hugging so tightly that he could barely breathe. Paul hadn't known that Ruth, two years his junior, was so strong. When Ruth finally released Paul, Aunt Betty grabbed him tighter before he could get a good breath. While being squeezed, Paul realized that the three of them were alone in the house. Grandfather and Uncle Adolf must have been taken. Hilda had been right.

"Sit down, boy," Aunt Betty said to Paul. Paul followed his aunt's request and pulled out a kitchen chair.

Aunt Betty told Paul a story much like stories being told all over Germany and Austria on that day. A group of SA men, Hitler fanatics, arrived in the middle of the night and banged on the front door. Adolf opened the door in his coat and house slippers. They took him right then, before he even had time to put on shoes and socks. They took Grandfather Levi away, too. Grandfather Levi was confused and pretended not to hear the shouting. He would not be rushed and insisted upon putting on a real coat, and shoes and socks. Still, they took the old man away as if old men were arrested in the middle of the night for snoring.

Cousin Ruth was crying. She scooted her chair next to Paul and he put his arm over her shoulders. Aunt Betty, done with the story, began to worry aloud about poor Adolf with no socks or shoes. What will become of him? Where are they taking him? For how long? When will he get socks so he doesn't freeze?

"What happened at your house?" Cousin Ruth asked Paul. "Is Uncle Julius alright?"

Paul told his cousin and aunt that he saw his father in the hospital just an hour before, that his father was still healing from surgery. Then he told Ruth that he had been expelled from school. "Which is fine by me. The *schlechte* Brockmeier can pick on someone else now."

Ruth said, "After the ruckus last night, *Mutti* kept me home today. I suppose I'll never go back." Then she started crying.

"What's the matter?" Paul asked.

"What will happen to my father?"

"Paul," asked Aunt Betty, "Would you mind going to the jail? See if you can give Adolf a pair of socks? Maybe you can tell what is going on."

Paul nodded yes, though he wasn't sure why. Going to the jail sounded scary. He'd never been inside before. It hadn't been a place he thought he'd ever go. Meanwhile, Ruth asked what happened at school. Who had told Paul never to come back? His teacher or the principal? Was Paul sure that Ruth was expelled, too?

"The principal said, 'All Jewish children are expelled from German schools.'" The finality of those words was starting to sink in. What would he do all day? What was he supposed to do all year? What was his life supposed to be? And, what would happen to his family if his father got taken away...to who knows where?

Aunt Betty returned with a small bag of socks and shoes. Paul took the bag from her, and Ruth opened the door for him. At the bottom step, he turned back and waved to his cousin. Ruth looked so small in her blue dress against the side of the large slate house. When Aunt Betty came up and shut the door, Paul suddenly felt like crying. Seeing how upset Betty and Ruth were made him realize that his situation was no better. The only difference was his two older sisters. Paul realized that being the youngest wasn't all bad. Lucie and Hilda were faster than him at asking questions. They would know what to do and say better than him. Ruth had no one. Paul felt sorry for his young cousin. He hadn't realized until now, that with her blue eyes and light brown hair, she looked like Hilda. Paul resolved that he would try to get to know Ruth better. She might like having someone in her life who could act as an older brother.

As Paul reached the street where the jail was located, a large truck rumbled by and stopped in front of the jail. Paul stopped walking, not wanting to arrive at the same time as criminals or guards or SA men. He waited at the corner, watching the truck. Soon Paul saw a man in an SA uniform walk out of the jail and stand at attention in front of the truck. Another man in an SA uniform, who had been seated in the cab's passenger seat, climbed down from the truck's cab. The men saluted each other. Then the driver jumped down from the cab. He unlocked the back of the truck with a key. The two other men stood by as one of them shouted, "*Heraus!* Get out!"

Watching from a safe distance, Paul studied the men getting off the truck. He didn't know all of them, but he knew most. These were the Jewish men from small villages just outside Berleburg: Arfeld, Elsoff, and Schwarzenau. He had seen some of these men at the Berleburg synagogue. Paul recognized Heinzy Kahn, a boy with Down Syndrome who was about Lucie's age. Heinzy followed steps behind his father just as he did in synagogue. What could the Nazis want with Heinzy?

Paul remembered that he was carrying socks and shoes for Uncle Adolf. He knew he should be brave and go into the jail. But his feet would not move in that direction. His heart was beating too fast. He knew he'd never muster the courage to speak to anyone in the jail. He couldn't accomplish the errand. He wouldn't know what to do if they took him as they'd taken Heinzy. His parents already had enough on their minds. Paul quietly backtracked and ran home.

When Paul walked into the kitchen, Lucie was in the middle of telling her account of going to Tante Adele's. Paul couldn't tell if her heart was beating as fast as his was, but Lucie was speaking in an unfamiliar choppy voice. Yes, she was frightened. He could tell. Tante Adele's window had already been broken and the apartment was cold. But Tante Adele refused Lucie's help. She didn't want Lucie to stay. She said Elisabeth Bald would be by later and Lucie should leave her alone. Lucie didn't know what to do. She felt terrible leaving. "Adele was just sitting in her wheelchair. She looked so sad and alone. But what could I do?" Lucie shrugged.

"If she wanted you to leave, of course you had to leave," Mother said.

"I'm worried about her, too," said Hilda, agreeing with Lucie. "She's all alone."

"It's terrible that Adele can't walk," Paul entered the conversation.

"Yes, it is a tragedy," said Mother. "But let's focus on today. She is safe in her house and Elisabeth is supposed to come by. Is that what had you upset Lucie? Or was there something else?"

"It was everything. This town is being turned upside down. Nothing is normal. I walked by the synagogue on the way to and from Aunt Adele's. I saw Frau Stern cleaning up outside of her house. She had me come in." Frau Stern's husband was Albert Stern, the local Hebrew School teacher. They lived next to the synagogue. Lucie continued her short sentences. "Outside the synagogue there was a mess. A huge mess. Pews, the chandelier, prayer books, even my Simchat Torah flag that I made last week. All of it had been taken from the synagogue and thrown into the street."

"Oh," Paul gasped. "The prisms I saw at school today. My classmates each had one. Those must have been part of the chandelier."

"*Schrecklich*. Terrible," said Mother. Hilda nodded in agreement.

"When inside the Stern house," Lucie continued, "Frau Stern told me her son Alfred had fled. She had no idea where, or what might happen if someone turned him in."

Hilda asked, "Where do you think Alfred Stern has gone?" But before anyone could offer any ideas, they heard a knock on their kitchen door. Mother and the three children looked at each other.

Might that be Alfred?

Mother called out, "Who's there?"

"Gertrude, from next door."

Mother opened the door to the neighbor girl, Gertrude, who was in Hilda's class at school.

Gertrude's face was red. Paul thought maybe she ran across the small space between their two houses quickly, so as not to be seen. Gertrude's family was not Jewish. Paul was surprised when Mother did not ask Gertrude to sit down – she usually preached the necessity of good manners – but then again, perhaps Gertrude didn't want to be here and would be happy to get back home.

"Mutti and I heard your window smashed last night. Terrible. Is there anything we can do? Mutti says you can use our phone if you need to call someone. Come anytime." Having delivered her message, Gertrude waved, turned to the door, and let herself out.

Paul was about to tell Mother and his sisters about his errand. Uncle Adolf's socks were still in his pockets. Normally, someone would have noticed and asked about them. But then there was a loud pounding on the front door, just like last night.

"Who's there?" Mother asked in a sing-song voice betraying her fright.

"Open up!" came a now familiar bark of SA men. Mother had barely begun to open the door when six uniformed men strutted in. Two men marched upstairs. Another two scrutinized the living room. Two more men went into the kitchen.

Paul watched the men in the living room open the linen cabinet. The old cabinet was made of highly polished old wood. Mother was so proud of its contents, her *trousseau* of tablecloths and napkins she had embroidered when she was Lucie's age. Mother treated the linens as if they were jewels. Everything was perfectly pressed and folded so the monogram faced up. But now these goons, the only word Paul could think of for these men, were treating Mother's things as if they were garbage. These two men in pressed green woolens stomped up and down on Mother's linens, undoing all her sewing, ironing, and folding. One goon, with a Hitler-like mustache, had a smile like a young boy jumping in a mud puddle. Or, maybe a pig.

Paul turned to Mother. Her face was proud, impassive. Paul wondered if he, too, was able to mask all his worries and fears. Why were these men ruining their belongings? Why had they broken their window?

The SA man with the Hitler mustache lifted the Oriental rug facing the couch. His partner searched under the couch. Paul had forgotten that he stashed his home-made toy soldier collection under the couch in a cigar box. Mother didn't want him playing war with these "lead shot monstrosities." He hadn't even thought about them recently. But Hitler mustache shouted, "Ah hah!" as he spotted the cigar box. He grabbed the box and pulled it from under the couch.

The other SA man lifted the lid of the box and examined the crude soldiers. Paul trembled. Would they take him to the jail? Could Mother stop them? Could she do anything for him? These were just toys, home-made toys. Paul meant nothing by them. They were just silly toys. What could be so "Ah hah!" to the SA?

Paul looked up – he had been staring down at the floor – to see Mother and his sisters looking at him. He realized he had been shaking and holding his breath. Paul wondered when he'd begin to breathe normally again.

Finally, the six SA men signaled to each other that they completed their inspection. The one with the Hitler mustache, the one who found Paul's box of toy soldiers, led the rest of them out the door. Paul watched him, wishing he'd trip and fall, spilling the soldiers out along the sidewalk. Maybe he'd even break his nose. But no, the men got down the front stairs without mishap. They marched away two by two, just as if they had been toy soldiers.

Mother shut the front door once they were half a block away. She turned back to the children with tears in her eyes. "What a mess," she said, then sighed. "Let's clean this back up." Hilda and Mother started to sort the linens. Paul and Lucie straightened out the couch and rug. Many of the dishes in the kitchen were broken. Mother cried as she put them in a pile to take out to the garbage. Then she returned to the living room.

Mother fluffed the couch pillows and put them back in their place. She sat down and motioned for the children to join her. The four of them stared out the hole where their living room window had been. Hard to believe it had been less than a day since the window was broken, less than a day since they were kicked out of school, and only a few hours since Paul visited the jail (which he had still told no one about). Now their house had been examined and vandalized by Nazi goons. No one spoke, all of them leaving unsaid the big question: What next?

After *Kristallnacht,* Grandpa realized that what his friends had said about the Nazis not taking root in Berleburg was wrong. The madmen ruling the country were getting stronger, not fading away. His friends could not protect him. In fact, he was no longer sure they were his friends. Someone in a position of authority took pity on Grandpa's irascible 78-year-old father, Levi. He was allowed to go home from jail and remain with his family. Grandpa's younger brother Adolf received no such compassion. Like most of the Jewish men over sixteen, he was sent off to Oranienburg to pay his debt to the Reich with forced labor.

A few towns over, Grandma's only remaining sibling who had not already fled Germany, her brother Julius, was also rounded up. The Jewish men of Frankenberg/Röddenau were sent off to Buchenwald. The SA rank and file in this area were especially brutal. Grandma's brother was beaten up even before he got to Buchenwald. A Jewish teacher of Frankenberg, Ferdinand Stern (no relation to Albert Stern, the teacher in Berleburg), was murdered. Journalist Karl-Hermann Völker found this photo of boys posing on Ferdinand Stern's destroyed car. Was this supposed to

Kristallnacht destruction of Ferdinand Stern's Car
Courtesy of Karl Hermann Völker
Photo provided by Horst Hecker to the US Holocaust Museum

be fun? Or were the children being instructed in how to be men-
acing and cruel?

Grandpa, too, was going to have to serve his time for the crime
of being a Jew. He was lucky that his doctor refused the orders of
the SA to turn him out of the hospital. That gave him a little time
to plan for his family. The options and opportunities were few, but
less than a month after *Kristallnacht*, Grandma and Grandpa had
a plan in place.

In December 1938, Dad and his sisters were told that they would
be moving to Belgium to live with their aunt and uncle, that they
would go to school there, and that eventually (in more than a year)

Grandma and Grandpa would meet them in Belgium. Then all five of them would immigrate to the United States.

I can picture myself at ten. I enjoyed tromping through a field, forest, or swamp looking for butterflies and frogs. I played with friends after school. I watched the popular children's programs on television and listened to the hits on the radio. I did my homework. If my parents had told me that they were going to send me away to a foreign country for an uncertain length of time, I would probably have looked as frightened, confused, and melancholic as Dad in this picture.

Paul Krebs, age 8?

CHAPTER NINE
Poker Face

I never doubted Dad's love for me or his intention to be a good father, but some days he just wasn't there. On a good day, Dad came home from the farm singing "What's New Pussycat" or whistling the jingle from the Oscar Mayer Wiener commercial. He'd regale us with stories, telling us about a daughter of one of his customers who trained a calf to come when she whistled. The calf was no longer small, but it still ran across the field when the girl whistled. I loved this story. Our dog, Pudgy, never came when we called, unless it was dinnertime and her food was being put in the dish.

Other days, though, Dad seemed like grumpy Jackie Gleason on *The Honeymooners.* If I asked him a simple question like, could he take me to the movies with my friend, he'd shout, "You can walk!" Mom said Dad was being sarcastic and I should ignore him. Then I'd imagine Dad was trying to be like Jackie Gleason on *The Honeymooners* or Fred Flintstone. Comedians were allowed to be loud and rude. It was funny.

Grandma didn't think Jackie Gleason was funny and she didn't like it when Dad was rude. She'd yell at him in German. More than once, she told Dad to be nicer to me.

Although I laughed at Fred Flintstone, I wanted our family to be like *My Three Sons* or *Leave it to Beaver.* On those shows, there were silly misunderstandings. No one stayed angry all through dinner. About the same time that the first of my friends' families got a color television, I came to realize that the black and white shows I enjoyed were oversimplifications. No one I knew lived in families as easygoing as the Cleavers. Life was not that simple. People's emotions were complicated.

During our evening card games, Dad imparted wisdom on how to deal with difficult people. The trick was to master the poker face. You do not smile if you get a great hand in Rummy. You do not frown, or throw your cards on the table, if you get the queen of spades in Hearts. You keep your face still and play the cards you are given. Look down at your cards and unload that queen of spades in a surprise attack. Or frown for a hand or two and then play all your best cards. Don't let your face tell your strategy. Then, maybe then, you'll get lucky.

At first, I thought the poker face was just about cards. Even there, I struggled with keeping a neutral expression. Then I noticed that Dad practiced the poker face many times a day such as when he was driving, or watching television, or when I tried to speak with him about something. Was Dad always hiding what he really thought about things? What hand did he have? What was he keeping from me?

CHAPTER TEN

King of the Road / The Auction

I was still eating my breakfast at 7:30 in the morning when I heard Dad open the garage door. Seconds later his booming voice shouted, "Everybody ready for the OU-CK-SHUN?" That was Dad's attempt at humor, an exaggerated imitation of Grandpa pronouncing the word "auction." There was no school, perhaps it was spring break, and Amy and I were going off with Dad for the day. He had the truck, already loaded up with cows, parked in front of our house. We three ran down the driveway.

At age eight, I was finally big enough to climb into the truck by myself. Dad lifted Amy in and then went around to the driver's seat. The AM radio had only three options. As usual, Dad had it turned to *News on the Hour*, which was really news every fifteen minutes with maybe a song or two and a commercial or ten in between.

"Can I pick out a different radio station?" Amy asked. "How about the top 40 station that Mom lets us play?"

"Don't touch the controls!" Dad sounded snippy already. "The controls are for the driver. How many times do I have to tell you that?"

"Jeech," Amy said, "You've probably heard the news ten times today."

"C'mon, now," Dad said. "Let's try to have a good time. We're going to the OU-CK-SHUN." Neither Amy nor I laughed. After the news ended, Dad told Amy she could change the station.

"Let's see what I can find," Amy said, twisting the dial. A very crackly Roger Miller sang "King of the Road." By the third stanza, we were all singing along, Dad off key. It was hard to tell if in fun or he really couldn't hold a tune as Mom always said. Amy and I an octave higher. Amy shrieked when she heard *Beep, beep, beep, beep, beep, beep. News on the Hour.* "Oh, no. Why are we still on the news?" She tried to change the station, but Dad slapped her hand away.

The newscaster's voice crackled, "The *MV Bremerhaven,* a West German cruise ship, capsized in the harbor. We await a casualties report. The East German government denies any involvement."

"Is that the boat you came on?" Amy asked.

"No, no. We came on the *Villa de Madrid.* It was a Spanish boat, not a German boat."

"Oh," she said.

We drove along a creek, past the fish hatchery, and through woods. We stopped at a train crossing for a long cargo train to pass. It wasn't raining, but the sky was overcast. Around 11:30 Dad finally pointed out the auction house. "We made it! Who's ready to buy some heifers?"

"I am!" Amy said. "Can I pick one out?"

"Do you think you know how to pick out a good one?"

"No," Amy admitted. "But I can try."

"Isn't that Uncle Adolf's truck?" I asked.

"Right you are." Uncle Adolf's truck was red, with ALBION CATTLE on it.

After Dad stomped down on the parking brake, he came around to the side door and opened it for us. Before I climbed out, I looked down to see Dad standing in the middle of an enormous puddle shaped a lot like Lake Ontario. His work boots were submerged practically to his ankles. He swung me out over the puddle to dry land, then did the same with Amy. Amy yelled, "Uncle Adolf!"

"Are you here to steal my cows?" Dad asked Uncle Adolf with a smile, once we four were all standing together.

"Yesssss, sssssssir," said Uncle Adolf. "I'm going to buy all the good ones."

"And what do we call someone who does that?" asked Dad, looking towards Amy and me.

"A *goniff*!" said Amy smiling.

Uncle Adolf laughed.

"Goniff. Goniff. Goniff," Amy said.

"But you're not really a thief, are you?" I asked.

"Yes, I am."

After a bit more banter, Dad said he had cows that needed unloading and that we girls should wait with Uncle Adolf. I stood there with my hands in my pockets, looking around. A couple of other cattle dealers walked towards us, speaking German to Uncle Adolf. I had no idea who they were or what they were talking about. Finally, Dad returned and gestured for us to follow him.

The bottom floor of the auction house had the cows in different sized pens. That all the calves were together made sense. But I could tell no differences between the animals in the other half dozen pens. I saw only a sea of black-and-white creatures all crammed in together. How Dad was going to select the one, two, or twenty new cows to bring back to the farm, was a mystery. Dad's answers fell along the lines of "I can tell." I couldn't tell and I couldn't guess how he could. I wondered if Grandpa had given Dad such vague explanations.

"Who's hungry?" Dad asked after we left the area with the cow pens. He led Amy and me to a brightly lit room with a couple of diner-style counters. Dad pointed out three empty stools in a row and lifted Amy into a seat.

A waitress put down a water glass for each of us. "I see the Krebs Brothers staff has grown. Three of the usual?"

"Yes, three slices of apple pie. Girls, do you want your pie plain, with cheddar, or with ice cream?"

I made the bad choice of asking for cheddar cheese, like Dad. The cheddar dampened both the sweetness and the tartness of the apples. I should have picked ice cream, like Amy. But Dad would have been mad if I peeled the cheese off the top. He didn't believe in wasting food. So I alternated eating the top crust with the cheese and the bottom crust with the apples separately, not loving my solution.

"That was delicious," Dad said to the waitress when she returned with the bill. Amy ate all her ice cream but only a bit of pie. Dad finished her food and then led us out of the diner and into the large auditorium for the auction.

The auctioneer, a man maybe Dad's age, wasn't wearing typical cattle dealer coveralls and mud boots, or overalls, or some other outfit that would be thrown in the wash at the end of the day. Instead, the auctioneer wore a shiny black suit, a starched white shirt, and a string tie. He stood behind a podium just to the left side of the auction floor. Holding a small microphone, he chanted, "Who'll give me one, give me one, give me one, give me two, give me five, give me ten, give me seven," and so on until "SOLD. Thank you, number 75. Aren't you a big spender!"

I spotted Uncle Adolf talking to a bunch of men. Uncle Adolf still had his hat on, and he was tapping his cane on the floor to make some point. Even though he was a head shorter than the rest of the group, he seemed to command their attention. At some point, Jerry Miller, who had a farm near our house, broke out laughing. I wondered what Uncle Adolf's joke was about. He always had a joke about something. Amy must have been watching them, too, because she pointed them out to Dad.

Dad was too busy watching the auctioneer to turn around. He picked up a pen from his shirt pocket. The auctioneer caught his signal. Dad bid against another cattle dealer for a minute. Then he said, "Let's go, girls." I think he won the bid, but I wasn't sure. Did he get a good deal?

Back in the empty truck—no, Dad didn't buy any cows, and we didn't stay long enough to find out how much Dad's cows sold for—we headed back home. I asked Dad if we could stop at the fish hatchery in Caledonia. A friend from school had visited and said it was a lot of fun watching all the little fish swim in the creek. Dad didn't answer me, not the first time and not the second.

Amy asked, "Is Uncle Adolf really a cattle thief?"

"What do you think?" Dad snapped. I had no idea why Dad got so grumpy. I thought everything was going well. I silently looked out the car window. The news came and went a few more times. There was still no explanation for why the *SS Bremerhaven* capsized. Dad whistled along when "King of the Road" came on the radio again. But by then, Amy was asleep with her head on my shoulder. I watched the fields and creeks we passed. Dad sang off-key all alone.

Mom was in a good mood when we got home. She made roasted chicken for dinner and ate with Dad, Amy, and me. (Often Mom stood at the sink washing dishes while the three of us ate.) She chuckled when we told her about running into Uncle Adolf. Amy asked if Uncle Adolf was a cattle thief, and Mom told her no. Then Dad snickered. Though Dad told Mom that we'd all had fun, he said he was too busy for us to come with him again this week.

When I tried to fall asleep that night, the bouncy music and sad lyrics to "King of the Road" came back to me. "No phone, no pool, no pets. I ain't got no cigarettes... I'm a man of means by no means. King of the road." I struggled to make peace with the song's concept. Did the singer really want nothing but to be alone? Or was the song a cry for the baggage of home? I wondered which made Dad happier: time alone in the truck? Or time with me full of questions, needs, and opinions? I also wondered which option would appeal most to me once I grew up.

CHAPTER ELEVEN

On to Mechelen

After *Kristallnacht*, Dad, then nine-year-old Paul, and his two older sisters knew that their parents were sick with fear. Mother and Father wrote or called every relative near or far to let them know what happened and to plead for help. Though the family no longer was allowed to have a telephone or a radio, Mother was able to use the Bald's phone to call her oldest sister Mathilde in Mechelen, Belgium. She also called her sister Martha in Amsterdam and her sister-in-law Selma, who lived in the old family house in Röddenau, Hesse, the next province over.

Mother found out that when her brother Julius tried to say goodbye to his young daughter in the middle of the night, he was hit in the ribs. Then he was taken to prison. Selma sounded frantic. How were she and the girls supposed to manage without a husband/father, business, school, and no front window? Mother told her to stay in touch, that they should help each other.

But Mother's sisters outside of Germany were fine. Belgium and Holland may have had antisemites in their governments, but they weren't ruled by Nazis. There had been no window breaking, no mass arrests of Jews, nothing to worry about. Mother also sent letters to the rest of her family now living in the U.S. Perhaps one of them could help. The Krebs family didn't have an appointment to get visas until May 1940, which was over a year away. Perhaps someone could help get their date moved up.

Father decided that helping his brother Adolf was his first priority. Adolf was the sort of person who attracted trouble. With his short stature and hunchback, people picked him out of a crowd. And with his quick tongue, Adolf could get under anyone's skin. Father had heard that at the Oranienburg Camp, Adolf and the other Jews from Berleburg were required to lay railroad ties. Father couldn't imagine Adolf doing this for long without getting shot by a prison guard for insubordination. Father learned about a program to get German Jewish men visas to England. Father sent off an application (with a large application fee) on Adolf's behalf. His hope was that Adolf would reach England, and then procure visas for Betty and Ruth.

Three weeks after Kristallnacht, just a day before Paul's tenth birthday, Mother announced over lunch that she had received a telegram from Aunt Mathilde. Paul didn't have a clear image of this aunt. Mother and Father had too many sisters for him to remember all of them.

Mother said, "The three of you will go live with her in Belgium."

"What?" Hilda sputtered. Paul's potato formed a lump in his throat and would not be swallowed.

"When did you decide this?" Lucie said, indignantly.

"Germany is no place for children. You cannot go to school. All you can do here is get into trouble."

"And what am I going to do in Belgium?" asked Lucie.

Mother wiped her eyes. "Your Aunt Mathilde will take good care of you. She has room for all of you. You'll be safe."

"Have I ever met her? Who are her children?" Paul asked.

"Of course you've met her," Father said. "She is your mother's oldest sister. You met her at all the big family parties in Röddenau. Her husband Hugo owned a big furniture factory in Frankfurt. Now they live in Belgium. Belgium has a king. No Hitler. You can all go to school." Father lowered his voice and spoke quickly when he said Hitler's name. Who knew what was overheard these days?

You can't be too careful if you're Jewish.

Mother continued. "Your cousins Anneliese and Doris Bachenheimer from Röddenau will travel with you to Belgium. And in Mechelen, your Aunt Mathilde has another daughter, Lore. There will be plenty of children. You will have fun."

"Lore is stuck up!" Lucie shouted. "I don't want to live with Lore!"

"Lore is at finishing school. I don't think you'll see her much. But you will have Doris and Anneliese. You like them."

"How long will we be there?" Hilda asked quietly. She sounded frightened.

Father mumbled something about Americans and visas. Paul was about to say that the family's date to visit the American Embassy in Stuttgart had been set for 1940, more than a year away, when Father said, "Aunt Mathilde will take you to the American Embassy in Belgium for visas. We'll meet you in Belgium."

Mother looked at Paul. "There will be a boy at Aunt Mathilde's, too. He is Uncle Hugo's nephew, Horst. He's a year younger than you."

"Let me get this straight," Lucie snapped. "We're going to Belgium without you. And we're to live with Aunt Mathilde, Uncle Hugo, cousins Lore, Doris, Anneliese, and Horst. Do they have a palace?"

"I grew up with eleven siblings. Who sounds stuck up now?" Mother said. Mother kept to herself that there was one more person descending on Mathilde and Hugo, Hugo's elderly father who had brought Horst and was staying on indefinitely. Yes, the house would be crowded. But neither she, nor Lucie, was in any position to complain. Then Mother remembered how someone from the Jewish Agency had advised her to speak to the children. She said, "Think of this as an adventure!"

"Yes," Father said. "You are all going on an adventure."

Paul got up to use the bathroom. He thought he might be sick. As he walked, he repeated, "I am going on an adventure," several times under his breath. Adventures, he thought, could be good or bad. He hoped the new adventures would be more fun than going to the jail to bring Uncle Adolf his socks or getting expelled from school.

When he returned from the bathroom, Paul found Lucie and Hilda looking through old schoolbooks in the living room. "What are you doing?" he asked.

"We're trying to find out something about Mechelen. Come see, I found it on a map." Hilda backed up so Paul could look. Lucie pointed to a city roughly mid-way between Antwerp and Brussels. When Paul nodded, Hilda said, "It is the fourth largest city in Belgium, called Malines in French." Paul nodded again. He was more concerned with the fact that he was leaving than about where he was going.

The following morning, Paul awoke to Lucie and Mother arguing downstairs in the kitchen, again about the conceited Lore Lindheim, and how unhappy Lucie would be.

Father came into Paul's bedroom before he could go downstairs. Father told Paul that he had been a soldier in Belgium during the Great War. Paul shouldn't worry. Belgium looks a lot like Germany, Father said, only with fewer hills. Father also said that Uncle Hugo had many friends and business associates, that there might be parties at the house, and that Paul might meet some important people. In short, Father was sure that Paul would learn a lot.

Later that day, Mother received a fat envelope with details of the children's trip, the *Kindertransport*. On December 13th, Mother was to drop the children off at the Jewish Welfare Service Agency on Rubensstrasse in Köln. They would be accompanied by the Red Cross on a train from Köln to Brussels.

Paul accompanied Mother and his sisters to the Bald's house next door so Mother could call Aunt Mathilde with the travel details. Uncle Hugo would drive to Brussels to meet their train. Uncle Hugo's car was big enough to fit all the children and their luggage. Although Gertrude Bald and her mother left the room for the phone call, the pair returned as soon as Mother set the phone in its cradle. They had been crying. Paul didn't understand why. The Balds weren't going away. He was. What did they have to be upset about?

At Aunt Adele's house, she wasn't the only one who cried. Lucie and Hilda cried, too. Ditto at Aunt Betty and Cousin Ruth's. Paul was the only one who wouldn't cry. He would not let himself.

On the drive from Berleburg to Köln, Mother insisted upon going over the children's itinerary one more time. Paul knew that she was just talking to try to keep from crying. He worried that she would cry, and then he would cry, and then he wouldn't be able to say goodbye.

Father's voice trembled a bit as he described when they would see each other again in Belgium. Once all the visas were secured, he and Mother would be in Belgium to meet them. Then they all would travel to America, far from the Nazis. They would all start over there. But first, they would enjoy their time in Belgium.

Father missed the turnoff for Rubensstraße. By the time he found a good place to turn around, Paul saw Father's hands shaking on the wheel. Father found a parking spot close to the Jewish Agency. Then the five of them walked into the office together, each child carrying a heavy rucksack with clothes, a book, and lunch for the train.

Inside the Jewish Agency, two women greeted the family. They reviewed each child's documents. Then they gave each child a cardboard tag for their luggage. They ushered the family to a small room where other children sat with their luggage. Paul realized that this was where they would say goodbye. When he and his sisters left that small room, it would be without their parents.

CHAPTER TWELVE
The Kindertransport

After *Kristallnacht*, Dad went on a *Kindertransport*. When I said these words out loud as a child, they turned into train cars in my mind. I could imagine Grandma and Grandpa waving goodbye to their children in Köln. I could see Dad and his sisters sitting stoically in their seats as the train pulled out of the station, heading west for Belgium.

I never met anyone outside of my family who'd been on a *Kindertransport*. Most of my classmates at Hebrew School were the grandchildren or great-grandchildren of immigrants. I was well into my twenties before I joined a group of children of Holocaust survivors. Most of the others in the group had parents with stories completely different from Dad's. Statistically, most offspring of children who went on *Kindertransports* lived in England, which was the terminus of the journey for roughly ten thousand children. The number of children who wound up in Belgium, the Netherlands, Switzerland, or Sweden was much smaller. As the Nazis invaded Belgium, the Netherlands, and Sweden, children who'd come on *Kindertransports* may have been forced into hiding or sent off to concentration camps.

Grandma talked to me many times about how terrible she felt sending her children off to her sister's. Grandma had studied to be a nursery schoolteacher: she loved children. She loved *her* children. She said, "No mother should ever have to send their children away. It was the worst day of my life. But what could we do?" Then she'd look at Grandpa, both of them with moist eyes.

"Every day the children were gone, I wondered, would I ever see them again?"

Noting that she had changed from we to I, I asked "Where was Grandpa?"

"He was gone. Forced to do construction work. Slave labor. I had to send food and clothes. They gave him nothing. First, he was near Berleburg and then they sent him away. When he came home, he had no more meat on his bones. *Schrecklich.*"

This application for Dad's travel documents shows a sober young boy. Was the photo taken two days before, or a week after, his tenth birthday? What is the look on his face? An attempt to hide his fear? Is he in shock? Or is he trying to hold in his emotions?

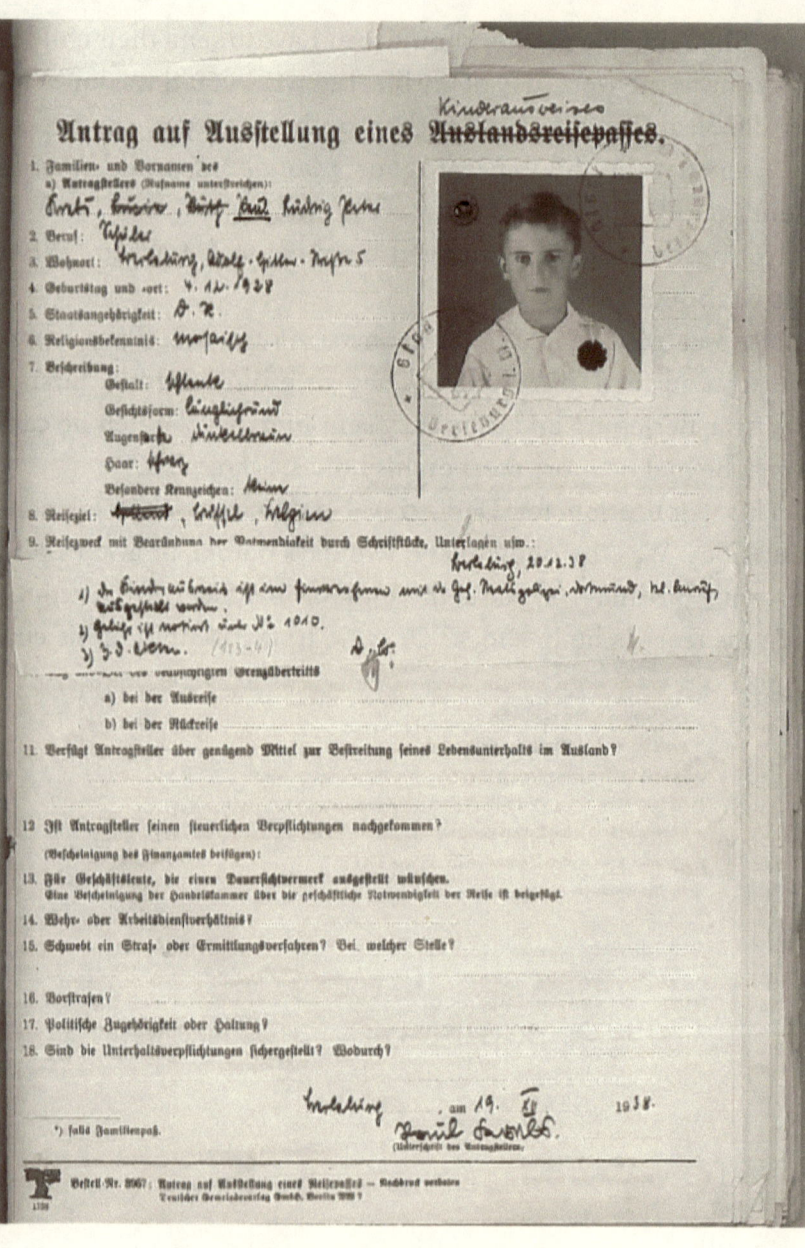

Passport Application, Paul Krebs, December 12, 1938
Courtesy of Stadtarchiv Bad Berleburg

An article I found on the internet about the *Kindertransports* to Belgium described a 2020 museum exhibit in Köln.[6] A photo of the exhibit shows a wall of head shots from children who went on *Kindertransports* from Köln to Belgium. I look for a familiar face—maybe Dad or his cousin Doris—but recognize no one.

One girl looks like Anne Frank. A boy has a serious look as if he wanted to be looking through a microscope or reading a history book. Another boy could have had a sign that read "class clown" under his picture. I wonder how these children fared in Belgium. How many of these children found their way to the U.S., England, or elsewhere prior to the Nazi invasion? How many died during the invasion? How many were ultimately deported to concentration camps? How many, like Dad, made it out alive? What kinds of traumas did these children experience?

Courtesy of Roland Kaufhold
Website caption says, "Some children were the same
age as the students you see on the picture wall today."

I also wonder about the teens in the foreground listening to the docent. What are they learning? How are they affected? Will they

---

[6]https://www.juedische-allgemeine.de/gemeinden/zuflucht-in-belgien/

ask their parents and grandparents questions at home later? Will any of them leave the exhibit imagining a story like the one Dad and his sisters tell me? Will any of them ask the docent about the young boy who is hidden behind the woman with the white scarf? That hidden photo is of my dad.

CHAPTER THIRTEEN

Crossing the Border

Paul had thought Mother and Father would say goodbye to him at the Köln train station, a huge building where he imagined that could watch the trains for distraction. In this fantasy, Paul would have led his family to the correct platform for the train to Brussels. He'd lead his sisters to their compartment. He'd find his seat and wave out the window to his parents. No one would notice his fears or tears.

As it turned out, Paul and his sisters said goodbye to their parents at the Jewish Agency building about a mile from the train station. Paul studied his shoes, not wanting his parents to see his tears. He was both afraid and sad to say goodbye.

Mother pulled Hilda aside, but not far enough for Paul to miss her words of advice, "You are a wonderful girl but look out for your younger brother. He doesn't know as much as you. Make sure he doesn't get lost on the train or in the station before you meet Uncle Hugo."

Father hugged Lucie tightly and said, "Lucie, you are so brave. You're the leader now. Show your aunt and uncle you are tough stuff, smart, talented. Be helpful and cooperative. Make me proud!"

Father picked Paul up a foot off the ground so they could look into each other's eyes. "Where is your smile? Let me see it, son. When I see you again, you'll have grown into those big teeth. You'll have to teach me Flemish, or French. Then we'll learn English together!"

Then it was time for Mother and Father to leave. The children had to board the bus to the train station. Although Paul hadn't noticed Cousin Doris in the agency office, she got in line for the bus right behind him. She looked red in the face and her eyes were bloodshot. Paul wondered where her sister Anneliese was, but it was his turn to climb on. He hoisted his rucksack a bit higher on his shoulders and followed behind Hilda.

When the bus arrived at the train station, someone from the Jewish Agency led the children to their train car. Each car had four compartments with six seats each. Paul let Doris sit next to Hilda. He took a seat beside Lucie, the four travelers facing each other. Two other children were ushered into the compartment, two girls who looked a bit older than Paul. They sat facing each other on the end by the door. Paul was glad to be traveling with children older than him. One young boy, perhaps a three- or four-year-old, had cried the whole bus ride. Paul would not have wanted to sit next to him or by one of the other very young children who didn't know enough to blow their noses by themselves.

As the train pulled out of the station, Hilda asked Doris why Anneliese wasn't there. "Someone in the district office decided only one Jew could go. Who knows why. Since I'm older, Mother thought it would be better for me to go. She really wanted both of us to go. Perhaps she needed to bribe someone to get a permit. With Father away, she didn't know who to approach or what to do."

"You're with us now," Hilda said. "We'll stick together." She put her arm around Doris. Paul watched them draw together, then he stood and went to the door of the compartment to see who was sitting where. He saw the woman from the Jewish Agency sitting in the next compartment. She sat next to the boy who had cried on the bus, as well as three other very young children. Each of these children wore a tag on their lapel with their name, age, and the name of the person planning to meet them in Brussels. In the same compartment, Paul noticed a woman with a Red Cross hat. She was trying to get a young boy interested in a stuffed animal. The boy wouldn't take it.

As the last large streets of Köln narrowed into smaller country roads cutting through pastures, the train picked up speed. Father had shown Paul their route on a map. The big stop between Köln and Brussels was Aachen, at the German-Belgian border. At that stop, Father said, the children would have to go through customs. German officials would stamp their passports to indicate that they were leaving, and Belgian officials would grant them entrance to their country. This was official business. Mother insisted that Lucie carry all the children's documents in one bundle. She had gone over the documents with Lucie until Lucie told her to leave her alone. Father smiled and said he was sure Lucie appreciated how serious a matter this was, and that she would ably take care of things.

Paul, his sisters, and his cousin looked out the window as the train moved westward to the German-Belgian border. The landscape in this part of Germany didn't look much different from Berleburg. Lucie had been sure to let them know they were now in the Rheinland, no longer in Westfalen.

Eventually, a conductor walked down the aisle announcing Aachen in ten minutes. The woman from the Jewish Agency got up and began to circulate to the different compartments, making sure everyone had their documents on their laps. Doris pulled hers out of her rucksack. Lucie handed Paul's and Hilda's documents to them as she had been told to do. The two other girls in their row had been clutching their documents in their laps during the entire ride.

A German passport agent in a stiff suit of green wool with an official *Adler Hackenkreuz* (eagle-swastika) insignia on his lapel came to the entry of the children's compartment. Lucie gestured for Paul to sit up straighter. When Lucie began to answer the agent's questions for everyone in the row, the passport agent told her that they were all old enough to answer for themselves. Paul imagined himself calmer than he felt. He didn't stutter when he gave the man his full name, Paul Peter Ludwig Krebs. The man looked from Paul's passport to his face half a dozen times. Finally, he stamped Paul's passport and moved on.

The Belgian agent wore a similar wool uniform, but in blue with a red collar. He quickly inspected the same set of documents for each child and kept moving. When he was several aisles away, Lucie suggested that they might have lunch when the train started moving again. She mouthed, but didn't say out loud, "We'll be done with the Nazis!" Out loud she said to Paul and Hilda, "We'll have another hour before Brussels. Pass me your documents."

When the train left the Aachen station and passed into Belgium, Lucie lifted her arms in triumph. "We made it!" Everyone in their compartment smiled and opened their rucksacks. Collectively the children had egg or wurst sandwiches, cut up apples, and thermoses of milk with coffee and sugar. Doris showed everyone that she had a large parcel of *Apfelkuchen* (apple cake), enough for all of them to share. Even though everything looked delicious, Paul didn't feel like eating. Since saying goodbye to his parents, he'd had a lump in his throat. Perhaps it was a cold coming on. Perhaps it was fear and sadness. Either way, he worried that if he tried to get food past the lump, he might vomit.

The conductor came through to let everyone know that they would be arriving shortly in Brussels. The woman from the Jewish Agency got up and began counting the children again. She told everyone to be sure to take all their belongings. Anything left on the train would be gone for good. Lucie told everyone to look under their seats and be sure that they didn't lose a pen, a hat, or anything else. When the children got off the train, the woman from the Red Cross stood just outside their train car. Her job, it seemed, was to match children with the adults who had come to get them.

Paul did not recognize Uncle Hugo, but Lucie shook his hand and said hello. Uncle Hugo was not as tall as Father, but bigger of belly. It looked to Paul like he'd eaten a few too many slices of *kuchen*. But he stood straight and looked closely at the paperwork the Red Cross worker wanted him to sign. After signing, he gestured for the children to follow him. He didn't ask their names or offer to help anyone with their luggage, which Paul knew Father would have done. Paul wondered if there was a rule here that adults should not talk to children.

Lucie must have been uncomfortable with the silence because she started answering the questions they knew Father or Mother would have asked. "The trip was fine; no one bothered us. Our parents send their love. We are happy to be here." She smiled a bit. But Uncle Hugo didn't notice because he hadn't turned around when she spoke.

"Yes, yes," Doris agreed. "Thank you for having us. My parents send their love, too."

Uncle Hugo led them to another train platform. Paul had thought they'd be picked up in a car. But it turned out that they were getting on another train. Uncle Hugo gestured for everyone to get in the second car. Lucie went first. But with no one to tell her whether to turn left or right, she stood still. Doris piled up behind her. The conductor, speaking an unfamiliar language – was it French or Flemish? – pointed to the right so Lucie and Doris walked that way. Then Hilda and Paul followed. When Uncle Hugo got on the train and showed the conductor their First-Class tickets, the children had to walk back the entire length of the car. Two women sitting together made faces at Paul. Maybe they didn't like hearing Uncle Hugo speaking to them in German.

On the hour-long train ride from Brussels to Mechelen, Uncle Hugo pointed out a few things: a village on a hill in the distance, a church with a very tall spire, and a town with a famous restaurant. It looked a lot like the countryside they had passed through all day long: some forested areas, some pastures, some towns. The big difference was that the hills in Belgium were barely hills at all.

As they approached Mechelen, Uncle Hugo told the children that the city was a trading center, a bit like Amsterdam with its canals and row houses. "Though we don't have a canal view from our home, the canal is just at the end of our street." Then Uncle Hugo had a lot to say about canals. Canals connect rivers. Canals were dug by hand and enlarged over the decades as barges got wider and longer. Now canals and barges were standardized. Uncle Hugo listed a series of cities that were all connected by the waterway to Mechelen.

Remembering that Uncle Hugo had a furniture business, Paul asked if he shipped his furniture by barge. This made Uncle Hugo smile a bit.

"It depends. Could be barge or train or truck, depending upon where it is going. We still sell mainly to Germany, which goes by truck or train. But I am trying to expand our markets in Belgium and the Netherlands. Next year I plan to try to sell furniture in France and Switzerland. Maybe the United States, too."

"Are you moving there?" asked Hilda. "We are moving there as soon as we get visas."

"Maybe, maybe," said Uncle Hugo. "Right now, I am making a living here."

"My brother Fritz is in New York," added Doris.

"Yes, yes, I know," said Uncle Hugo. "He wants to go to medical school."

When the train stopped in the Mechelen station, Uncle Hugo led the children to a taxi stand. He ordered the driver to take the group to Auwegumstraat. As promised, the taxi driver took a route along a canal, then turned onto Auwegumstraat. "This is it!" said Uncle Hugo, pointing to a black door in the middle of the street. Once Paul was out of the car, he wondered how he'd ever find this house again. The entire street was comprised of red brick row houses, most with black doors. Other than the canal on the corner, how would he find "his" door.

A woman a bit smaller than Mother but with a similar erect posture opened the door that Uncle Hugo had pointed to. She clapped her hands. "You've come! You've come! Right this way!" She stood in the doorway ushering first Uncle Hugo, then the children, into the house and up the stairs. Hilda thought she should kiss Aunt Mathilde, but no cheek was offered.

The top of the stairs opened into a dining room on the right and a living room on the left. Uncle Hugo went to stand next to a stooped man with a cane. "My father," he introduced the children. "His name is Siegfried Lindheim. You can call him Uncle Lindheim." Uncle Lindheim smiled at Uncle Hugo and then the children. "And this fine young man is my nephew, Horst. We call him Freddy."

"I'm eight," Horst said.

Paul offered, "I just turned ten."

"And that's why you two will be sharing a room," Aunt Mathilde said. "Unfortunately, there are only so many bedrooms. Uncle Lindheim will be with you, too."

"Follow me," Freddy gestured to Paul. "I'll show you where you can put your things." Paul followed, thinking it might be nice sharing a room with another boy...but Uncle Lindheim was sure to snore. Freddy took Paul to a room with three beds crammed in. There was barely room to walk by the beds to get to the clothes armoires.

"Should I unpack now?" Paul asked.

Freddy shrugged. "I think we're supposed to eat dinner now." Paul put his rucksack on the bed that Freddy pointed out to him. Then Freddy said, "My parents are coming next month to get me. How long will you be here?"

Paul shrugged. "We need visas."

"We're going to England."

Paul was glad when Aunt Mathilde called them to dinner. The way Freddy puffed out his chest earlier, he was not acting like someone Paul's junior. Paul would have expected Freddy to ask questions about toys or books, not to grill him about his parents. "My parents are coming next month. We are going to England," sounded like bragging to Paul.

Dinner was exactly what Mother would have made on a cold

damp afternoon like this: stewed beef, boiled potatoes, and sad winter green beans. Paul couldn't eat much. None of the children, except Freddy, ate much.

Aunt Mathilde commented, "It is a shame to waste food. I know your mothers expect you to do better!"

Paul tried another bite. But he had that lump, still, in the back of his throat. Should he tell Aunt Mathilde that he felt sick?

After the dinner dishes were cleared – by a maid! – Aunt Mathilde cleared her throat. "I want to talk with you about school." Paul gulped. School already? He'd just arrived. He didn't even know the street name or number yet.

"As you know," Aunt Mathilde continued, "my Lore goes to a finishing school. She lives there during the week and comes home every Friday. You'll see her then." Paul watched Aunt Mathilde smile when she said Lore's name. "Horst goes to the boy's elementary school for now." Aunt Mathilde glanced at Horst without smiling. Then Paul heard her pronounce his name very sharply. "You will attend the boy's Atheneum." Atheneum sounded like Paul might have to study Greek. What could he be in for?

Aunt Mathilde went on to say the names of the schools that Hilda, Doris, and Lucie would attend. Paul had stopped listening. He was still imagining what Atheneum would be like. How many languages would he have to learn? What if his new Belgian teacher made him wear a dunce cap?

Lucie asked if they would be starting tomorrow (Wednesday), or the following Monday. Paul was relieved to hear that they would not start until after the New Year. By then, Paul thought he should be able to find the house on his own. He started to relax, a little, and sighed. Hilda smiled at him. Paul smiled back.

Uncle Hugo cleared his throat. "My advice to all of you is to use your ears. Listen carefully to your teachers in school and the other children on the playground. Lose your German accents as soon as you can.

"Try to sound like you are from Mechelen. Try to blend in. Me, when I talk, they know I am German immediately. It is impossible for Mathilde and me to sound anything but German. On the other hand, with Lore, they detect no accent."

What a strange family, Paul thought. Lore was off at school, Aunt Mathilde must have a book of behavior rules somewhere in the kitchen, and Uncle Hugo loved the sound of his own voice. Uncle Hugo was droning on about the relations between Belgium and Germany going back to before the Great War. Blah, blah, blah, the Kaiser. Blah, blah, blah, Hugo's regiment in the Great War. Blah, blah, blah, the Iron Cross he was awarded. Paul knew Father had one too. Blah, blah, blah.

"Between my accent and my Iron Cross, the Belgians see me as a potential Nazi collaborator. It keeps our immigration status up in the air. Meanwhile, Herr Hitler threatens to invade any day now."

Invasion? That got Paul's attention. If Hitler was going to invade Belgium, why did his parents send him here? Did Uncle Hugo know something Father didn't about Hitler's plans?

Paul started to cry. He had been away from home less than a day. How was he going to live here with this lump in his throat and these strange people who spoke calmly about a Nazi invasion?

"This has been a long day for all of you," Uncle Hugo said. "Perhaps I've tired you out with my talking. You will be fine once you settle in." He addressed his last sentence to Paul.

Paul looked at Freddy, who smiled at Uncle Hugo as if he believed him, that everything would be fine. Maybe, Paul thought, it would. Maybe Freddy's parents would come next month. Maybe Paul's would come the month after. But Paul wasn't sure that the lump in his throat, and the queasiness he felt throughout his body, would go away until he saw his parents again.

CHAPTER FOURTEEN

Party on Long-Gi-land

Towards the end of elementary school, an excerpt from Anne Frank's diary was included in our class reader. Mom and Dad had a worn blue cloth-bound copy of the book at home, but I had only examined the cover and title page. My reading teacher, Mr. Green, asked us to raise our hands if we had heard of Anne Frank. Knew what happened to the Jews during World War II? Knew what a concentration camp was? My face felt hot. Was I blushing? What was I feeling?

I knew the outline of Anne Frank's story. Was there a Jewish girl in my generation who didn't? The first American edition of the diary was issued five years before my birth. An adaption of the diary for the theater opened on Broadway three years later, and Shelly Winters won the Academy Award for her portrayal of Mrs. Van Daan in the movie version in 1959.

It is quite possible that my hand was the only one up in the air for Mr. Green's questions. I don't remember if I offered my fifth-grade knowledge to the class or if Mr. Green provided the outline of Anne's life. It was bad enough telling the Chanukkah story, which, like every Bible story, may or may not have been true. But Anne was a real person, a girl only a few years older than us, when she was forced to go into hiding...and then killed in a concentration camp.

It crossed my mind that one of my classmates might say something positive about Nazis. Or be dismissive of Anne. Or treat her diary as fiction, silly, laughable. What was I going to do if this happened?

During spring break, just before our class read Anne Frank, we were invited to a party at Aunt Hilda's new house on Long Island. If the party wasn't specifically a housewarming party, then it was a party for Grandpa's birthday. Aunt Hilda liked throwing parties, which were often timed to end a visit by my grandparents at her house. We'd drive from Spencerport a day or two before the party, do some stuff in Metro New York – perhaps a museum, shopping, visiting my mom's sister and family – then after the party, drive Grandma and Grandpa back to Spencerport.

One time when we had visited Aunt Hilda's, my sister Amy, who'd been complaining of car sickness the whole drive on the Long Island Expressway, puked on Aunt Hilda's carpet before she'd even taken off her coat. Aunt Hilda told this story so often that I was not surprised when, upon arrival, she pointed us around the house to the backyard. No tour of the new house until after the garden party.

As we generally came early to parties, no one else had arrived. Even Grandma and Grandpa were still in the house. I circled the backyard, looking at the trees and bushes planted around the perimeter, wondering if the pale-yellow blooming flowers were honeysuckle or something else. It seemed like I had time to explore every leaf on every tree and still I was wandering alone in the backyard. What were my cousins doing in the house? Why was no one coming out for the party?

I wanted to see my cousins' new bedrooms, find out what they were reading, watching on TV, listening to on the radio, and wearing...all the stuff that wouldn't be coming to Spencerport for another year or more. I'd already exhausted my limited topics of civil conversation with my parents or sister on our eight hours in the car the day before. I was beginning to feel sorry for myself and began another inspection of the trees.

After what felt like an hour but was probably less than ten minutes, guests began arriving. I chatted around the soda siphon machine with a few cousins close to my age. We mixed ourselves orange, grape, and even chocolate sodas. Then we filled our plates with wurst, potato salad, and cucumber salad. Too quickly, I'd run through our topics of mutual interest. I just couldn't seem to click into the fun-party groove that everyone around me seemed to have found, or so I imagined. I felt grumpy. I felt self-conscious. I felt lonely. I thought maybe Aunt Hilda would let me in the house now and I could help with the party, like her daughters.

Grandma grabbed my arm. "Isn't the food out of this world? Did you try my potato salad?"

"Von-Tastic!" I said to Grandma, smiling and mangling the English word to sound German. Grandma beamed. I wasn't sure if it was because I'd complimented her salad, or if she'd picked up on the joke.

"Such a beautiful girl," Aunt Frieda said, pinching me on the arm and drawing me to her. I gave her a kiss on her uplifted cheek. As usual at family parties, where you'd find Grandma, you'd find Aunt Frieda. She didn't look like Grandma that much, but they both dyed their hair the same auburn color. They were constantly locking arms, telling each other stories, sometimes with their heads right next to each other so no one else could hear. While Grandma told me she didn't believe in favorites – not sisters, not children, not kitty cats in the barn – she spoke about Frieda and her husband Max all the time.

It was Frieda and Max who had been Grandma and Grandpa's lifeline out of Germany. Uncle Max came from a village where the Nazis had asserted themselves early. Frieda and Max had applied for and received visas years before Grandpa and Grandma. Once in the U.S., Frieda and Max collected funds from New York relatives to help pay for Grandma and Grandpa's expenses. They had called the Joint Refugee Committee regularly. They kept their ears to the ground about escape routes out of Germany. Plus, once Grandma and Grandpa arrived in New York, Frieda and Max set them up in their apartment building. As teens, Dad and his sisters were constantly in and out of Frieda and Max's apartment, always with Frieda and Max's sons. Grandma often told me, "Frieda and Max couldn't do enough for us. We wouldn't be here without them."

After Aunt Frieda released me, I looked at the rest of the people sitting at the table. Grandma asked if I knew everyone. I pointed to the one man at the table and guessed Uncle Otto, the only brother's name that I knew. He had visited the farm once, come by train with his little Dachshund, Schnitzel. I remembered Schnitzel sitting in the house on Uncle Otto's lap. In general, Grandma believed that animals belonged in the barn, not the house. Our dog Pudgy was certainly not allowed in Grandma's house. But Schnitzel got a pass. Maybe it was because Uncle Otto would not travel without Schnitzel. Or maybe Grandma liked Schnitzel more than she let on. Or maybe Grandma couldn't resist Uncle Otto's smile. He and Aunt Marga, his wife, both had faces that seemed very warm when they smiled.

Now that I'd identified Otto and Frieda, I was at a loss as to the rest of the table occupants. Who were these people with prominent foreheads, noses, and chins? Grandma's other sisters? What were their names? I was supposed to know...but didn't. Trying to find an entrée, I asked, "Who's the oldest sister?"

"What an impolite question to ask!" commented one sister sharply. She did not have Uncle Otto's warm smile. Neither did she pull me toward her for a kiss like Aunt Frieda. She made a face like Grandma when she tasted something that she didn't like.

"I'm the oldest one," said Aunt Frieda. She motioned around the table. "Then Paula; then Martha; then Lina, your grandma. Anni is the youngest, but she lives in Memphis. And Mathilde, who died, was the oldest." The unsmiling one who called me rude was Aunt Martha.

Uncle Otto looked at Aunt Martha and joked, "I sometimes forget who the boss is."

"Don't be ridiculous," said Aunt Martha.

Then a bald man with a mustache walked over. I had noticed him smoking cigars earlier with Grandpa and Uncle Max. He wore highly polished cowboy boots and a heavily starched bright white shirt. He put his hand on Aunt Martha's shoulder and said, "Who are you giving hell to now?"

Then everyone around me was speaking German. I could only stand there smiling, pretending to understand what was going on when I had no idea. I would have to wait until the next day to find out the name of the bald guy with the cowboy boots. When I described the boots, my sister knew exactly who I was talking about. He had three children who were sitting at our table.

"Did no one introduce you?" asked Grandma, making me wonder if, when she started speaking in German, it was as if I'd vanished, which I suppose I had.

Amy asked, "Is he a cowboy?"

Dad laughed. "No, he's in commodities. He just got back from Brazil." Amy and I played twenty questions about Mr. Cowboy Boots, eventually learning he was Aunt Martha's son Walter and a year older than Dad. Because he was in commodities, like his father before him, Uncle Walter had traveled many places, and was doing very well. Then Dad dropped the bomb. Walter, his older brother, and both of his parents had all been in a concentration camp.

The conversation paused as Amy and I tried to process this information. Until then, I had been under the impression that everyone who went to a concentration camp died. I wasn't sure what to ask.

Eventually, Grandma filled the silence with her version of a story appropriate for Amy and me. Grandma's sister Martha (the sourpuss) had moved to Amsterdam because her husband had been fired from his job at a bank in Berlin for being Jewish.

"Like Anne Frank," said Dad.

"What do you mean?" I asked.

"Anne Frank's family moved to Amsterdam. Lots of German

Jews moved to Amsterdam."

Grandma continued, "Eventually all the Jews in Holland were sent to Bergen-Belsen, a concentration camp."

Another moment of silence.

"My sister Martha and her whole family survived Bergen-Belsen. But they don't want to talk about it."

"What about Anne Frank?" asked Amy.

"Only her father survived. Everyone else in the family died."

Another moment of silence.

"Bergen-Belsen," I said the word out loud, trying to imitate the German pronunciation.

"A concentration camp," Amy said.

"Did Aunt Martha's family hide, too?"

"No," said Grandma. "They were very lucky to survive the camp. Very lucky!" Grandma said those words like she was still trying to convince herself that this was true. Some of her family had not been very lucky.

If I hadn't been so self-conscious, so afraid of my classmates' reactions, I might have told my class about Uncle Walter and Aunt Martha. I met relatives who were in the same place at the same time as Anne Frank.

But I couldn't do that. I couldn't really do the reading assignment. It wasn't that the language was so difficult. It wasn't even that I was afraid of how my classmates might react. It was my own reaction that scared me. I didn't want to let my imagination carry me to Anne Frank's secret attic. I didn't want to hide. I didn't want to write in a diary because I had no friends. I didn't want my life interrupted by world events out of my control. And I didn't want to contemplate my death in a cold place surrounded by guards, barbed wire, and machine guns. Or a gas chamber.

If I read the assigned passage at all, I read it at supersonic speed. And I never took down the blue cloth-bound book from Mom and Dad's shelf. Maybe I wanted to believe that if I never read through to the book's conclusion, Anne might have been lucky like Aunt Martha and Uncle Walter, might have made it to America, might have been at a party like the one at Aunt Hilda's.

CHAPTER FIFTEEN

Hamlin Beach

During the early years of my childhood, I saw little of my Aunt Lucie. She and Uncle Stan lived abroad first in Japan and then in England. She'd visit the farm for a week every summer or so. But in 1968, Stan was offered a job teaching Buddhism at Yale, a big job per Grandma. (I later learned that Stan had been considered for the position years earlier but was turned down because of a Jewish quota.) Lucie, Stan, and four-year-old David moved to New Haven, Connecticut. Dad and I looked on a map. New Haven was about the same distance from Spencerport as from where Aunt Hilda lived.

Coincidentally, Lucie's arrival back in the U.S. corresponded with the onset of puberty for me. While I understood the mechanics my body was about to undergo, I in no way felt eager or prepared. Mom still insisted I dress in hand-me-downs from a "big boned" cousin. These were well-made timeless clothes, and she didn't need to spend good money on a new skirt just because I wanted hot pink instead of navy blue. Now if I slimmed down, maybe I'd "need" something new. In addition to commenting on my weight, Mom thought I behaved like "a bull in a china shop," at-home messaging designed to reinforce "sit down and shut up," which was a regular refrain of teachers in the 1960s. I felt "Girls just wanna have fun!" as Cyndi Lauper wrote two decades later. I was not going to go gently from childhood, even if longed to be seen as mature and knowledgeable.

Aunt Lucie and David arrived for a week on the farm just before I was to start the sixth grade. Amy and I had just come back from overnight camp. Mom and Dad had sent us there to make Jewish friends. I failed. I never figured out who went to which school and what the established pecking orders were. I read *The Yearling* again. It was a thick volume and reading it took up a lot of time. I also borrowed comic books, something Mom otherwise forbade.

One day, Mom offered to take Lucie, David, Amy, and me to Hamlin Beach on Lake Ontario. One last beach day before school! Here is a photo I took before we piled into the car to go home at the end of the day.

Aunt Lucie, standing on the right, is wearing a red sun dress belted at the waist. She has on aviator sunglasses, and a book tucked under her arm that might be a biography of Golda Meir. Lucie is almost certainly wearing an Israeli sun hat. Later this

Left to right: Cousin David, Sister Amy, Mom and Aunt Lucie, summer 1968

same year, Dad took us all to Israel. Four sunhats arrived several months before the trip to help get us ready.

I was still too young to carry a book to the beach with me. I liked running in and out of the water, climbing the bluffs to the caves, and getting soft-serve ice cream cones. Sitting on the sand getting a suntan and reading a book were not for me. But I did want to use Mom's camera. This photo was one of my first experiments focusing people in a camera's frame. Maybe Kodak had just come out with their new Instamatic model, the kind where you didn't need to stretch the film from spindle A to B but could just drop in a cartridge and snap the back closed.

Hamlin Beach was less than ten miles from the oldest Kodak plant in Rochester. Starting a summer or two earlier, dead fish had begun to wash up on the beach all summer long. These were silver looking glistening things, perhaps five inches long. I remember being both sad and afraid of the carcasses. So many of them. Aunt Lucie picked one up by the tail and asked, "What happened here?"

"Ignore it. Fish die," Mom said.

David and Amy wanted to swim right away. Mom said she would watch them. I wanted to go look for the caves a bit west of the beach. Aunt Lucie said she'd join me. I told her about a time several weeks before camp when Aunt Erna joined us at Hamlin Beach. Seeing all the dead fish, she began to throw them back into the water. Then she announced she was not swimming here. Lucie and I smiled at each other. Then Lucie asked, "Have you heard of Rachel Carson?"

"Nope," I said.

"She wrote a book about how humans overuse chemicals and that this overuse can harm animals and plants."

When Mom opened the container to place a new film cartridge in her camera, the cartridge gave off a bad smell, a chemical smell. I visualized a school of silver fish swimming into those chemicals. "Yuck."

"It's a real problem."

Then she went on to ask me what I liked in school, what I liked doing after school, and who my friends were, easy questions to answer. I could tell my aunt was well-meaning and wanted to make a connection. But my failure to make Jewish friends over the summer was all I could think about.

Aunt Lucie must have noticed my reticence and attributed it to early-onset adolescence. She began talking about how difficult it was for her as a teen. Some of her story sounded like what I'd heard before from Aunt Hilda and Dad. Lucie had been kicked out of school in Germany and sent to Belgium. But her story was also different from Dad's. The teachers at her school in Belgium were nuns and pressured her to convert to Catholicism. Meanwhile, her aunt didn't understand children and treated all of them meanly. She had been miserable.

"Which aunt?" I asked.

"Come to think of it," Lucie continued without answering my question, "The first time your father and I went to the beach, we were in Belgium. Your father must have been about your age. Did he tell you about that?"

"I know he can't swim." We both giggled at this.

"Aunt Mathilde was Grandma's sister. We lived with her. She took us to the beach once, not too far from Dunkirk. Have you heard of it? There was a famous battle there."

I pointed to Lucie that we had to climb a set of steps to get to the cave. I didn't want to interrupt her story.

"I'd never seen the ocean before. In Berleburg we just had streams and lakes. I couldn't believe that all you could see was water. It looked endless."

We were standing in a small cave by now looking out on Lake Ontario, which to me looked endless. I knew Canada was on the other side of the lake but that was miles from here, much farther than I could see.

"We were all having such fun. The sand, the sea, the waves. Such fun." Lucie paused. She was looking out, but not seeing the same lake I was looking at. "And then, that awful Mathilde wanted us to nap under blankets. Who expects a teenager to take a nap on the beach? She knew nothing about children."

"This isn't the ocean," I said.

"But it is beautiful," Lucie said. Then she grabbed me in a bear hug. "You are a wonderful girl, bringing me here."

We walked back to rejoin Mom, Amy, and David. Amy and David were making sandcastles at the water's edge. Grandma had bought David a red pail for the task. He said he was making a castle that I'd never heard of, but one that he'd visited earlier in the summer before he moved from England to Connecticut. I went into the water by myself. There was a lifeguard on duty, so Mom said it was okay. Aunt Lucie sat down by Mom. Perhaps she read the Golda Meir book then.

When it was time to go, Mom said yes to me taking the picture. In the picture she seems to be attempting to smile. Maybe I hit the shutter too soon. Maybe she was giving me some other instruction. Or maybe she had not enjoyed the day at the beach as much as she'd hoped. Maybe she had counted on chatting with Lucie, and instead Lucie had joined me for a walk to the caves. It wouldn't have been lost on Mom what everyone in Dad's family said about me even before Lucie moved back to the U.S. I was Lucie's spitting image. Now here she was...and without a daughter. Mom could very well have found it a challenge to smile.

Here is a photo of children who seem to have no difficulty at all smiling. These are radiant children on their first trip to the ocean. It is the summer of 1939, the summer just after *Kristallnacht*, the summer before the Nazis invaded Belgium. These children are from the left: ten-year-old Paul, my dad; fourteen-year-old Lucie; eighteen-year-old cousin Lore; and twelve-year-old Hilda. I'm not sure if this photo was taken before or after nap time. Of course, nap time – either cruel or an outdated rule of safety – was only a small part of the story.

Left to right: Paul, Lucie, Lore, and Hilda, Summer 1939

CHAPTER SIXTEEN

Lapwings

Mathilde Lindheim and her daughter Lore sit at a table for six at the outdoor terrace of the Seaside Cafe in Westend, Belgium. Mathilde is proud of the sophisticated young woman Lore has become. At age eighteen, Lore is self-composed and self-contained, content to read a novel while Mathilde savors a cup of coffee. The other four – her not so self-composed nieces and nephew – have returned to their spot in the sand. Mathilde loves looking out towards the horizon, that place – how far away is it? – where the sea meets the air. Between here and there, the sea laps the sand, waves crest and fall, and there, there, is the line where everything seems to merge. Mathilde takes another very small sip of her coffee, so delightful. She cannot bear to drink it quickly; she wants this quiet moment to last and blend into another one. Mathilde has pulled off a vacation!

It is July 1939. Mathilde's husband Hugo said he couldn't get away. She took the children and left him in Mechelen with his work. He is always working. When he's not arranging matters at the furniture factory, he's reading the newspapers or talking business and politics with his associates. What can she do? As he likes to remind her, vacations, and other fine things, those don't come free.

Mathilde doesn't consider herself, or Hugo for that matter, to be political. But, as Hugo always says, politics drives business. If the

Nazis hadn't made him sell his factory in Frankfurt, they'd be enjoying their wonderful old house on Lersnerstraße. What a beautiful house with its magnificent moldings and high ceilings, wallpapers selected by Mathilde, and specially designed furniture made at Hugo's factory, the largest furniture factory in Frankfurt. It was a bit of a brag. But why not? The Lindheims had a lot to brag about!

That was then.

Mechelen, Belgium, has small-town charms, but none of the excitement of a real city. Frankfurt had the Schumann Theater, with different musical shows almost every night. There were modern artists painting and glittering costume balls. The Jewish community was large with several synagogues, not just one small building with an ancient rabbi. Not that Mathilde had ever been particularly religious. In Mechelen, the largest building in the city is a church. Some days it seems half the women in town are dressed in nuns' habits. And the languages! Mathilde's schoolgirl French is not enough to carry on a conversation more profound than asking the price of beets. The French speakers don't want to speak Flemish, and vice versa. No one wants to speak German (although Mathilde suspects many people can speak it). She can't blame them. Most Belgians are still angry with the Germans for the Great War, and everyone is worried about Hitler's schemes. Mathilde could tell them a thing or two about Hitler. After all, she lived under the Nazis; she is here because of the Nazis.

Mathilde takes another sip of her coffee, cold now. Then she looks past Lore out to the sand. Yes, the poor refugees, as she calls her nieces and nephew, are still there, doing what she instructed them to do, lying on their blankets covered with their towels, trying to keep from getting sunburns or drowning themselves.

Ach no, no, no. Mathilde should not be taking care of young children anymore. The youngest of the bunch, her nephew Paul, still wets his bed. How her sister could send her a bed-wetter, she has no idea. The girls are not so bad, especially Doris, who follows instructions from time to time.

Mathilde takes the final sip of her coffee and scans the horizon. Where is it, that illusive horizon? How far? Ten miles? Mathilde pictures her doctor smiling and saying, "You cannot live without breathing. You might as well enjoy it."

One child is plenty. How many times did she say this to Hugo when he suggested they try for another? Mathilde was the oldest girl in a family of twelve. Maybe she didn't help raise her older brothers, or even the next two siblings born right after her, but that still left six! She was always wiping a nose, tying a pair of boots, ironing a dress, combing someone's hair, or helping someone learn how to write their last name, B-A-C-H-E-N-H-E-I-M-E-R – 12 letters! Why did they have to have such a long name?

It's *deja vu*, as the French say. She's got Lucie, Hilda, Doris, and Paul, the poor refugees, country bumpkins all, just when Lore is finally able to act like an adult. They are making her crazy, just when she wants to enjoy her last peaceful year or two with Lore.

Mathilde squints at the horizon. Could she swim that far, swim away from poor Doris? Poor Doris! Mathilde can't avoid giving her the news forever. She must tell her. She'll have to face the weeping, the deflation on her face, and who knows what else.

Mathilde takes in the kids again. Yes, Doris is the most sensitive of the bunch. She's not loud or demanding. She pays attention to what is going on. She tries to follow the rules. There, Doris is looking at Mathilde. Mathilde lifts her hand and waves at Doris.

The other three, the Krebs siblings, are starting to disobey. Lucie is digging in the sand, her shoulders uncovered. Paul is lying on his side, no blankets, watching Hilda tickling Doris' feet and making her squirm.

They are all of them trying to have fun. This is a vacation, after all. They seem happy. Are they happy? When should Mathilde break up this happiness and tell Doris?

Maybe Mathilde should go to the sand and tickle Doris too. Let her have a long, good laugh, and then when the laughing dies down, break the awful news.

Mathilde can't remember now how she learned of her own father's death when she was the exact same age as Doris, just fourteen. It seems so long ago. And the way her mother asked Mathilde to help, telling her it was her duty (just like now, she has taken in these children because Mother would have told her it was her duty, would have been furious otherwise). But looking at Doris now, she sees a girl, a girl laughing with her cousins, a happy girl. A girl at the beach. Mathilde hates to ruin this vacation. They all deserve a vacation, don't they?

While Mathilde can't remember hearing the words, "Your father died," she does remember Father being sick. He never seemed strong and vigorous, like Hugo. He always had to watch out, to take care. He seemed like an old man, though he was only 46 when he died from a heart attack.

Is it just her memory, or did it rain every day that summer of 1906? Mathilde shivers a bit remembering the damp and cold. She would lace the boots of the younger children to go out into the rain. How many times did her youngest sister Anni kick her? She wanted to slap that girl more than once.

Mathilde should have been like Doris, smiling and joking, playing with cousins. Mathilde should have been allowed to have fun. Mathilde wishes the world were not so hard.

Why did Julius, Mathilde's brother, Doris' father, die? She really didn't understand the letter her sister-in-law sent. Perhaps she was too distraught to make sense. Liver cancer. How could a man as invincible seeming as Julius, a man who fought on in the Great War even after being shot in the chest, die at age 52? His heart was not weak like Father's. He had been strong and healthy when she last saw him two years earlier. How could he have lost his health so quickly? Could it have been from the beatings? If your liver is pummeled, can that give you cancer?

Poor Doris, the last she saw her father he was being ordered out of his house seven months ago now on *Kristallnacht*, last November. Was Julius beaten that night? If not, when? Where? What happened to her poor brother? Her mother's favorite.

Mathilde tries to breathe but finds a catch in her throat. Mathilde has been good to Doris. She knows she has, even if some days she lacks patience. There was that beautiful cake that Mathilde made for Doris' birthday, the one with raspberry jam. They all – she, Hugo, Lore, and the rest of them – sang "Happy Birthday" to her. They gave her cards. They laughed. Mathilde tried to make it up to her niece that she wasn't home with her mother, father, and siblings.

Mathilde looks again out to sea. The horizon line, that blur where the water and the air meet, is still out there, far away, or maybe not so far.

Lore looks up at the sound of birds chirping, and notices how they have just landed on the sand. "See the curly feathers coming out of the back of their heads? I think they are Lapwings."

Mathilde can't see any plumage, but she hears short bursts of sounds as if the birds are commenting to one another. Perhaps they are saying, "The best fish are over here." Or, "My plumage is nicer than yours!" Or perhaps just "Here I am!" like when Lore was a baby. "Here I am, alive!"

"Lapwings?" asks Mathilde. "Who taught you about lapwings?"

"There was a picture in our hotel room of one. Didn't you look?"

"I guess not. I guess I was distracted."

"Don't worry, Mother, now you know! My cousins are playing in the water," Lore points. "Should we join them?"

"Yes," Mathilde says, standing up. "We're on vacation. Let's show them a good time."

CHAPTER SEVENTEEN

The War Correspondent

By the time I was in my teens, I had questions for Grandma and Grandpa about Germany almost every time we got together. In school, history was far and away my favorite subject. While classmates complained about memorizing dates, I visualized a ladder of human time on earth. Dates were rungs on the ladder that corresponded with stories. I loved a good story.

With the backdrop of America losing men in Vietnam to no discernable end, I wanted to know how Grandpa felt about being on the losing side in World War I. Grandma hated talk of war, and Grandpa's English was lacking, so I learned a lot more about Germany's depression in the 1920s than I did about Grandpa's service to the Kaiser. (Per Dad, Grandpa served on both the Eastern and Western fronts as a replacement soldier.)

I heard a lot about Grandma and Grandpa's lovely but cut-short honeymoon because the suitcase of money they'd brought for expenses didn't last long. Then I heard about their wonderful house in Berleburg, Grandma's trousseau that she spent years embroidering, the prosperous cattle business, their friends both Jewish and Gentile, parties, good food, and celebrations, all lost because of that madman Hitler and his followers.

I could see my grandparents were conflicted. They had to hate Germany: it had sent them fleeing, left them penniless, and killed off beloved family members. But before Hitlertime, as Grandma called it, there were good memories, love, warmth, hope. They were loyal Germans. It was hard for them to reconcile life before, life during, and now this chapter they were living with me in a different country with a new language.

Dad, on the other hand, had not one good word for his country of origin. In fact, Dad had not one good word for his continent of origin. To him, every country in Europe had a deep-rooted antisemitic history. Between the aristocracy and the church, children grew up blaming the Jews of Europe for their problems. Individuals who were kind to Jews were few and far between. If he never went back to Europe, that would be fine with him. He still couldn't sleep through the night. So what if the castle in Berleburg was pretty? So what if they had a nice house? You could find pretty and nice anywhere.

Most of my conversations with Grandma and Grandpa took place in their kitchen. Grandma needed to keep her hands busy with something: peeling apples, washing dishes, stirring a pot of something on the stove, darning socks. Grandpa played board games with Amy and me: Chutes and Ladders, Checkers, or Mill. Grandpa was only allowed to beat us once or twice before Grandma yelled at him to let us win.

Part of the reason that I rarely won Mill was because I was always thinking of my next question. What were they doing while Dad and his sisters were in Belgium? How did they feel? Tell me again what happened at the embassy; I still don't understand. The American doctor was a Nazi?

"We had bad luck," Grandma said. "If our appointment with the American Consulate in Stuttgart had been in February or March instead of May 1940, we could have gotten to the children. We could have immigrated from Belgium. That was our plan."

Grandpa closed his mill, and I lost the game. I didn't mind.

Grandma continued. "But our appointment was in May. Hitler

invaded Belgium on May 10, 1940. It was war. There was no way to find out if our children were alive or dead."

Grandma's anxiety from May 1940 had never really quieted. Her voice quavered and it made the hair on my arms stand up. If someone had asked me to run out of the room, I'm not sure I would have been able to get up. Grandma was stuck in Germany. Dad was stuck in Belgium. And I was glued to the kitchen chair.

Some months later, Aunt Hilda was visiting. She tried to engage Dad about his feelings while he was in Belgium. She said she had been sad and afraid and lonely. She was worried that she'd never see her parents again. I looked at Dad and wondered what he'd say. He was wearing his poker face. Maybe he'd say nothing at all.

But then Dad found his voice, "May 10, 1940: We were awakened in the middle of the night to Nazi planes flying overhead. They knocked out most of the Belgian Air Force before they got any planes off the ground...." All eyes turned to Dad. I was proud and impressed by his authoritative tone, as if he had spent May 1940 in Belgium as a war correspondent instead of an eleven-year-old boy.

Aunt Hilda and the rest of us turned toward Dad as he began talking.

Chapter Eighteen

Walking Toward Dunkirk

Paul heard a knock at the door. Aunt Mathilde went downstairs. She didn't let the person in, so Paul looked out the window. He wondered what they were saying to each other. He wondered if the neighbor, or whoever it was, knew what had happened the previous night. It had been terrifying. Luftwaffe planes strafed Mechelen. The war against Belgium had begun. How would it end? Paul's whole life people had spoken to him about war. Father and his uncles had been soldiers for the Kaiser. But now, young German men didn't want Jewish soldiers in their ranks. They hated the Jews. What did they want with Belgium?

Soon Aunt Mathilde came back upstairs. She told Paul, his sisters, and his cousins that Mechelaars were leaving their homes. They had been through German invasions before. They would not be safe. Aunt Mathilde said they might have to leave. What if the Nazis dropped bombs on their street? What would they do?

"But where are they going?" Paul asked.

"They are walking towards France," said Aunt Mathilde.

"Why France?" asked Hilda.

"The French have a big army. They should be able to hold back the Germans. We can find safety behind the lines."

Aunt Mathilde didn't seem to know how far France was, but more concerning, she didn't know what had happened to Uncle

Hugo. He hadn't been home in over a day. He'd been arrested before, taken in for questioning from his office. Someone in the Mechelen police department no doubt had a list of Jews. But what they'd want with Hugo, or where they might take him, Mathilde hated to consider the possibilities. Lore didn't want to leave the house without him. Who could blame her? But Mathilde's mind was set. With or without Hugo they were leaving in the morning. It wasn't safe here anymore.

As if reading Mathilde's mind, Lucie said, "It isn't safe here. Maybe we should leave immediately." As if to underscore her point, Luftwaffe planes flew low overhead, and the house vibrated. Paul didn't disagree with Lucie – he was afraid – but he wondered how his parents would find them in France.

Lore said she would pack a suitcase for her father, but Aunt Mathilde said no. Just the basics. "Pack only what you can carry in your rucksack. We'll take the bicycle and carry our food on it. Don't pack too much."

"What about Father?" Lore had tears in her eyes.

"Let's start packing. Maybe he'll arrive home before we're done," Aunt Mathilde said again. Paul didn't know what to think. Did his aunt know the way to France? Where would they go in France? How would Mother and Father find him? Paul wished his parents were with him. Mother would tell him what to pack. It's May. Summer was coming. How long would they be gone? Paul pulled clothes out of his drawer. He put underwear and socks in the rucksack. Then he tossed in a rag-tag assortment of his clothes.

On Sunday morning, May 12th, they set out: Paul, Aunt Mathilde, Cousin Lore, Cousin Doris, Lucie, and Hilda. Lucie and Hilda argued almost immediately about who should push the bicycle. They were so busy arguing with each other that Paul couldn't hear the discussion amongst several of the neighbors about which way to walk to avoid the Germans. The Belgian Army was, if Paul heard right, trying to hold the line, less than 15 miles away. How long could it hold? Could the Belgians fight back against the Germans?

Were the French on their way? What about the English? Could several armies together push back the Germans?

Paul looked around the streets as they began to walk out of town. He followed his sisters, who followed Aunt Mathilde. His cousins Lore and Doris right behind him. He could hear Lore crying, probably because Uncle Hugo hadn't come home. They joined a long line of people walking. Some had bicycles, some wheelbarrows, some just bags filled with clothes. Paul had never seen anything like it.

The family slept their first night on the road in a small church near Berg. Paul wondered if they'd walked more than ten miles. In the morning, they ate the last of their sandwiches packed at home. They still had a bit of provisions – cheese and boiled eggs – but Paul wondered what they would do after that. He pushed thoughts of his parents from his head. Otherwise, he'd start crying and he wasn't sure he'd be able to stop. Aunt Mathilde wouldn't have anything more reassuring to say than they were doing the best they could. How far to France, he wondered.

On May 13th, Paul slowed down his walking pace to watch a dog-fight between a V-formation of three RAF Hurricanes versus the Luftwaffe Finger Four. Two of the RAF Hurricanes received fire. Paul watched two British airmen parachute from one plane into a nearby field. One man's parachute didn't open properly. He thudded to the ground. The other two British planes turned around and the Luftwaffe gave chase. When Paul heard explosions, they came from far away. Paul hoped the British were able to outfly the Nazis or shoot them down. Hilda just stared at the parachutes in the field, unable to look away. Aunt Mathilde told the children that they had to keep walking, that there was nothing they could do for the men, that the Red Cross would come. Hilda and Doris were both sobbing. Eventually, Lore put her arm over Doris's shoulder, and Lucie hugged Hilda. Then the group moved on. Paul wished someone hugged him but no one did.

The good thing and the bad thing about the Belgian country-side, Paul realized, was how flat it was. Paul could walk in even measured steps. There were no hills to tire him out. But there were no peaks to look down from. It was unclear if they were making any progress at all. Just after a small sign for the town of Aalst, Red Cross workers had set up tables where they were serving soup. Aunt Mathilde said the soup would be their main meal this day. The family ate near the Red Cross workers in a group with many others.

On May 14th, the family was handed sandwiches and hot water for dinner at another Red Cross stop by the side of the road. A man that Aunt Mathilde had spoken to earlier in the day encouraged them to walk to Oudenaarde, a town he said was large enough so there might still be provisions for sale. After finishing their sandwiches, they continued walking. As the last of the light faded from the sky, the group settled down in a field. They hadn't made it to the Oudenaarde. But Aunt Mathilde tried to calm the children by telling them that they should be able to walk there by the time shops opened in the morning. Paul put his head on his rucksack with his coat as protection for his back. As he tried to sleep, he overheard a man say, "The British will save us."

Another man responded, "From your lips to God's ear."

A woman said, "If the British don't save us, we'll die. The French army is nowhere to be seen. What happened to them?"

Paul saw French soldiers earlier that day, lots of them. Maybe one hundred. Unfortunately, they were being taken prisoner by the Germans. None of them had their weapons. They walked with their heads down. Not a one looked at Paul. He wondered what was wrong with them. Why hadn't the French beat back the Germans? And how far were they from the border?

In Oudenaarde, the following morning, Aunt Mathilde sent Lore to buy bread. She was able to buy only a small loaf. They divided up the loaf for breakfast and ate it without either butter, jam, or something hot to drink. The people that Aunt Mathilde spoke to said to go to Dunkirk. They should head toward the coast. Dunkirk. Dunkirk. Everyone is headed to Dunkirk. The family followed the signs in that direction.

About a mile out of Oudenaarde, the Luftwaffe was back. *Buzzz*, then *Rat-a-tat-tat*. Paul could see no soldiers around at all. Were they firing on civilians? Paul noticed three women on the other side of the road. Their heads were covered and they wore black habits. Nuns. They had stopped walking. Paul, meanwhile dove into the ditch as he heard more guns being fired from overhead. The nuns held up wooden crosses towards the plane. Paul watched them pray. But he couldn't hear them. The firing was so close. Paul put his hands over his head and closed his eyes. He felt nothing as he heard the planes continuing past his spot. *Rat-a-tat-tat* again in the distance. Paul wondered, *Did the women dive toward the ditch at the last minute, or were they gunned down?* He hesitated. He didn't want to look.

"Get MOVING right now!" Mathilde snapped. "Let's go! They may come back!"

That night Aunt Mathilde didn't let them stop to sleep. They walked all night long. Paul was in some state between consciousness and sleep. He thought he heard Father telling him to scan the horizon. Scan the horizon. Stay with the group. Watch your comrades. Keep your center of gravity low. Paul imagined that Father was here with him walking to Dunkirk. Father knew Belgium. Father was here. Father survived. Father wanted Paul to survive. Scan the horizon. Watch your comrades. Keep your center of gravity low. Keep moving.

In the morning, another small Red Cross table, staffed by two workers, offered the family coffee and bread. Paul wanted to eat it, but his stomach hurt. He took a few bites then passed the rest of the bread to Hilda when Aunt Mathilde was looking away. He didn't want her to get mad at him. He noticed some people walking past them, but also a few people looking like him – poor refugees – walking back from where he just came. This was, Paul later mused, when he first realized that they were not going to make it to Dunkirk. Germans were everywhere. People were confused as to where to go. Aunt Mathilde made them keep walking.

That night there was no food for dinner. They slept in a hay loft near Anzegum. For the first time, Aunt Mathilde apologized. She had no food to offer anyone. She had no idea what was next, where they would go in the morning. She was sorry. All they could do was keep walking. Walking to safety. That is, if safety could be found.

Paul's stomach was still hurting. He wanted to drink water. But they had no water, and he had no glass. Why was he so thirsty? The next thing Paul knew, he vomited. He was supposed to be going to sleep. He was supposed to be nestled in the straw in the hay loft. But Paul vomited on his sister Hilda. Now Hilda was crying. Crying and crying. Her hair. Her hair was disgusting. How could she wash her hair? She needed to wash her hair. Paul said he was sorry. He was sorry.

"I'm sorry, too," said Aunt Mathilde. She had located scissors in her rucksack. "Turn around," she said to Hilda, and then she lopped off Hilda's braids.

"My hair!" Hilda cried. "My hair!"

"There is no other option," Aunt Mathilde said unsentimentally. Paul wanted to hug Hilda, to make her feel better, but she pushed him away. Paul's stomach was still hurting. He didn't know what to do.

Even though Paul didn't remember falling asleep that night, in the morning he woke up to German, a gruff soldier's German. "There may be people hidden here. Where?" Paul heard objects – Guns? Shovels? – pressing into the straw in the barn below the hay loft. There was only one cow in the barn. Would the soldiers come up to the hay loft? Would they be found? Paul held his breath. He pinched himself, hoping it was a dream. It was not. Then he heard a soldier climb up the ladder to the hayloft. He heard the poking sound again. If the soldier came into the hayloft, they would be found. What would happen to them then? Would they be taken as prisoners? Sent back to Germany? Shot on the spot? Paul continued to pinch his arm. Dream? Dream? No.

"Empty," he heard the soldier say.

Paul wanted to sigh, wanted to sit up, but it was still too soon. He knew he had to wait until the soldiers left the barn. He had to be silent. So silent. Invisible.

Finally, Paul heard the barn door open, then close. He heard German being spoken outside the barn. Yes, it was outside the barn now. Still, he waited. Silent. Invisible.

That evening, miraculously, the family made it to Menin. France, they were told, was across the bridge. The bridge was guarded by the Germans, who were not letting anyone go through. Or they could continue to Dunkirk, where the British were still fighting with the Germans. Dunkirk was another two or three days of walking. Aunt Mathilde told the children that in the morning, they'd see what happened. In the meantime, they all had to sleep. They were at yet another farmer's house for the night. Paul wondered if Father would let strangers sleep in his barn. Paul thought he would. Father would help people.

Hilda and Lucie pumped water for the family and some French soldiers who were garrisoned at the same farm. Paul's stomach was feeling better. He ate bread and water for dinner. He didn't throw up. Paul overheard Hilda tell Lucie how she felt safer knowing the French soldiers were close. They would have no problems tonight. Paul wished Hilda would sleep next to him, but since he'd thrown up on her, she kept close to Lucie. Paul took a spot next to Aunt Mathilde. It seemed like he'd been walking a month or two. But it was still May. May 1940.

Paul awoke to German again. He understood the soldier's command. The soldier was asking someone – the farmer or his wife? – about French soldiers. "Where are the French soldiers?"

"Nein. Non. Nichts," the farmer's wife said. "Nein." Paul wondered what would happen if the German soldiers came into the barn.

"Bicycles?" asked the soldier.

"Nein," said the farmer's wife again. Paul had seen bicycles the night before. What would happen if the German soldiers found the bicycles? Had the farmer's wife hidden them somewhere since last night, when they were just behind the barn?

The German soldier must have trusted the woman because Paul heard his footsteps going in the other direction. Once again, they had been lucky. What would have happened to them if German soldiers came in the barn?

An hour later, Paul and his family were in a queue to cross the bridge to France. The line wasn't moving for now, but Aunt Mathilde said she was hopeful. It was just over there. From France they could get word to the children's parents. From France she could find Hugo. Everything would be better in France. It was just over there. Paul was silent, waiting, hoping, waiting.

Then he spotted another Luftwaffe plane. Would they be bombed right here along the border? Was this it? There was nowhere to take cover. Not again. This was terrible. But when the plane came closer, it dropped leaflets, not bullets. Little pieces of paper fell from the sky. Paul picked up a leaflet written in Flemish and read it.

> *The Belgian army has capitulated.*
>
> *You are now cut off.*
>
> *More than 500,000 soldiers have deposited their arms.*
>
> *As the Poles in Poland, the Norwegians in Norway, the French and the Belgians in Belgium had the honor of holding the positions so that the English had time to retreat. You must give up your arms or die. You will better serve yourself and your country by living for Belgium rather than by dying for England!*

Propaganda was Paul's first thought. He had recently learned that word. This could not be true. Or could it?

Lucie picked up a different leaflet in written in French, and with a map of the country. It showed Dunkirk, Bruges, and Lille as *Les Alliés*. The rest of the territory on the map was marked *Les Allemands*! Lucie ripped it up. "Nazi lies!" But as she said this, groups of people who were in front of them in the bridge line turned around.

"This cannot be," said Hilda.

Lore started crying. Then they all cried. Lore, Doris, Paul, Hilda, Lucie, and Aunt Mathilde. They had walked all this way for nothing. Paul looked around. Even though people who stood between him and the bridge were leaving, he couldn't see the other side. He couldn't see safety. Where France should be was now Germany. Germany was certainly not safe. He knew that much. He might only be eleven. He might be smaller than when he left Mechelen, having walked all this way, vomited, and eaten very little, but he wanted to go on. He wanted to walk to safety. He didn't want to think about what the Germans would do to him. A country run by Brockmeier, his old nasty teacher, and Brockmeier's ilk. Would he ever see his parents again? Were they still alive? Where were they and could they find him?

"I'm sorry to say this, children," said Aunt Mathilde after she wiped her face with her hanky, "but it is time to return home to our house in Mechelen." Paul listened to the first part of her sentence, but then turned away. He had never felt at home in Mechelen. He had never felt free since Hitler. He would never feel safe.

CHAPTER NINETEEN

Thanksgiving in Connecticut

Once Aunt Lucie, Uncle Stan, and David moved to Connecticut, we began going there for family parties and holidays. Like Aunt Hilda, Aunt Lucie wasn't coming to Spencerport except maybe for a week in July or August. Dad wasn't buying four plane tickets to New York or New Haven, so every few months, when there was a family party or get together, we set off by car for the east. Dad was usually happy driving the New York State Thruway through central New York, even into Albany, but once we got within a hundred miles of metro New York, the complaining about congestion and city drivers would commence. It turned out the Connecticut drivers on the Wilbur Cross Expressway were no fans of their turn signals. Between the narrow lanes, curved roads, and trees overhanging the signs, Dad was twitching with frustration by the time we arrived at Aunt Lucie's.

Dad gladly accepted a Scotch from Uncle Stanley. "May as well," he said, as he sank into the brand new deep green velvet couch and pronounced it com-fort-A-ble, poking a bit of fun at his mother's accent. I didn't really know Uncle Stanley. He always had work when Aunt Lucie visited the farm, or so he said.

"Stan!" Lucie shrieked. "It's not even four o'clock! You'll get drunk."

Uncle Stan and Dad clinked glasses. Then Uncle Stan started talking about his students, who had been to the house the night before to discuss their various lines of research. "Back when I was a student in Japan, we would never have left the professor's house if there was still Scotch in the bottle."

"Nice bottle," Dad commented.

"Why don't the rest of us get snacks in the kitchen," Aunt Lucie suggested. "Let's have a little sandwich, shall we?"

"We won't be able to eat dinner if we have sandwiches," said Mom.

"Maybe some cookies then? We have the most wonderful Italian bakeries in New Haven." Aunt Lucie knew Mom. Mom liked coffee and cookies. Aunt Lucie, David, Amy, and I had open-faced sandwiches followed by cookies. Occasionally, I'd hear Dad and Uncle Stan laughing. It seemed like we were having separate parties.

Although Mom said we didn't need dinner, Aunt Lucie insisted we go to their favorite Chinese restaurant. We all ate tons of food, many dishes that I'd never heard of. Uncle Stanley wrote out our order in Chinese. He said he couldn't speak the language, but he knew how to write the names of the dishes he wanted: fiery pork, beef with vegetables, and a few seafood dishes. He and Aunt Lucie also did a lot of bowing to the restaurant staff. No one bowed at Chinese restaurants in Rochester, I said. Aunt Lucie said in Chinese culture you bowed to show thanks and appreciation. When I tried to bow to her, she smiled and bowed back.

Back at the house after dinner, we all sat on the com-fort-A-ble couches in the living room. Uncle Stan took out the Scotch again. "Time to settle in for the evening," he said. "Who's joining me?" Uncle Stan looked in my direction and asked, "How about some Amaretto. Sweet almond liquor?"

"I like almonds," I said.

"I'll bet you do," said Stan, "One glass coming up." Then upon handing me a small cordial glass filled to the top, he said, "Sip it slowly."

"So, what did you think of your trip to Israel?" Uncle Stan asked me.

"It was great," I said honestly. "It was my first time out of the country, other than to the Canadian side of Niagara Falls. I loved it."

"Ah," said Uncle Stan who seemed to study me now, "A Zionist like your father."

Now I was confused. Uncle Stan's tone seemed mocking. I'd imagined him treating me like one of his college students, with the Amaretto and his serious-sounding inquiry about my trip to Israel. Wasn't everyone in my family a Zionist? Everyone talked about Israel, bought bonds, planted trees, hushed the room when the name Israel came over radio or television airwaves. It was, I thought, who my family was, just like we all had dark hair, skinny legs, and ate open-faced wurst sandwiches with mustard and pickle.

"Did you not drive by a Palestinian refugee camp? Didn't you see how poorly the Palestinians were treated?" asked Uncle Stan. "Like second-class citizens, no?"

I opened my mouth. I wanted to say something about our visit to the West Bank, how I observed the outrage of Palestinians in Hebron. How I had been afraid. But I couldn't seem to formulate a sentence.

Dad must have seen my look of confusion. Or maybe he and Uncle Stan had already had this argument earlier in the day. Dad said, "Israel is the only democracy in the region. And it's not like any of the neighboring Arab countries treat their Jews with respect." When Stanley tried to reframe the debate by describing how his colleagues in Japan thought about events in the Middle East, Dad wouldn't be talked down. Dad concluded asking, "How can a self-respecting Jew not support Israel?" Or maybe he said, "Only a self-hating Jew wouldn't support Israel!" Or even, "What are you, an antisemitic Jew?"

Scotch was poured. Scotch was drunk. Dad and Stan grew no closer to ceding a point.

Eventually, Aunt Lucie joined the scrum, seconding every point that Uncle Stan made in a higher decibel range. I made only a remark or two before I understood that I would need to quote the *New York Times* or a thick historical volume to be respected even slightly by Lucie and Stan. Dad didn't care that his sister and brother-in-law didn't take his comments seriously. Or, if he did, he showed it by raising his voice, not backing down.

When Uncle Stan got up to refill liquor glasses, Aunt Lucie made the oddest comment. "You know who you remind me of?" she said to Dad accusatorily.

"I can't read your mind," Dad said sarcastically.

"Hugo Lindheim! That's who."

"Hugo Lindheim? What do you have against that poor man?" asked Dad.

"Who is Hugo Lindheim?" I asked. Dad and Lucie glowered at each other, both of them scrunching up their eyebrows and looking down their noses. "Who is Hugo Lindheim?" I asked again.

"A capitalist with his head in the sand," said Aunt Lucie angrily. "We had to live with him in Belgium."

"Hugo Lindheim," I repeated, trying to figure out exactly who he was.

Finally, Aunt Lucie answered me. "Mathilde Lindheim was Grandma's sister. Hugo was her husband. He thought he knew everything because he was rich. Just like your father. Rich people think they know everything."

Dad rich? I thought. *Your house is bigger. Your furniture is nicer. You lived in England and Japan. Dad's been in Spencerport all these years.*

Aunt Lucie had a lot more to say about the Lindheims, though I never got the connection to Israel, if there was one. While Grandma and Dad were clear that the Nazis had ruined their lives, Lucie seemed to blame her aunt and uncle for ruining her life. Aunt Mathilde knew nothing about teenagers. She treated Lucie worse than the help. She never said a kind word to her. She said nothing when Cousin Lore acted stuck up. And Uncle Hugo knew nothing about politics. If he had.... Lucie quieted for a split second.

"What happened to them?" I asked.

CHAPTER TWENTY

Back to Berleburg

When Dad wanted to, he could capture an audience with a story or joke. He liked a good punchline or ironic twist. But I often had a hard time getting Dad's attention. Aunt Lucie, at least when we spent time together, seemed happy to answer my interminable questions. She seemed eager for me to learn about her favorite subjects. Aunt Lucie had an advanced degree in Japanese Art History. She valued clarity, beauty, and elegance. She taught college students and was used to dealing with youngsters who couldn't quite articulate what they wanted to know. While she had a memory for chronology, she always referred me to Dad if I asked a question about something political or military. But because she was older than Dad, she remembered things in Germany going from normal to bad to worse. Dad never really had normal.

When it came to telling stories about the years in Belgium, Lucie's version of things started and ended with the same headline, "I thought I was going to be left behind to die."

As she spoke, I wondered, *What about school?* She, along with Dad and Aunt Hilda, reported having excellent educations in Belgium. And what about that day at the beach? Dad may have minimized his fears, but surely Lucie was exaggerating how terrible things were.

In my sophomore year in high school, I got training in rhetoric.

My European History teacher recruited me for our school's nascent Model U.N. Club. She encouraged me to lead our first delegation. She pushed me to organize and prioritize the points I wished to make. I started to understand the roles that exaggeration, rhetorical questions, fake naivety, sarcasm, and the like played in everyday discourse. I realized I could use these tools to my benefit.

I wanted to tell Aunt Lucie about the Model U.N. Club. She was always asking me about school, and I hadn't had much good to say about my freshman year. When we went to her house for Thanksgiving during my sophomore year, I'd already attended my first Model U.N., at Harvard no less. "How wonderful!" She punctuated my narrative about my role as Japan's representative on the Security Council. In an overnight emergency session, I had helped write and persuade others to pass a resolution to address a plane hijacking. Next stop, I thought, world peace.

"I can see you are passionate!" Aunt Lucie added, "Though politics is a dirty business. A very dirty business. But maybe it will help you get into college." If Mom had been there for that conversation, she might have called Aunt Lucie's remark a back-handed compliment. It wasn't the first time Aunt Lucie had said something in my presence that seemed flattering at first but was ultimately critical.

I segued to Aunt Lucie's time in Belgium, perhaps by asking her what she studied in Belgium when she was fifteen, the age I was. As I anticipated, she gave me an earful about awful Aunt Mathilde, miserly Uncle Hugo, and stuck-up cousin Lore. "I was sure they were going to leave me behind."

"When?" I asked. "When were they going to leave you behind?"

"I don't know. The fall of 1940 after your father and Hilda went back to Berleburg. I was stuck alone with those awful people."

"But why didn't you go back to Berleburg with Dad and Hilda?"

"I was too old."

"I don't understand."

"I was sixteen. I was no longer a child according to the Nazis."

"I still don't understand."

"I couldn't get a visa. Your father, Hilda, and Cousin Doris all went home. I was stuck."

Things were starting to click into place. Lucie's birthday was in August. Dad, Aunt Hilda, and Cousin Doris must have returned to Germany in the fall of 1940. They were children traveling with children's visas. Grandma had to pull strings to get Lucie a visa. Grandma had told me that story. But Lucie was left behind in Belgium while Grandma pulled strings. This was what Lucie was still so upset about.

"I knew if those miserable people got visas to Switzerland, or somewhere, they'd leave me behind. They treated me like a poor refugee, a second-class citizen, someone they had to put up with. They would have loved to leave me behind."

"But you were a teenager," I said gently.

"Maybe they would have found an orphanage."

"Good thing Grandma pulled strings," I said.

Lucie nodded. Grandma's "coup," as she described it to me, was that she persuaded the mayor of Berleburg, a childhood friend of Grandpa's, to write a letter on Lucie's behalf. Grandma told the mayor that if he allowed one sixteen-year-old girl back to Berleburg for several weeks, the entire family would get visas and leave forever. He would be recognized for helping to get rid of the Jews. All this, per Grandma, was a bit of a bluff because the family still didn't have visas to go to the U.S.

"I thought I was going crazy," Lucie said. "I had nowhere to go, nothing to do, and just the relatives for company. I have never felt more alone in my life. You can't imagine."

I was imagining though. I pictured Lucie in a small room pretending to read a book. She was cold, had drawn blankets all around herself. Maybe I pictured Lucie like this because often when I felt lonely and isolated at home, I sat in bed reading or pretending to read. I felt cold.

"But eventually, my visa arrived. I don't think my aunt and uncle believed I'd make it back to Berleburg. Aunt Mathilde took me to a store and bought me a brand-new traveling outfit."

Uncle Hugo trained and quizzed Aunt Lucie on how to answer the questions that she would certainly get asked. "A beautiful girl like you, surely you are educated. What political parties interest you and your parents?"

"We don't speak about politics at home."

"Do you have a favorite journalist?"

"I don't read the newspaper."

"Do you listen to the BBC?"

"I don't have a radio." Lucie had the script memorized.

Uncle Hugo accompanied Lucie to the Mechelen train station and said goodbye there. He had no ticket and was not let in. Once on the train from Mechelen to Brussels, Lucie followed Aunt Mathilde's advice and looked out the window. Five months earlier she had been walking through Belgium toward France. How different things looked now. The Germans controlled the whole country. German flags flew; police and military personnel wore swastikas on their lapels.

In the Brussels train station, Lucie switched platforms and got on a train heading east to Köln. She found a seat next to the window and looked out. She sat quietly until a conductor announced that they'd arrived in Aachen and all passengers needed to deboard for customs.

Lucie reached for her suitcases and grabbed her pocketbook. Two young SS men appeared and wouldn't take no for an answer. They wanted to help the young lady with her bags and insisted upon taking them from Lucie. She gave them a practiced smile. As they approached the customs building, Lucie reached into her pocketbook and took out her passport and visa. One SS man noticed the big red J stamped on the front of her passport. He dropped Lucie's suitcase as if it were on fire. The other man followed suit.

"This way, Fraulein." Lucie wasn't surprised that she was surrounded by a team of SS men in mere seconds. An unsmiling man cocked his head to the right of the main room. Lucie picked up her suitcases and walked where directed. She entered a private office with a large wooden desk. One officer took his seat behind the desk. Another officer gestured to Lucie to take the wooden chair facing the desk. Two more officers stood slightly behind Lucie. She could barely see them out of the corner of her eye.

The officer behind the desk began asking questions like the ones Lucie had practiced with Uncle Hugo. "Where do you come from?" "Who do you live with?" "Where are you going?" But these men kept cutting her off before she could answer.

Lucie tried to keep her answers short and bland. Then the man behind her started firing more questions. He had a whip that she could only see out of the corner of her eye. He slapped the whip on his boot. "What newspapers does your uncle in Mechelen read?" "What newspapers does her father read?" "Where does your uncle work?" "Are you carrying communist literature?" "What socialist books are in your luggage?"

Then the officers began to answer their own questions. They began to make up answers for Lucie. They told her that they had a sworn statement from her father that her uncle was a Communist. They told her that they had found anti-Nazi books in her Aunt Mathilde and Uncle Hugo's home. They insisted that she must have had pamphlets in her luggage. Snap, crack, Lucie heard the whip hit the man's boot.

Lucie looked straight ahead. She did not lie. She did not change her answers. So they instructed her to open her suitcases. The whip cracked again.

One of the men poked every item with a cane, picked it up as if it had lice or smelled, and then shook it onto the floor. The other man, still behind his desk, yelled, "Where are the pamphlets?"

They hailed a woman wearing a white nurse's uniform to the room. She instructed Lucie to remove all her clothes. It was February 1941. The room was freezing. It was a customs office in a train station. There were no blankets, little heat. The woman conducted something she called a *Leibesvisitation*. Lucie tried not to cry.

Lucie pretended that she was looking out of a window. Then there was shouting, and Lucie feared the train would leave without her. Where would she go if she were abandoned at the train station? She was shaking from the cold, the fear, and the humiliation.

Finally, someone knocked on the door of the room and shouted in, "Hurry up with that girl. You are holding up the whole train."

The nurse screamed, "Get dressed! You are holding up the train." Lucie somehow obeyed. Then she dragged her suitcases back out of the building, across the platform and back to the train.

As Lucie found her seat, passengers jeered at her, "You held us up, you dirty Jew. Now the train is late. Go back to Palestine." Lucie cried silently to herself. Intermittently she shook from the cold or the fright. She tried to hide this from the other passengers by looking out the window, watching the daylight fade.

I had wanted to hear Lucie's story. But now what? I could still feel her fright. I couldn't do anything about what had happened so many years ago. I struggled to find something to say that wouldn't sound stupid.

Finally, I said, "Your story should be in a book."

"No, no, no," she said. "I'm getting a Ph.D. in Art History. I'm too busy."

"Did you send a letter to Aunt Mathilde once you got back to Germany? Or did she ever write you?" I asked.

"You'd have to ask my mother," Aunt Lucie said bruskly. Eventually, I learned that Aunt Mathilde, Uncle Hugo, and Cousin Lore had all been sent to a concentration camp. Lucie was the last in the family to see them. And she would say no more. It would be years before someone suggested to me that Aunt Lucie's anger and evasiveness about her aunt and uncle might be survivors' guilt.

CHAPTER TWENTY-ONE
End of an Era

Grandpa died a couple of weeks before I turned sixteen. Though he was eighty, which was considered a ripe old age in 1973, it was still a shock to me. Grandpa had been our family's Moses. How would we go on without his wiles, intuition, planning, and good luck? It was his decision that the family, when they finally had the chance, should flee to the east from Berleburg to Berlin, right to the heart of the devil. Maybe he had a dream or saw a burning bush. Or more prosaically, he'd heard about people failing to escape from all the local cities, so he thought Berlin might offer more opportunities. Someone even mentioned a route to Shanghai.

Grandpa had always been a lucky man. He came home physically unscathed from the First World War, save for a hernia operation that didn't quite solve the problem. He had served on both the eastern and western fronts as a replacement soldier; according to Dad, replacement soldiers were the men sent in when half the unit had already been lost and they needed fresh soldiers. Also, per Dad, Grandpa had a great eye and was a terrific shot. In his seventies, he only wore glasses when reading. I'd been wearing them since I was eight. He had a voracious appetite, and he never said no to food until the last few months of his life.

If Grandpa didn't regale me with war stories (Grandma wouldn't let him), he enjoyed a good game of Checkers or Mill. If he didn't sing lullabies, he sat by my bedside when I got the chicken pox. If he didn't go to school plays or concerts, he listened when I sang him songs or played the piano for him. He let me tickle him and laughed uproariously. Whatever language gaps were between us, love broached them.

I went off to Israel for the summer of 1973. The Rochester Jewish Community offered its first (and maybe only) program for high school students to go study Hebrew and tour the country. When Mom and Dad asked me if I wanted to go and handed me the application form, I signed up immediately. At that point, Grandpa had indigestion. By the time I left for the trip at the end of June, Grandpa was going into the hospital for exploratory surgery. Dr. Grainer hoped to pinpoint and treat the source of Grandpa's pain.

When I returned, mid-August, I was told, "Grandpa has incurable cancer, but don't tell him. And don't talk to Grandma about it. It will upset her." No one was to use the word cancer (*Krebs* in German) around Grandpa and Grandma. Maybe magically, he'd live another year or two if we all willed it to go away.

Grandpa couldn't keep his food down. An hour after he ate, he'd vomit everything back up. The stench made me want to run from the kitchen and cry. It was a challenge to smile and pretend that Grandpa was getting better. I tried to talk to him about my trip, and my plans for the coming school year, my junior year of high school. Grandpa seemed too sick to listen.

He was so sick that he could no longer climb the steps to his bedroom. Dad took him to the Jewish Home every night to sleep. This also gave Grandma a break. I watched her stoically clean up the vomit. She looked mis-er-A-ble. With Grandpa at the Jewish Home at night, at least she could sleep.

Some mornings I went with Dad to pick Grandpa up. I liked pushing him in the wheelchair. I told Grandpa that in a couple of weeks, when I turned sixteen, I'd be getting my learners' permit. Then I could drive him in the car. Wouldn't that be great?

Then Dad was spending the night with Grandpa at the Jewish Home. One morning he reported that Grandpa wished to be shot in the head and put out of his misery. Several days later, Grandpa died at night. Dad said he had held Grandpa's hand when he died.

I don't remember much about the funeral. I felt numb and must have been somewhat shut down. I do remember the shiva at our house. Aunt Frieda and Uncle Max's sons Freddy and Kurt came from New York with enough cold cuts to feed the entire town of Spencerport. The rabbis from our synagogue, Brith Kodesh, one of whom had accompanied my trip to Israel, the other of whom had officiated my bat mitzvah, said a few prayers and chatted with my relatives. Although occasionally someone would pull out a hanky and cry, it seemed much like a party.

It was spring break when I first noticed the re-jiggering of our family's dynamic to fill the void left by Grandpa. We went to Florida (by car) to visit Grandma, our first time to that distant state. Grandma and Grandpa for at least a decade by now had flown off to Florida every winter. They rented the same apartment every year, one adjacent to Aunt Frieda and Uncle Max. This was Grandma's first year traveling there alone. Aunt Lucie and David, who had been flying down for years, had sleeping rights at Grandma's. Amy and I were sent to sleep next door at Aunt Frieda's, which was fine by me. Mom and Dad stayed at a hotel, which Dad worried was infested with bed bugs. We all went to the beach for a day or two, and then someone had the idea that we should visit Lion Country Safari.

We seven all piled into our sedan, which had seating for five. Grandpa's seat in the front was taken by Aunt Lucie with David wedged in. Amy, Mom, Grandma, and I were packed in the back. That was the decade of the lemon car. All kinds of random things wouldn't work. Either the car had no air conditioning, the AC was broken, or the system was under-designed to cool seven passengers in Florida heat.

We muddled through the hour-long drive to the theme park.

Even though Grandma paid – her treat! – Dad complained about the ticket prices. David read the brochure out loud as we followed the car in front of us into the park. "Rule number one: To avoid injury, keep your windows up at all times! Rule number two: Don't feed the animals!" There were more rules. But these did not have exclamation points.

We drove by a couple of elephants. Then the car in front of ours opened their windows to feed a giraffe. Dad opened his window. "Ah," he said, "What a *mehiyah*!" the only Yiddish Dad used. He was hot and relieved to have a bit of a breeze.

"The rules!" Lucie shrieked, with enough lung capacity for the entire game park to hear her.

"The people in front of us have their windows down," Dad said coolly.

"They are idiots!"

"Probably!" I watched the giraffe's head go in and out of the car.

"Look!" said Amy. "I see a lion!" Sure enough, a female lion was heading toward the car in front of ours with the open window.

"We're going to be killed! Put the window up!"

Dad raised his window, grumbling loudly that the lion was on Lucie's side of the car, and she had her window up. As she continued to shriek, Dad lost his cool and shouted, "You know nothing about animals!"

"Keep your window up!"

Although no one died either in our car or the car in front of ours, I was sorry we hadn't spent the day at the beach, where the breeze might have made their arguments float away, or I could have run into the water to escape. Instead, it seemed Dad and Aunt Lucie found reasons to antagonize each other for the rest of the trip: how Grandpa had set Dad up for life on the farm, the value of art history, which newspapers and periodicals were the most informative and which were propaganda, whether President Nixon should resign. If they came to a stalemate on any of these, they returned quickly to the Middle East, where their differences seemed less resolvable than the PLO and the Israeli Labor Party. I was glad to get back to school after that "vacation."

In the waning days of the following August, when Lion Country Safari had almost faded from memory, Aunt Lucie and David came to visit the farm. Dad worked all day, and Amy, Mom, Aunt Lucie, David, Grandma, and I spent a rainy day at the brand-new planetarium in Rochester. Another day we went to Hamlin Beach. Still another day, I was allowed to go with my friends to Letchworth Park and opt-out of family togetherness. But the final evening of Aunt Lucie's visit, Dad wanted to barbecue his famous steaks for his sister. These were blackened on the outside and still cool on the inside. Anyone who wasn't born in Germany or hadn't been eating them since their days in the crib, found them repellent. My family loved them. Or if they didn't, they kept their mouths shut. I'm not sure which category Aunt Lucie was in.

After dinner, the Scotch came out. Mom washed the dishes while Amy and David played outdoors. I sat in the living room with Dad, Grandma, and Aunt Lucie. As I was soon to start my senior year of high school, Grandma said wistfully that this would be my last year living at home. She was going to miss me. She pinched me on the cheek.

Dad said that I wouldn't be all that far away. He wanted me to attend one of New York's wonderful public universities. He'd received an excellent education at City College of New York, as had Mom at Hunter College. New York had dozens of four-year colleges. I could go wherever I wanted courtesy of his tax dollars.

"Foolishness," said Aunt Lucie. "You shouldn't send your child to a school based on price. You should send your child to the best school she can get into for her prospective field of study." Dad should support me in my efforts.

Grandma nodded along with both points of view diplomatically. Then she mentioned the names of the schools that my older cousins, Aunt Hilda's daughters, had attended. It was a mix of public and private schools in-state and away.

As I listened to the acrimony build, I remembered how Grandpa never tolerated this kind of arguing. He would bellow the word "Quiet!" which sounded more like "Quite!" Would this have stopped the squabbling? Thinking about Grandpa allowed me to tune out Aunt Lucie and Dad. I began to strategize a way to get what I wanted, which was to study international affairs in a real city, which only had three or four months of winter instead of eleven. I decided to visit the colleges of metro D.C., where half a dozen schools offered such programs. I wanted to determine my chances of getting in.

I took a Greyhound bus to Baltimore, where an aunt and uncle lived. I visited Johns Hopkins, Georgetown, George Washington, and American, and liked Georgetown the best: the campus was pretty, the coursework sounded rigorous and serious, and I liked D.C. with its free museums, theaters that promised student-discounted tickets, and internship opportunities on Capitol Hill. Although the Jesuit affiliation put me off, an admissions officer told me roughly ten percent of the student body was Jewish, a lot more than Spencerport.

I applied to these colleges, and several in New York. When the envelopes came that April, Mom and Grandma were delighted that I got into Georgetown. I remember Grandma offering me a small glass of schnapps to celebrate in her kitchen. Mom said I could go, not to worry about Dad. Dad was happy for me. He just had a hard time showing it.

I could see Dad trying to be happy for me. He smiled. He hugged me. But he also seemed sad, unsettled, or maybe wistful. I wondered if Grandpa might have helped Dad with this transition. Perhaps he would have told Dad to pat himself on the back, not just me. Maybe he would have reminded Dad that the farm wouldn't go under even though I wanted to go to a private school that would cost more than if I had stayed in New York and attended one of the colleges Dad had preferred.

Maybe Grandpa would have said something special to me, too: how even though I was leaving home, I'd be welcome to return. That Dad loved me and was going to miss me (even if he had trouble showing this). That my family would always be there for me in my heart, that they'd always wish me the best and cheer me on. That was what leaving home was: taking the good, learning the new, and moving forward.

CHAPTER TWENTY-TWO

The Cooking Gene

Mom did not like spending time in the kitchen, so after I learned cooking basics in my mandatory home economics class, a requirement for girls in Spencerport through the mid-1970s, I started bothering Grandma for an advanced course. The first two or three times I suggested cooking lessons, she pretended not to hear me. But as I got closer to leaving home, I wore her down.

We were sitting in her kitchen. As always, she sat with her back to the sink. I sat with my back to the porch, kitty corner to Grandma. The yellow Formica table must have come with the house, like the ancient pool table in the basement that no one ever used. Grandma's hands were busy peeling apples for an *Apfelkuchen* she was going to make the following day. "Why don't I come tomorrow morning and help you with it?"

"No, no, you don't get up so early. It will be too hot when you wake up."

Eventually, we agreed that if I was at her house by 7:30, she'd show me how to make an *Apfelkuchen* as well as a *berches*, which was a cross between white bread and challah. I had begun working at a donut shop and a day or two a week, I had to be at work by 6:00 am. Getting to Grandma's by 7:30 was no problem. Grandma sighed and asked me again whether I was sure. After all, my generation "had it *so* easy."

The following morning when I arrived at Grandma's, she had everything all set up. The apples were in one bowl, and she'd already put a bunch of flour in another bowl.

"How much flour did you put in?" I asked. Grandma shrugged. I had file cards with me. I guesstimated that she had four cups of flour. I wrote that down on my card.

"Okay," Grandma instructed, "Now you make a well in the flour, a little indentation. Inside the well you put the yeast, a bit of salt, and a bit of sugar." She explained how she used to add equal amounts, but she'd recently learned that too much salt was no good. After I poured the yeast, sugar, and salt into the well, Grandma filled the well with hot water from her kettle. "Not boiling," she said, "Hot." I dipped a pinky into the water. "Now we wait." I wrote down each step we'd done on the file card.

"You've got to trust your hands," Grandma said when I was done writing. "Start mixing by hand. Go ahead." As I blended the ingredients together, a yeasty smell permeated the kitchen. I liked the smell. It smelled like Grandma at work.

"Keep going," Grandma said. Then, several minutes later she said, "That looks right. How does it feel?"

I shrugged. She picked up a small piece of dough and pinched it between her fingers. It stretched out a bit. "If you don't like the feel, you add more of what is needed: flour or water."

While we waited for the bread and *Apfelkuchen* dough to rise, Grandma and I went to relax in the dining room, which I thought of as the TV room since I couldn't remember the last time we'd eaten there. Since Grandpa died, Grandma had expropriated his recliner chair. But before she climbed into the big chair, she fished around in her purse and pulled out a piece of paper. "I wanted to show you this letter that I got. But you can't read German. I'll try to translate it for you." She unfolded the letter and began reading,

My name is Lina Bachenheimer, and I was born in Röddenau on January 22, 1902. My father died when I was four years old. It was very difficult for my mother to raise all of us children alone, because I had eleven siblings. When I was six, I started school in Röddenau. I went there for three years. Then my mother sent me to the higher school in Frankenberg, which I am still attending. When I was in fourth grade, the Great World War broke out. My three oldest brothers had to go to war and the house felt empty. My brothers had fed and supported our family since my father's death. Now we lived in hardship. To date, I have completed two years of high school classes and will be 16 next year. But one of my brothers was killed last year and a second one this year in the Flanders battle. I cannot continue studying. I must earn a living now for myself. Therefore, I ask you, the Royal District Office, to assign me a suitable position. Sincerely, Lina Bachenheimer[7]

"What do you think?" Grandma asked. "Things weren't so easy when I was a child."

"Did you get a reply to your letter?"

"I didn't get a job."

"What kind of job did you want?"

Grandma shrugged. "The main thing was that I couldn't finish school. I had to help my mother." She paused a moment, and repeated, "Things weren't so easy." Grandma looked at me in earnest. "You see how good you have it? You're going to get a college education! I never got my education to be a nursery schoolteacher."

"You've always called me a lucky girl."

I suppose she picked up on my ironical tone. "Don't you feel that way?"

"I guess," I said, conceding the point, but not really feeling all that lucky. I spent far too much time brooding to consider myself lucky or happy. I could always find something to worry about: a test at school, politics, what would happen with my high school

---

[7]Hecker, p. 218, translation Jennifer Krebs with help from Google Translate.

friends now that we were all moving to different places and pursuing different interests. Why did no one in my family see my anxieties? Dad saw me as having everything I needed since he provided food, clothes, shelter, and love. Grandma saw that in addition to what Dad provided, I had ambition and dreams.

I looked down at my hands. I noticed several spots where dough that I hadn't fully washed off was drying and cracking. I rubbed a spot to try to remove the dough. I'd received a packet of information from Georgetown. A document in the packet listed the required courses for incoming freshmen. I knew of these requirements when I applied: one or more years of English, history, government, economics, philosophy, theology, and a foreign language. Only students who had passed AP exams would be exempted. Spencerport had no AP classes. That my Model U.N. advisor thought me brilliant might have gotten me into Georgetown, but it wasn't going to get me exempted from classes that sounded identical to what I'd done in high school.

"Your father had to work very hard for that money."

"I know."

"And look at Lucie. She had to work for everything she got. No one gave her anything. She is still working to get a Ph.D. She never stops."

"I know," I said, still trying to peel the drying dough away from my skin. I wasn't Lucie. I wasn't Dad. I was untested. I steered the conversation back to the present, back to the paper Grandma was still holding. "Who sent the letter?"

"My old friend in Germany."

"Who's that?"

"Her name is Elisabeth Bald. She took care of your Aunt Adele. We have been corresponding since the war ended."

"Why would she have that letter?" I asked.

"We left lots of things behind in Berleburg. Elisabeth must have found it. Let's go check on our dough now. Maybe it has risen enough."

Grandma got up and I followed her back to the kitchen. We stood together side by side staring at the two loaves of bread and a large apple cake. This was perhaps the last instance when Grandma and I were the same height. I had reached five foot six at around age thirteen, and she was just about to shrink back from it.

"Beautiful," she said, "just like you." Grandma pinched me on both cheeks. Then we slid the bread and cake into the oven.

I wrote down everything. I planned to follow the instructions again and again and again, until my hands knew how to do it. I wanted to leave behind some things from childhood, but I thought Grandma's baking lessons might serve me well in the coming years. Even if I didn't become a farmer's wife (perish the thought), who didn't like a slice of warm bread or a nice piece of apple cake?

CHAPTER TWENTY-THREE

Tante Adele Says Goodbye

Adele Krebs sat alone in her room, crying into her handkerchief. Her brother Julius would be coming by shortly with the rest of his family to say goodbye. She would be the last family member remaining in Berleburg. How had things come to this?

Julius' problems had been many. But somehow, he'd persevered. He'd had his business taken from him. He'd worked slave labor for close to two years, and paid good money on top of that, for a newly created Jewish tax. He'd missed his first appointment at the American Consulate in Stuttgart because war had broken out. But he'd been at the second one, with his wife, children, and our father. He got passports for all of them. Except Adele, who couldn't walk, and couldn't go to the consulate.

They were leaving today. In a few minutes. Adele cried again into her hanky. She wished she could get out of bed, but she even needed help for that. She needed to wait for Elisabeth Bald, who would help her. Adele hoped Elisabeth would come before her brother. Adele didn't want the family to see her in bed, without her hair combed, without her clothes.

Adele had visited doctor after doctor when she stopped walking. One specialist even performed surgery. Nothing had helped. Adele hadn't taken a real step in close to a decade. It was both infuriating and humiliating. She was always feeling sorry for herself.

Life was passing her by in this small forsaken town, in this wretched country.

Once she was in love, wanted to live in Dusseldorf, have a cosmopolitan life. She would be independent and chic. But God had other plans for her. That's what everyone said when she stopped walking. God must have other plans for Adele. What rubbish!

Not that Adele wanted her erasable father to stay behind in Berleburg – America could have him – but how was it that Americans would take him and not her? Adele didn't understand Julius' answer. Adele asked Julius at least three times. How did an eighty-year-old, far too old to work in America, qualify for a visa when she did not? What did he have to do to get that visa for their father?

Adele's hanky could hardly absorb the tears now running down her cheeks. When would Elisabeth come? What time was it? Adele looked for her watch. Only six a.m. The sun should be coming up.

And how did Julius get that visa for Lucie? Lucie told Adele that the American doctor said she had tuberculosis, that America couldn't accept a girl with tuberculosis, that she'd have to stay behind. Julius was advised, and then found another doctor (an old German doctor) who x-rayed Lucie. The German doctor said Lucie had nothing more than the common cold. The consulate gave the girl a visa.

While Adele would have been happy for Lucie's company – she was a spirited, intelligent girl who reminded Adele of herself at sixteen – Lucie would have been miserable if everyone left her behind...like Adele.

Adele hadn't listened to the rest of Julius' plans. Whether he would go east or west, north or south from Berleburg. What did she care? Today they were off to the train station. Today they were off to America. Today they were off to their new lives. And all Adele could do was feel sorry for herself.

Adele threw the hanky on the floor. All that she could control were her tears. She would stop crying. It was enough already. She would compose herself to say goodbye. She would maintain her dignity. She deserved that, at least.

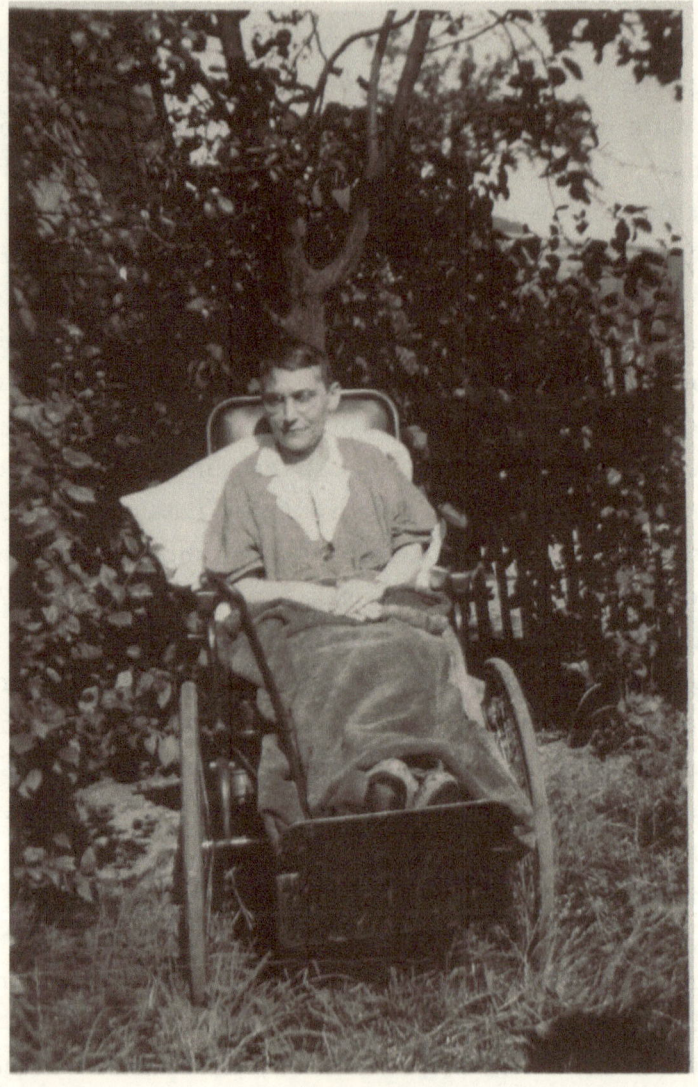

Adele Krebs, after 1933

CHAPTER TWENTY-FOUR

The Penultimate Train

While Aunt Adele cried in Berleburg, Dad, his sisters, his parents, and his grandfather Levi traveled to Berlin. In Berlin, with the assistance of the Joint Refugee Organization, they were able to board what became the penultimate train of Jews legally allowed to flee Germany on May 25, 1941. The train had many cars, but only one very overcrowded boxcar was for Jews. Guards stood at each end of the car, and no one was allowed in or out, even to go to the bathroom.

Someone from the Joint Refugee Organization met the train at its first stop outside of Germany, Paris. The Jews were allowed to get off the train and clean up. They were also given sandwiches to eat. My grandma and aunts would have loved to visit Paris under other circumstances. But this day, all they saw was the grey train station lined with swastika flags, which looked not so different from Berlin.

After Paris, the train traveled south until they arrived at the French-Spanish border in Hendaye. There, they de-boarded for customs. The Nazis took another opportunity to rifle through the family's luggage. They'd left Germany with very little: clothing, linens, some silverware, and the equivalent of three dollars a person. The customs agent now confiscated Grandpa's Iron Cross, a cherished memento.

Aunt Hilda told me Spain was unthinkably poor and full of children with outstretched hands begging for money or food. Flies swarmed around their eyes. By 1939, Franco had won the Spanish Civil War, and my family was concerned that if Franco joined the Axis, they would be sent back to Germany. They spent two weeks in Madrid, communicating with Hebrew Immigrant Aid Society (HIAS) and the relatives in New York, sussing out the best way to get to the U.S. Dad's most prominent memory was of being "eaten alive" by bedbugs.

Perhaps at the advice of the Joint Refugee Organization, from Madrid the family took a train to Lisbon, a port city, where presumably they could find space on a boat. There, Aunt Lucie went out to the docks in Lisbon with her father. Even though she'd studied no Portuguese, Lucie was as close to a polyglot as anyone in the family. They purchased tickets on the *Villa de Madrid,* which was setting sail to New York.

On the boat to the U.S., Dad's eighty-year-old grandfather ate nothing but bread. While the rest of the family suffered from upset stomachs, vomiting, and ptomaine poisoning, the voyage was easy for the old man. He spent much of his time on the deck of the ship, walking laps. When the rest of the family was not vomiting, they came up on deck and kept him company.

Dad deeply regretted not sticking to his grandfather's diet, but he was a growing boy and couldn't turn down food. Aunt Hilda said that while they were at dinner, the crew rifled through their suitcases and stole things. By the third day, Grandma was in the ship's infirmary, where she spent the rest of the trip. An article from the *New York Times* of July 14, 1941, "617 War Refugees Jam Small Ship," describes the conditions on the ship as follows:

> Normally the ship accommodates 225 passengers...
> (but) three hundred passengers slept in temporary bunks
> constructed in between decks. A reporter who went down
> to inspect their quarters was talking to a group of them,

including a German physician and a former Vienna bank manager, when a small rat scurried along a water pipe running along the top of the compartment to which they were assigned. One of the passengers declared that rats were no novelty in the between deck sectors.

It was said that the cost of accommodations in these sections ran between $400 and $450. First-class passage cost $1,200, according to voyagers...

Captain Bruguera said the 6,942-ton liner carried a Swiss cargo transshipped to Barcelona from Genoa. He would not disclose the amount or the items carried, saying he had "orders" not to do so.

Dad called the "four-day refueling stop" in Las Palmas an attempt at extortion by captain and crew. While some on board had the funds to pay their share, others, including my family had to call relatives and HIAS for additional help. The *Brooklyn Eagle* had almost the same report, also avoiding a discussion of the extortion.[8]

Bearing the scars of German bombers which sank it while she lay in Barcelona Harbor during the Spanish Civil War in possession of the Loyalists, the refloated Spanish liner, Villa de Madrid, today was safely harbored at the foot of Columbia St. after an eventful ocean voyage...

After she left Barcelona on June 21 the vessel was held up at Gibraltar for 30 hours as British officers made a thorough search of the passengers and luggage, removing a Swiss physician, Dr. Noel Cornelius. Stops were also made at Lisbon, Tangiers, and Las Palmas, Canary Islands, where four days were spent for loading fuel.

Passengers on their arrival were bitter about the lack of accommodations. They were crowded into every available nook... The voyagers also complained of the lack of sanitary

[8]https://redhookwaterstories.org/items/show/1620

facilities and protested that they had paid from $350 to $450 for these accommodations. It was said first class passage cost $1,200.

The entire family felt incredibly lucky to arrive in New York. The crossing had not been easy. Grandma was so sick from the ship's food that she could barely walk. Someone had to help her stand to wave to her sisters who had come to meet her and bring the family to their new apartment in Washington Heights. Instead of going to their new homes, my family was sent to Ellis Island for quarantine.

"We thought we'd died and gone to heaven," said Aunt Hilda. "There was a fruit bowl on each table. In Europe, we didn't have much fresh fruit. And the infirmary was clean. Everything was clean!"

"It seemed almost like a vacation," Dad added. Over decades, Dad and his sisters quickly contradicted anyone who said anything bad about Ellis Island.

"So your grandfather never got sick?" I asked Dad. "Did he like life in the U.S?"

"He was not an easy person to get along with. He was supposed to live with my aunt, but she kicked him out because he was mean to her children. Then he came to live with us."

"He got along with Grandpa?"

"I guess so. Anyway, we had to take him in. He died shortly before his 81st birthday. Grandma's mother, Auguste, also died in the U.S."

Here is the obituary that my family placed in the *Aufbau*[9] in December 1943 for Dad's grandfather, Levi Krebs. Of note, his oldest daughter Adele's address is Theresienstadt.

And the obituary for Auguste Bachenheimer, July 21, 1944. Of note in this obituary is that the mourners include only her children living in the U.S. Those still in Europe, why were they not included? Were their whereabouts unknown, were they presumed dead, or were they saving words to economize?

Ein Tag vor seinem 81. Geburtstag starb heute unser lieber Vater, Schwiegervater, Grossvater u. Onkel

Levi Krebs

aus Berleburg, Westfalen.

Die trauernden Hinterbliebenen:

Julius Krebs und Familie,
667 W. 161. Str., N.Y.C.

Adele Krebs, Theresienstadt

Fritz Krebs und Familie,
Baltimore, Md.

Herman Hess und Familie,
562 W. 179. Str., N.Y.C.

Adolf Krebs und Familie,
London und Polen

Leo Lamm und Familie,
Baltimore, Md.

New York City

[9]The *Aufbau,* which my grandparents read religiously (mailed to Spencerport) is described by the Leo Baeck Institute: *Aufbau* began publication in 1934 as a newsletter for the German-Jewish Club of New York. By then the club was ten years old and its membership was steadily increasing. In the beginning, the newspaper contained mostly news about club activities, articles about Jewish culture and contemporary events, and helpful facts for Jewish refugees. Over time, its articles focused more and more on international events and especially the treatment of Jews in Germany. *Aufbau* became one of the leading anti-Nazi publications of the German press in exile. Many well-known personalities wrote for the publication, including Hannah Arendt, Albert Einstein, Thomas Mann, and Stefan Zweig. From September 1, 1944, through September 27, 1946, the *Aufbau* printed numerous lists of Jewish Holocaust survivors located in Europe, as well as a few lists of victims.

CHAPTER TWENTY-FIVE

Demonstrating Proficiency

Dad might have been anxious about sending me out of town to college, but this did not stop him from helping me move into my dorm room. Dad found the upper classmen too wimpy looking to entrust them with my trunk of clothes. He hoisted the trunk on his shoulder and charged up the stairs to the fourth floor of the dorm, one of the oldest structures on campus with no elevator. Our good-byes were quick, but with moist eyes.

I looked at my roommate and wondered how all this would work out. She was a French major and would be taking a different curriculum from me. We went to separate rooms for different language placement exams. But just like the packet a month earlier had suggested, we were both assigned to Introductory French, though my roommate was in a more intensive class for language majors. After my French placement test, I went to a series of welcome speeches for the International Affairs majors.

Dean: "A grad named Bill Clinton has just moved to Arkansas and announced that he is running for attorney general. If you want to follow in his footsteps – and I imagine one of you might! – you'll need to graduate top of the class, get a Rhodes Scholarship, get into Yale Law, and then move back to where you've come from!"

My stomach rebelled at the thought of living in Spencerport again. I'd just been freed!

Provost: "The foreign service is VERY selective. Just because we accepted you doesn't mean you're the stuff for the foreign service. Most of you will find other things to do. We have a job placement office. Make sure to visit it."

I wondered if he was having a bad day or was just a cup-half-full kind of guy. It didn't seem like he was setting a "You can do it!" tone. I made a note to steer far from this man.

Although my first year went well enough – I got along with my roommate and classmates, did fine in my classes, found part-time employment, and availed myself of every movie, play, and museum show of interest – I liked the reality of Georgetown far less than what I'd anticipated. I groused about the lack of dorm rooms for upper-class students, the dearth of assistance finding paid internships, and the stale perspectives of some of my teachers and their teaching techniques. But mainly, I was out of sorts because I hadn't found my group of kindred spirits. I wasn't a preppy or someone always at the library. I wasn't interested in joining the school paper, a singing group, or a sorority. I tried the Model U.N. Club but found it too nerdy. The Jewish Students Association was run by male students only. I hadn't even found a group of dedicated complainers. Where were they?

By the middle of my second year, I had talked myself out of the foreign service. I didn't have the right temperament or politics. I was not preppy, rich, conservative, or smug. What was I going to do when I graduated? How would I figure this out?

Two of my cousins had studied abroad. I thought I might find a route to my future self away from Georgetown, far away. Besides, I needed to pass a proficiency exam in French to graduate. (Something else on my list of grievances against Georgetown: Why wasn't passing one or more upper-level classes in a foreign language enough to show proficiency?)

My French teacher, Madame H, made a very sour face when I asked her to write a recommendation letter for a junior year abroad program. Though I thought I was speaking clearly and making eye contact, she looked at me like I was daft. Perhaps I'd conjugated the verb in the past tense instead of the future. No matter how many times I tried to make myself understood, Madame H's lips remained pursed. Finally, she began speaking to me in English. I explained (again) that I needed a recommendation letter to get into a study abroad program.

"You are not proficient."

"That is the point," I said in English. "I want to study in France so I can become proficient."

"I am not sure you'll succeed. Let me discuss this with the department chair."

A week later, I approached Madame H again and asked her if she had written my recommendation.

"I don't think you should go. But the department chair said that if you enroll in his program in Dijon over the summer, you'd qualify."

"You'll write me a recommendation letter?" I wanted to study in Tours, France, on a program with Rutgers. That program advertised living in a French dorm (not with a family) and classes with French students at the University of Tours (not a separate all-American program). The program was competitive, and I wanted to get in.

"I'll write something." She gave me the barest hint of a smile, hardly a ringing endorsement. I thanked her profusely.

Now I had to get my parents to say yes. My cousins who had studied abroad had gone to Israel, which Dad would have had to agree to. But I'd been to Israel three times, and I wanted to go to France. I needed to pass the French proficiency exam.

Dad listened patiently as I made my case over the phone. I rambled on about my grades, my teacher, and the proficiency test. To pre-empt a speech from Dad about French antisemitism over the centuries, one of his favorite topics, I rambled on about Leon Blum. I must have read a book about him that semester. He had been the French prime minister, then imprisoned by the Nazis, then a mover and shaker in post-war French politics. "We've never had a Jewish president here!" I concluded. When there was silence on the other end, I asked, "What do you think?"

"I'll think about it," said Dad.

"Sounds great," said Mom. Maybe Mom was worried that I'd call Aunt Lucie and she'd call Dad up and yell at him again.

I saw my departure that summer as a fresh beginning. When my European classmates couldn't understand my nickname, Jenny, I started introducing myself as "Jennifer, like the Donovan song." This at least brought a smile, if not the full chorus of "Jennifer, Juniper..."

The Georgetown program funneled a cohort of roughly thirty students into an intensive French program that attracted students from the Americas and other European countries. My main teacher was a poet. He helped us build our vocabularies by reading poems out loud and then asking us for other ways to say the same thing. We laughed, something that rarely happened with Madame H.

I took the lunchtime seminar with Monsieur M, the Georgetown French Department chair. He had a reputation as a reactionary tyrant in D.C., rarely giving out A's, and making men wear ties and women dresses or skirts for his 8:00 a.m. class in French 101. Monsieur M didn't require a dress code for class in Dijon. He leaned on his desk and smoked cigarette after cigarette during his lectures on the French language over the past hundred years. He smiled, answered questions, and seemed perfectly amiable. No lip pursing. He seemed generous in his grading, or perhaps I had finally started to get the hang of French.

Mom and Dad planned to come visit me over Spring Break, but Aunt Lucie wrote that she was coming to France the last two weeks of August, just when the Dijon program ended. Why didn't I join her and David? This seemed perfect. I had almost a full month between the end of the Dijon program and the start of my year-long program in Tours.

Aunt Lucie had recently completed her Ph.D. in Art History. She arrived in France with my cousin David, then 13, and an agenda to photograph Romanesque churches. Apparently Lucie's university had a deficient photo library of these churches. She had a new Nikkormat camera weighing several pounds, and she was going to take lots of slides. She had rented a car for us to travel from Paris through Burgundy, down the Rhone to the Mediterranean, and then across to Toulouse. From there, we'd drop the car and take a couchette back to Paris.

This all sounded fine. I didn't have an agenda, or an international drivers' license. I was happy to navigate, as was David. One day we went to the beach, but otherwise David and I received a private course in Medieval Art History. In the stained-glass windows and tapestries, Lucie explained, people learned Bible stories and how to pray. For those who were not devout, an array of tormented faces looked down from the church's entry, crowds of sinners waiting to be judged by God. "Look at those cowed faces!" Lucie exclaimed. David and I ran up the stairs of a bell tower and looked down on the town covered by a morning mist. The fields looked carved up, perhaps as they had been several centuries earlier.

We had long meals, largely *ménus du jour*. I drank copious amounts of wine, perhaps too much the night that Lucie apologized to our waiter for "losing her French" and letting me order for her. "I used to be quite proficient," she said to David and me once the waiter left.

Perhaps it was the word proficient that stuck in my craw. I still had the French proficiency exam in my future. "You speak fluent English, German, and Japanese. Why are you always apologizing about not speaking French?"

"If I'd had a normal education, I'd speak Flemish and French. I was ROBBED of my education."

"I don't understand," I said.

Now Lucie raised her voice, "I had to work for every single class that I took. No one paid for me. I've had to work to pay for everything. You understand nothing. And what are you going to do with your degree anyhow? You know nothing about the world."

I drank a sip of wine. She sounded so bitter, so angry. Was she mad at me? Grandma and Grandpa? Dad? The Nazis? I didn't know how to respond.

David stepped in and saved the evening (at least for me). He asked what we were going to do the next day. Lucie smiled and turned to answer him. We were going to visit the Papal Palace in Avignon. Did we know that there were French popes during the Middle Ages? (I did, but I let Lucie tell me all about it.)

Several months later, back at Georgetown, I took my French proficiency test. Luck of the draw, Madame H was administering my test, which called for me to read and summarize an article from *Le Monde* on Valéry Giscard d'Estaing's economic positions. I found the article boring and had forgotten most of it by the time I was called in. When Madame H asked me to summarize Giscard's industrial policies, I could offer only that he wanted industries to prosper, not which industries, nor where. She refused to listen to what I wanted to tell her, about what fun the department chair was in Dijon, about my classmates in Tours, about the books I'd read, the museums I'd visited, or the fact that I made life-long friends, both French and American. She was all about Giscard in *Le Monde*. I was mediocre once again. *Tant pis*, as the French said.

CHAPTER TWENTY-SIX

Visiting Berleburg

My aunt and cousin were not my only visitors during my junior year in France. My parents and sister came for spring break. Prior to their arrival, I spoke to my parents by phone and was surprised to learn that Dad wanted to visit Germany after our time in Paris. It took me a minute to respond to him. Up until now, he mentioned Germans or Germany only when he was discussing scoundrels, louts, antisemites, and fascists.

Now Dad said, "It's right next door to France...if we're coming all that way, we may as well go."

I repeated, still disbelieving, "You want to go to Germany?" I hoped I didn't sound confrontational. Though I hadn't considered going to Germany with Dad, I 'd already spent a few days in Trier, and a week in Stuttgart. I had felt surprisingly comfortable in Germany. In both situations, visiting new friends associated with my program in Dijon, I made sure to mention that I was Jewish and that Dad had been born in Germany. I got into long discussions. My friends' parents were roughly Dad's age. Though the parents might have "forgotten" their participation in Hitler Youth, like Dad, they had been too young to join up as soldiers. My friends expressed confusion, shame, and remorse about the rise of the Third Reich and its lethal agendas. Too many of my peers back in the U.S., it seemed to me, seemed disinclined to look at the legacy of slavery and genocide against Native Americans in our lives. The entrenched poverty of peoples of color, and their disenfranchisement, spoke to enduring problems that my generation should combat. When teachers and classmates shied from discussions, I was sometimes disheartened and other times angry. Here, my German friends were eager to discuss evils from the past and how we should improve things.

Dad further elaborated, "I was thinking we could go to Berleburg."

"Berleburg?" If I didn't sound incredulous, I certainly was surprised that Dad wanted to go to Berleburg. What had changed? How had he gone from disinterested in visiting Europe to wanting to visit Berleburg, his hometown, of which he'd never spoken a word of praise?

I wondered if Grandma had put him up to this. Grandma occasionally produced pictures with smiling faces. Dad didn't say she had. He just said he wanted to visit. Another mystery for me.

Grandma, Paul, Hilda, and Lucie, 1930

I met my parents in Paris. I'd looked forward to showing off my French, and my knowledge of landmarks and how to get around. It turned out that being the family tour guide was not simple. Even what I imagined to be incontrovertibly magnificent – Notre Dame, Ste. Chappelle, the Louvre, walking along the Seine – were "boring" or "okay" to some. Other complaints such as hotel room size, portions at dinner, and the difficulties of understanding a menu, put me on the defensive.

I was relieved to pass the tour guide baton to Dad in Munich where he could order food, ask for directions, and decide whether to take the subway or catch a cab after visiting one of the famous *Münchner Biergartens*. All that beer! Good thing he picked the cab. Maybe, I thought, Dad was right to come to Germany. Maybe, for our family, Germany would be more fun than France.

After a few days, we headed off to Berleburg, a full day's drive from Munich. I sat up front to help navigate. While we drove through the Black Forest, I had a creeped-out feeling that had nothing to do with Hansel and Gretel or a witch's curse. It was the trees, which were brown and scraggly. They were dying. Though I'd heard of acid rain, I hadn't seen such devastation in the U.S. Thankfully, we were only in the wasteland for an hour or so before the landscape became scenic again. Eventually, we arrived in Berleburg. After Paris and Munich, it was almost jarring to go from the countryside to the town's center in less than a minute.

"Which one was your house?" Amy asked as Dad jumped out of the car. Dad pointed at the house in front of us. Like all the houses on the street, the house was tiled with black slate shingles that shimmered in the sunlight. I'd forgotten that the houses looked dark in the various postcards and photos that Grandma had shown me over the years.

As I stepped out of the car, I saw a woman run from the neighboring house and wrap Dad in a tight hug. "Booby, Booby, Booby!" she mumbled into his shoulder.

Mom, Amy, and I looked at each other, confused. A second woman appeared looking like an older version of the first woman.

She brushed away the first woman and continued the same chant, "Booby, Booby" with tears running down her face.

When the hugging subsided, Dad introduced us to his former neighbors. The one about Dad's age was Gertrude. The older woman was her mother. Their family name was Bald.[10] Mom, who had a year or two of German while in school, managed a greeting. Dad introduced Amy and me, and we smiled and waved. Gertrude and her mother continued to cry, pulling handkerchiefs out of their pockets.

Dad gave them a quick update on how everyone was doing in the U.S. Grandma, it seemed, sent Christmas cards every year. They had heard about us, at least Grandma's version which probably cast us all with angelic glows. They nodded and wiped their eyes when they heard that Lucie had recently received a Ph.D. in Art History. She had always been smart. They clapped their hands and smiled broadly when Dad said that he and Uncle Irv were business partners, still *Viehhändler*.

I pointed to Dad's old house, which looked almost identical to the Bald's – two stories, clad in black slate, which is an exterior finish common in the region. The house looked solid, somber. Perhaps if children tumbled out the front door, or there were tchotchkes glued to the windowpanes, it might have looked more inviting. But the curtains were pulled and there was no sign of life.

Dad inquired as to the current residents and Gertrude suggested that we knock. A tired-looking semi-disheveled man with an arm in a sling eventually arrived at the front door and opened it a crack.

Two or three years ago when Dad and I reminisced about this trip, I remembered that the man in Dad's old house rebuffed us when we asked to come in. Dad, however, remembered being served coffee. I thought the coffee came an hour later at the Bald's

---

[10]This Bald family, who lived next door to my dad as a child is unrelated to Elizabeth Bald, who took care of my great aunt Adele.

house. I remembered a table set with three beautiful cakes and freshly brewed coffee. I don't think the man in Dad's house could have managed that.

With no referee for our disagreement, Dad and I moved on to the other highlights of Berleburg. Did I remember the duck pond? The Jewish cemetery? The *Schloss,* or castle, owned by the *Fürst,* which can be translated as duke, prince, count, or even king? When I expressed surprise in the 1970s to learn that Germany still had nobility, Dad said that Germany had no guillotines in the eighteen or nineteenth centuries, just concentration camps in the twentieth. "Those," Dad summed up, "were not for the aristocracy."

Dad and I couldn't finish our reminiscences of the trip without revisiting Dad's getting locked in the guesthouse. "That crazy hotel," he called it.

"You were very upset," I said

"Crazy, crazy," Dad shook his head. He had a far-away look in his eyes. "What was wrong with those people? How could they have a policy to lock the front door at night?"

I remembered that morning in March 1978 when I heard of Dad's escapades. Unable to sleep, he had wanted to take a stroll around town at five or six in the morning, hours before the guesthouse served breakfast. When he found the front door locked, he had tried every trick he could think of to open it...unsuccessfully. He had waited in the lobby until seven, when someone had finally arrived to open the place back up.

When I sat down for breakfast, I found a very cranky father seated across from me. As he described his efforts to leave the guesthouse, I could see why he was so upset. Dad had been trapped again by the Germans. It must have been déjà vu, and not in a good way. Had the guesthouse owner known that Dad was an insomniac and early riser, perhaps he might have mentioned the door locking policy. But most guests, I was left to believe, didn't want to get in some fresh air before seven a.m.

On the last night of the trip, there was sparring between Dad and me. I said what a great year I was having, and how much I liked studying abroad. I made friends, traveled, and studied art and history, in addition to French. I meant to sound appreciative. But Dad grumped, "What are you going to do after you graduate? I'm not going to support you forever."

I hadn't imagined that he would. I felt hurt. I thought Dad was assessing me like a cow that wasn't penciling out for him. Maybe a whole herd of cows with mastitis. I had no quick comeback. I sulked for the rest of the evening.

As I took the subway from our hotel near the airport into Paris after my parents and sister left, I ticked off all the jobs I'd had since I first drove tractor for Dad. I'd babysat, picked cherries, helped move a college library, and sold donuts, ice cream, and burgers. I'd had three internships. One of them even paid me a little. I was not lazy. But I didn't know what I wanted to do, who I wanted to become, or where I would do this next piece of growing up. One thing was certain though. I was not going back to Spencerport.

Second Visit to Berleburg

In March, during my last semester of college, Grandma sent a letter inviting me to accompany her to Berleburg. I called Grandma when I got the letter. Of course, I'd love to go to Germany with her. She told me this would be my graduation present, and that she would arrange for tickets and get back to me.

A few weeks after Grandma invited me to Berleburg, Aunt Lucie came to Washington D.C. for the annual conference of Art History professors. She stayed in a hotel with her friend Tsedenka but invited me to tour the Freer Asian Art Collection with her. There she proceeded to give me a crash course on Buddhist Art. She had just signed a contract to write an introductory book on Buddhist Art. Why not practice a few explanations on me?

Over lunch at the museum, Aunt Lucie said she'd heard about my upcoming trip to Germany with Grandma, and that she'd like to join us if I didn't mind. I didn't think I was the right person to ask, as Grandma had invited me. But I said, "Absolutely!"

Graduation came and went, and I began packing for two weeks in Holland and Germany. I flew to Amsterdam from Washington D.C. I met Grandma and Aunt Lucie at Schiphol Airport. Almost as soon as we got through customs, Lucie began sniping at Grandma, asking questions snidely. Silly arguments over whether Grandma should carry her passport or leave it at the hotel, what pair of shoes to wear, or when we were going to have lunch. I gave Aunt Lucie the benefit of the doubt for a day or two. She'd slept poorly. She drank too much. Grandma wasn't walking fast enough. Then I had to wonder why she'd wanted to join us in the first place.

Thankfully, when we arrived in Berleburg, Lucie's surliness diminished. We were staying at Elisabeth Bald's house. (Not the Balds who lived next door to Dad as a child. Rather, the woman who took care of Grandpa's sister Adele.) Elisabeth lived with her daughter Elspeth, Elspeth's husband Ernest, and their son Ulrich. They greeted me like a long-lost friend and commented over and over how much I looked like Lucie. Had I not been so annoyed with Lucie, I would have accepted this as a compliment. Instead, I bristled. I didn't want to look like her or act like her. I didn't trust her mood swings. Was she Dr. Jekyll or Mr. Hyde?

One morning shortly after our arrival, I was to go hiking with Ulrich. Though he was twelve and had studied English only a year or two in school, he was to be my tour guide. Ernst dropped us off at the entrance to a park at the top of a hill just outside of town. The trail down the hill towards town was lovely, and Ulrich tried to teach me the words of the berries we passed on the forest floor: *Himbeeren, Erdbeeren, Stachelbeeren.* I repeated the words like a mantra trying to memorize them. Raspberries, strawberries, gooseberries.

When we weren't chatting, I was aware of internal discomfort, an emotion I was having trouble naming. It didn't just seem to be about the arguing between Lucie and Grandma. It was about something else. But what? I was on vacation. I was done with college. I had finished on time, with a respectable degree, and lots of information in the field of International Affairs. I should be feeling a sense of accomplishment and pride. I should be enjoying myself, having a vacation. Instead, I was feeling – what was it? – hollowed out, sad? Rudderless? Hadn't I been looking forward to this day for years? I had no more papers to write. No teachers to please. And all my parents wanted from me was for me to earn enough money to support myself. How difficult was that? Why was I feeling depressed?

At the end of our walk, when the trail deposited us near the town center, I asked Ulrich if there was a stationer. I wanted to purchase a notebook. I thought I would try to organize my thoughts to get a better idea of how to set my life on course for the next chapter. I picked out a notebook with a translucent orange-red plastic cover. I carried it home, unsure what I'd devote the notebook to as college was in the rearview mirror.

Back at the Bald house, Ulrich and I learned of the afternoon's plan. We were going to visit Röddenau, the town where Grandma was born. When I'd been to Berleburg last year with Mom, Dad, and Amy, we hadn't gone to Röddenau. In fact, we never even talked about the fact that Grandma grew up in a whole different town in the next province. Ulrich's father Ernst would drive Lucie, Grandma, Elisabeth, and me to Röddenau. Ulrich and his mother, Elspeth, would stay home.

I enjoyed the car ride. Ernst was giving us the scenic tour through quaint villages with old mills, half-timbered buildings, and the like. We crossed several creeks and then pulled off the road and went inside a simple one-room church. Eventually, Ernst parked in front of a large corner house that Grandma had directed him to in German.

"Our house!" Grandma exclaimed. Then she covered her mouth. In an echo of last year's trip with Dad to Berleburg, a small woman ran out of the house next door and grabbed Grandma. "Karolina, Karolina!" Grandma said over and over. I'd never heard of Karolina, but she and Grandma were kissing each other like long-lost friends.

After Grandma and Karolina separated, they each grabbed for a hanky. Karolina seemed to recognize Lucie and gave her a hug. She looked at me and asked Lucie if I was her daughter. Grandma explained that I was Paul's daughter. "Little Paul!" Karolina remarked as if he were still ten.

This was about all I could follow in German. I listened to long exchanges and could only guess about what they were discussing. I was especially confused because so much of the discussion was about Julius. Why, I wondered, were they talking about my grandfather who had never lived in Röddenau?

At one point Lucie took me aside and explained that Karolina had worked for Grandma's mother and then Grandma's brother. Or maybe Karolina's mother worked for Grandma's mother, and Karolina worked for the brother.

Röddenau Visit 1979: Grandma, Karolina, other neighbors

This photo, taken by Lucie (or maybe me), appears in Horst Hecker's book on the Jews of Frankenberg (*Jüdisches Leben in Frankenberg*, 2011). Thanks largely to Horst Hecker's book, I have a reference for the many discussion points that so confused me that day. What I came to understand, which the Hecker book describes beautifully, is that the subject of conversation was not my grandfather Julius Krebs. Grandma was talking to Karolina about her brother Julius Bachenheimer. Grandma's brother Julius was the only one of three brothers who returned home from the Great War. As his oldest brother was already living in New York, Julius became the *pater familia* of the Röddenau Bachenheimers. He ran the family cattle and dry goods business, took care of his mother and offered consultations, blessings, and assistance to his younger siblings (some of whom barely remembered their father).

Once the Nazis came to power, the Röddenauer Bachenheimers had trouble. A long simmering grievance turned into a lawsuit against Julius. Fritz was not allowed to enter any local high school. In the spring of 1938, Julius sent Fritz and Auguste (his son and mother) to New York. As a child, I only met Fritz Bachenheimer once or twice. But, I remembered what Grandma told me about him: Fritz had "accompanied his grandmother" to America. I was now accompanying Grandma back to Germany, something laden with historical significance for her.

By Kristallnacht, Julius and his wife Selma still hadn't secured immigration papers for the rest of the family which included three daughters. The youngest, Hilda, was only a year old. The older two were roughly the ages of my aunts. Doris went on the Kindertransport to Belgium with Dad and my aunts. Anneliese was supposed to go to Belgium, too, but for some reason this didn't happen. *Schade, schade, schrecklich.* There was not a dry eye amongst us, even though in my case I understood very little.

As I listened, I realized that I should have written notes from this trip in the little notebook that I'd purchased earlier. The story was bigger, and more complicated, than what I'd heard earlier during family gatherings. Perhaps learning the story of Grandpa's brother was why Grandma wanted me to come with her on this trip. She didn't want to forget him, his wife, and daughters. She wanted me to know her birthplace. She wanted me to remember those who were not as lucky as me.

CHAPTER TWENTY-EIGHT

Children of the Holocaust

I filled the first two pages of my Berleburg notebook with a family tree of my father's side of the family that I made the day after the trip to Röddenau. Grandma had an amazing memory for who married whom, maiden names, and birthdays going to her second and third cousins, as well as Grandpa's whole family. My tree followed the method that I learned in ninth grade. I'm not sure if it was part of the New York State curriculum or if my teacher had taken a genealogy course and decided to share. In those days, long before the Horst Hecker book, Geni.com, or Family Tree Maker, this tree became my guide to remembering what I learned in Berleburg and Röddenau.

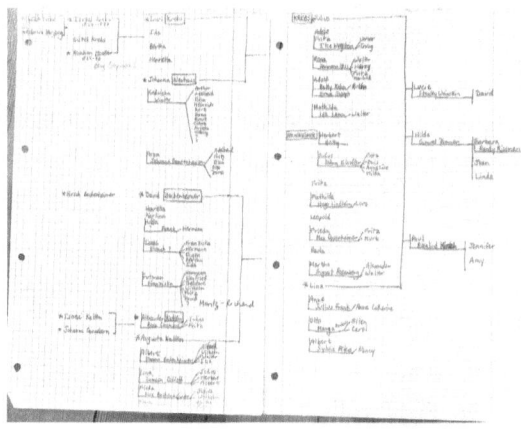

A page from my notebook, June 1979

Grandma found the tree interesting, but, she told me, "Your writing is so small. I can't read it." Aunt Lucie already knew who everyone was. She didn't see the point. That day, and the days and weeks that followed, I came to realize that the three of us were haunted by the past in different ways (as were all my living relatives). Aunt Lucie and Grandma had come to Berleburg looking for answers beyond what the German government and Jewish organizations had provided after the war.

Looking back from the 2020s to 1945, when the war ended, Europe was in disarray. Government office buildings throughout the continent had been bombed, burned, or looted. Germany became two countries with competing governments. Some civil servants were disinclined to release public records. There was no Wikipedia. No information was digitized. How were people to know what happened to their loved ones?

Except for Aunt Adele who was sent to Theresienstadt, the *model* concentration camp, all my relatives who didn't make it out of Germany were assumed to have been killed at Auschwitz, the largest known extermination camp. At least this is what I was told as a child.

Elisabeth Bald did her best to answer our questions – she had much to say about Aunt Adele, who she took care of – but she knew very little about what happened to other family members not in Berleburg. Grandma and Lucie were frustrated that the actual fates of those they had known and loved were out of reach.

I imagined that someday I'd get to the root of things, that I'd make Grandma and Aunt Lucie proud. I just wasn't sure how and when.

I liked doing research. I'd spent a good deal of time my senior year of Georgetown doing research into the Paris Commune of 1871 at the Library of Congress. I put in job applications there even before I graduated. Finally, shortly after I came back from Berleburg, I got offered a job. Since I had neither a Ph.D. nor a master's degree in library science, I didn't qualify to do independent research. But, I did qualify to be a library technician in the Congressional

Research Service. I received a month of training and was then deployed as a fetch-it for members of Congress and their staffs.

The LOC, as we called it, was beginning to adopt computers. We library techs got computer training in searching for periodicals, case law, and a beta version of their card catalog. We didn't talk about keywords in those days. It was Boolean logic: names, dates, places, topics, and the like.

Chatting one day with one of the library gods, a.k.a. a full-time subject matter expert, I mentioned my recent trip to Berleburg. She was a voracious reader, not only in her field, Iran's scientific achievements, but more widely. She suggested that I read Helen Epstein's *Children of the Holocaust*, which had just come out in paperback. I had read a review but been hesitant to buy the book. I decided to get the book so I could have another chat with her.

I struggled then to read the book, and still struggle with it now. For starters, Dad never considered himself a Holocaust survivor. He'd been in the U.S. before most Jews were sent off to camps. Anyone who survived that experience was, to his mind, a Holocaust Survivor. Or someone who hid in a forest, cave, or cellar. Or someone who faked an identity and somehow got through. A very small number of people. Not Dad. He may have had a terrible childhood in Germany, endured two years in Belgium (including fleeing the Nazi invasion), and had other harrowing tales to tell, but he was not a Holocaust survivor.

If Dad was not a survivor, then surely, what Helen Epstein wrote about herself, and her interview subjects wasn't totally germane to my situation. Or was it? Maybe agreeing with Dad on this was causing me to split hairs. Maybe I should be taking notes, reflecting deeply, discussing with a therapist, or finding a group at a local synagogue where others were interested in the topic.

I couldn't. It was just like my attempt to read Anne Frank's diary as a child, too hot to handle. I couldn't do more than skim the book. Nor did I did look for people with whom I could discuss the book. Not even my sister or cousins.

Instead, I kept ruminating on what happened to Aunt Adele. How awful it must have been for her to have been left behind. How haunting it must have been for Grandpa to leave her. This single story seemed the pebble thrown into a pond that sent ripples out to Lucie, Hilda, and Paul, and then to my generation. Leaving a loved one behind because she couldn't walk and couldn't get a visa. It seemed unspeakably sad and painful.

Lucie kept Adele's picture in her stairwell. "I think of her whenever I climb the steps to my bedroom." In the early 2000s, she spoke to a class at the academic high school in Berleburg about Adele and Elisabeth Bald, who cared for her until she was deported to Theresienstadt,

A truly heroic Berleburger was Frau Elisabeth Bald, geboren Wahl, at whose parents' house we Krebs children celebrated Christmas. Elisabeth was my Tante Adele's most loyal friend. At the height of her career, Adele was in charge of the Edeka Geschäfte, Berleburger branch, whose offices were opposite the old Bahnhof. When she was fired in 1933 for being Jewish, Adele's shock was so great that she collapsed on her way home and remained confined to a wheelchair[11] until her arrest in 1941-42. Adele died in Theresienstadt. Elisabeth Bald, disregarding all threats, took the Jewish woman into her house, during the height of the Nazi period, and stood by her. She knew the meaning of Zivilcourage and acted upon it. Once she even had words with the Ortsgruppenleiter whom she asked for eine Kleiderkarte für Adele. When he said Juden seien keine Menschen, and therefore needed keine Kleiderkarten, she contradicted him in no uncertain terms. Intelligent and straightforward, as was her manner, Elisabeth argued with the authorities to the extent that

---

[11]The story about Adele collapsing after being fired was debunked by Rikarde Riedesel, the Berleburg archivist. She found records from the Edeka that Adele wasn't terminated until several months after she stopped walking.

[12]Lucie Krebs Weinstein, Reminiscences of my Childhood in Berleburg, Johannes Althusius Gymnasium, date uncertain.

they advised her husband to file for divorce. But that was in vain, her husband stood by her.[12]

Poor Elisabeth Bald: She, too, had a palpable guilt that I remember from the time I spent with her in Berleburg. As did her daughter, son-in-law, and grandson. More ripples on the pond. Finally, I took out a pen and started writing about Adele.

CHAPTER TWENTY-NINE

An Argument

Part I: Thanksgiving at Lucie's

While at Aunt Lucie's for Thanksgiving, I thought I'd show her a piece I'd written about Aunt Adele. After many attempts to write something about my relationship to the Holocaust, I thought I had something different or inspired to say. I had gone from writing after work and on weekends into a writing program. My friends had seen promise in the piece on Aunt Adele. Several had suggested I publish it. Others had suggested I turn it into a book.

I brought it to Aunt Lucie, hoping for encouragement. Mom and Dad were tepid about my writing, though when I told them I was taking a course, they offered to pay for it. I thought maybe Aunt Lucie might intervene on my behalf, telling Dad to leave me alone while I finished a book.

Or, I thought, maybe Aunt Lucie would say, "I can see now why you didn't want to go to graduate school. It is not your path. I'm so proud of you having found yourself." (Over the past few years, she had been very concerned about me "finding myself," which I supposed was one way of saying finding a career path.)

I handed Aunt Lucie a copy of *Short Black Hair* and left her in her living room to read it. While she read, I went to the kitchen to help take some dishes out of the dishwasher. Or maybe I helped myself to another glass of something.

When I went back to the living room, Lucie was shuffling through my pages and looking lost in the couch cushions. Was she looking for something in particular? Was she collecting her thoughts? I wondered if I should leave the room again and come back later. Instead, I studied the artwork above the fireplace, of a young woman holding an umbrella with the rain at her back. I took another sip of my drink.

Finally, Lucie invited me to sit next to her on the couch. Once I was seated, she began her critique. I sat next to her for a very long time and was uncomfortable every minute.

Part 2: Lucie's point of View

Sometimes, you cannot do enough for people. I just cooked and served a big Thanksgiving dinner, and still that niece of mine, Jenny, wants more. She has asked me to read her "prose poem," whatever that is. She is in a writing program. She wants to be a writer.

The piece is called, "Short Black Hair." Maybe it will be funny—her new haircut certainly is.

I'm an art historian, not a literary critic. I'm not sure why one writes a prose poem and not an essay. I enjoy essays and books of non-fiction, though, from time to time, who doesn't like a good novel? My friend Hanna wrote a searing novel about growing up in Prague. She wrote it in German and then translated it to English herself. It sold quite well. But her second book was panned. It is tough to be a writer.

As I read, I wonder why this girl didn't take my advice to go to graduate school. Oh yes, it was that fool brother of mine who blindly did whatever our father said and is bullying his daughter the same way. Money isn't everything! And that sister-in-law, a Stepford Wife, who never stands up to my brother. Who would have thought that they'd become such conventional bores?

Jenny would be happy as an academic. Like me, she is smart and a good student. She remembers things. A few years back, she pulled up a fact that took Stan by surprise. Stan was saying some-thing about Trotsky, I think, and Jenny had an anecdote about Trotsky's time in Mexico City, his friendship with Diego Rivera and Frida Kahlo. Jenny had this funny tee shirt on with a picture of Frida on the front, as if she were advertising her expertise. She said she'd just read a novel about their love triangle.

Stan laughed and said, "Ah yes, the widely speculated Trotsky-Kahlo affair."

"It makes a great story!" said my niece. Then she turned to me and told me that I should read it. Maybe I will...and maybe this prose poem, sitting on my lap, is baby step number one to a book length work.

I read along. There is some rhythm. A bit of wit. It is not terrible. It is a start. I am trying to think what I want to say to Jenny. I visu-alize her swimming out in the ocean, going far beyond safety. The waters are deep. I am not feeling comfortable anymore. In fact, I am feeling very uncomfortable with what she has written.

I see my mistake. I should have taken "Short Black Hair" with me up to bed. I should have read it at my leisure and taken notes. I should be giving her my thoughts tomorrow. But now I can't. She is sitting there looking like a puppy, wondering if she'll get a biscuit or a rap on the snout.

I think of my students at Southern, what a poor education many of them have had. Like me, they are the first generation to go to college. They have all finished high school, a luxury I didn't have. But the European educational system was excellent. Once I learned Japanese, I had no trouble keeping up with my college classes in Japan.

Many of my students at Southern want to be teachers. When I first started teaching at Southern, they gave me a textbook and told me that first-year art students needed to be familiar with everything in the book. When I met the students, I realized that they didn't need to know everything in the book. Most of them were only tak-ing Art History because it was a requirement. The students didn't know Norman Rockwell from Botticelli. Many of them had no interest. Music History 101 was already filled.

Ten weeks into the class, I could see that many of them still had not been moved. Not by Gericault. Not by Picasso. Not by Koubou Daishi. The only thing that moved them were those awful Renoirs. The man couldn't even paint a human body, just dreamy looking skin tones on fairies. Oh, well. I did the best I could.

I tried to talk about my early experiences with art. We had nothing in Berleburg, and I grew up during the war, so we did not make trips to any galleries in distant places. We barely even had photos in our textbooks. That was it in Germany, black and white photos in textbooks.

The first time I saw an oil painting was in Belgium. The nuns took us to the Mechelen Cathedral, St Rumbold's, to make sure that we learned our catechism. While my classmates prayed and took communion, I looked around. The Madonna and child. The way she wept for her child because she knew eventually, he would die. And she was placed directly under a vault. My eye followed the lines, seemingly up forever. I was transported away from my situation, my terrible, terrible situation, by art and architecture.

I like talking to my students about cathedrals, specifically, the genesis of a multigenerational work of art. The artists and architects who begin the project know that their children's children's children will be the ones who see it through to fruition. In the case of St. Rumbold's, the first stones were set in 1200, and still today, the tower is not complete. It is on the next generation to complete it, to fine tune the vision, or leave it as is until someone takes up the challenge.

It is not lost on me that my niece has a vision like this of our family history. I am talking to her about her prose poem. I'm not sure what I'm going to say. I'm just talking. I hear myself say the words, "I can see what you are trying to do. You are trying to tell the story of our family and place yourself in it."

As the words leave my mouth, I am shaking with anger. Why? I haven't a clue. It starts with a bit of a face flush. And then takes over my whole body. Perhaps I have traveled back in time to my niece's age, twenty-two.

Or perhaps I am sixteen? My father says that I cannot finish high school. I must get a job and start supporting the family. We have loans to pay back. We didn't get to this country for free.

Yes, that is it! My niece had the nerve to insinuate this incident into the story. I am not sure if I ever discussed this with her. Maybe I did once, over some dinner in France when I drank too much wine and was feeling especially warmly towards her. That evening when I ordered veal head not knowing that they'd bring an entire skull to the table. What else did I say that evening as I looked at this poor dead creature? Did I talk about my sex life?

That doesn't give her rights! She cannot tell me how I felt. She cannot tell me why I did what I did. She wasn't there. The nerve!

I cannot even listen to myself talk. I have competing soundtracks in my brain. This girl will drive me crazy! I hear myself say, "How dare you?" I sound like a lawyer on a bad TV drama.

Fury was my guide from age sixteen to age...well, I don't know. Maybe it still is. Fury at the Nazis, fury at my parents, fury at my aunts and uncles for what they did and didn't do. Mathilde and Hugo! Selma! Frieda and Max. Those awful jobs Max sent me to. Terrible. I was regularly fired. And all I wanted to do was finish high school. Why could no one see that? Why did no one help me?

Art was my escape. You didn't need a high school degree to enjoy art. I could admire the buildings of New York. I could enjoy several hours in the Met or the Modern for the same price as going to a movie. And there was always window shopping. I eventually learned how to dress mannequins and help design store windows.

When I met Stan at a political meeting, I realized my luck was starting to turn. Art and Stan pulled me away from my anger and despair. But it is still here. That anger is sitting on my shoulder right now.

From the look on her face, my niece is terrified of what I'll say next. She, who has had everything given to her. Lucky, lucky, lucky. What has she to complain about? What has she to worry about? She should find her own God-damn subject and leave me out of her writing!

Where is Stanley? He is good at talking to students who have abandoned reason. He could help me clean up this mess I am making.

Stanley? When I met him, I was immediately struck by his dazzling intelligence. He was handsome, too. We met, like so many couples we knew, at a political meeting. We both wanted a better world, one that spread the wealth to the many. One that eschewed persecution of minorities. Yes, we were communists. But we didn't follow along blindly. We both had enough of things when Stalin's excesses became public.

Stan was interested in all things Asian. It started when he was a boy and the Japanese bombed Pearl Harbor. His response was to read everything he could find on Japan. He got himself a Japanese language textbook and quickly taught himself to read it fluently. He never learned math or science, but he could learn any language that interested him. By the time the Korean War came along, and Stan was drafted, they sent him to Tokyo to translate documents.

Listening to Stan, even before he was drafted, I started dreaming of Japan. I'd spent my childhood in Europe watching it destroy itself. New York was incredible, but it was a place for rich people. There was no equality. My choices as a girl without a high school degree were limited. I wasn't even a citizen.

I married Stan, and after he was done with the army, I met him in Tokyo. Stan enrolled in Komazawa University and finished as class valedictorian. Then he transferred to the University of Tokyo to get a masters' degree in Buddhism. He was so happy. He finally came into himself. He loved studying Buddhism. The texts, the languages – the more esoteric, the closer it crept into his heart. I was glad that he liked whiskey. Otherwise, I think he might have disappeared into some of his texts. But he loved spending the evenings talking and drinking with his professors and other students. I loved this, too.

Was I happy in those days? Yes! We studied, talked, went to parties, museums, bookstores. I loved it.

I went to Tokyo Geidai and studied art. Of course, I'd had to study Japanese first. Japanese was not easy for me. It didn't come quickly. But I became conversant after I started making friends, good friends, ones who I still visit every year when we go to Japan. Five of us women art students became particularly close. It was a relief to have friends again.

My niece has condensed my Tokyo years into two lines. I point out the lines to her, and say, still hot with anger, "This is all wrong. You understand nothing about me!"

I don't put that much stock in psychologists. Half of what they say is common sense. But I do wonder if my niece is going through some phase that I don't understand. The tears are running down her cheeks. I suppress my anger and suggest, "Maybe you are on a path that will take you somewhere with this writing. What do you think about that?"

A phase? Maybe not. Maybe this is who she is.

A lesbian. Really? Is that why she is turning all these stories on their head?

I encouraged Stan to apply to get his Ph.D. in the U.S. By now, my parents had paid off the relatives who got us out of Germany, and they had moved out of New York City to the farm somewhere west of nowhere. Then they talked my brother into working on the farm. What a mistake that was! He should have been a history teacher. He loved history. What a stupid thing, the cow business. I will never understand the allure.

My sister, too, married a dentist of all things. Living in Long Island and chasing the trappings of success. What happened to them? We got through that whole mess in Europe only to live in the suburbs and believe in this fatuous American dream?

But no, it is time to tamp down the anger. My niece is sobbing.

She understands my point. I pull her close to me and give her a hug. "I am just trying to help," I hear myself say.

"Yes," Jenny mumbles into my shoulder. I wish I could conjure up a happy ending for this girl. But for tonight, she picks up her pages and goes upstairs.

Part 3: If I knew then

Lucie was interviewee number six for the Fortunoff Video Archive for Holocaust Testimonies, which began at Yale University in 1979.[13] I don't remember her mentioning the interview to me in March 1980. Perhaps she kept it to herself because she wasn't sure the project would amount to much.

I never saw Lucie's testimony (or my dad's) until after 2000, when I was mailed a VHS tape of each of their interviews. It was clear that between the time Lucie and Dad were interviewed (1980 to 1999), the interviewers had improved their methods. Where Lucie's interviewers directed her towards clipped answers, or provided words, with Dad, they used a much more conversational style. Searching in the Yale archives, Lucie also requested a follow up interview in 2006, so she could provide information about a recent trip to Röddenau, the village where Grandma was born.

Maybe Helen Epstein, or another source, used the word *traumatized*, to describe the root of Lucie's oversized reaction to my poem, but I didn't see that. If I was coming from a place of *intergenerational trauma*, in my early twenties, I missed that too. But surely, Lucie and I were wrestling with the lingering effects of the Holocaust.

Dad had trouble sleeping because he was worried about the cows, the hay, the hired man, a fence falling down, or some other aspect of the business. Lucie took sleeping pills. Hilda never

---

[13]Lucie W. Holocaust Testimony (HVT-6). Fortunoff Video Archive for Holocaust Testimonies, Yale University Library.

slept. By the time I stopped growing, I stopped sleeping through the night.

Grandma was a worrier. I was a worrier.

During Lucie's interview with Yale, she twirls her ring or her watch. Dad holds his hands clasped. It takes great effort to sit still, to seem unperturbed by the events he is recounting.

I probably took Lucie's rebuke far too seriously. I'd seen Lucie blow her top many times in the past. Though she'd never let loose on me like that before, it wasn't that I was unfamiliar with her scolding holier than thou persona. And newly in the work world, the routine praise that came along for excellent test scores or writing a good paper, was absent from my life. I probably still seemed a bit like an untrained puppy looking for praise for doing something not all that amazing.

It wasn't till many years later that I understood that Lucie respected me for bucking the paths that she and my father wanted for me. She came to see that I made life and career decisions (or stumbled into them) that brought me satisfaction, were "good work," and brought love and joy to my family.

But after Lucie's rebuke, I let the (still un-named) family history project slide away. It wasn't that I didn't think about it. I couldn't stop myself. But I realized it was not the right time. I didn't want to spend my life arguing with people. Perhaps I knew that I needed more maturity. And perhaps my time at the Library of Congress helped me anticipate changes that would come with archiving, digitization, and ultimately the world wide web. I couldn't have known that passenger lists from trains sent to Auschwitz would be made public. But I must have anticipated that someday I'd have the time and volition to work on the project.

Would Lucie respect today's effort? I'm sure she'd quibble with much I've written. But I think she'd be happy to know that her legacy still resonates. That I am still turning over things she said, such as this dialog from Lucie's 1980 interview.

INTERVIEWER 1: You arrived in Aachen in Germany, in 1941.

LUCIE: February 1941. It was ice cold out. It was—there was snow everywhere. And then two SS men came to the car and were very polite and helped me with my suitcases. And they—and in fact, they spoke to me in French, and I answered in French. I was very naive. You know? They spoke to me in French, I answered back. So we went to the passport control. And when I pulled out my passport, which had a J in it, all of a sudden, they were astounded. They dropped my suitcases and were very rude to me and asked me what I was doing here, that I was breaking the law, and so on and so forth.

INTERVIEWER 1: You were a young girl of 16?

LUCIE: 16, yes.

INTERVIEWER 1: Entering Germany.

LUCIE: Entering Germany. Wearing a hat for the first time. [LAUGHS] I was—my relatives had dressed me up to look grown up for the first time. That's what I was aspiring to at the time. So anyway, then, yeah. That's right. First, they looked through my suitcases, or somebody else did. We had to go through this—

INTERVIEWER 2: Customs.

LUCIE: Customs. Through customs. It's funny. When I recall this, the German words seem to come out of my—more than the English ones do. Anyway, I went through customs, and then I had to be examined by this nurse, physical examination. They wanted to check that I wasn't carrying anything, weapons, or documents, all sorts of things they suspected me of. And then afterwards, I was called into this room. And I remember the room as an office, sort of. And I sat on a chair, and one sat on one side, and the other one sat on top of a table, there. And they asked me questions. They interrogated me for about two hours...

CHAPTER THIRTY
A New Direction

My parents were not happy when I told them my plan was to move to the west coast, Seattle or San Francisco. Dad grumbled about me not growing up. Mom detailed all of Rochester's virtues, as if I'd missed them all these years. My parents did not want me to leave.

My plan was not rational: I had no job offer, internship, year-long house-sit, or educational program. I was not moving to be with a friend or lover.

I was searching for an epiphany, my second. My first had come two years earlier just after I graduated college. I'd had several attempts at romantic relationships that had gone nowhere. I was unable to fall in love. I didn't understand why I kept pushing romance away.

Then one Sunday afternoon, I fell asleep on the living room couch. As I woke up, a clear voice commanded, "You should be with a woman."

"What?" I asked.

"You should be with a woman!" Where, I wondered, was this voice coming from? Who was speaking to me? What was going on?

I slowly sat up. As I looked around the familiar room, I turned the sentence over in my mind. I should be a with a woman. Really? Should I?

The next day, I remembered the word for such a revelation, an epiphany. My epiphany was that I should be with a woman.

I walked around for several months wondering what to do about this epiphany. Eventually, I told my parents about it. Mom cried. Then she argued with me, telling me that I could not be a lesbian. Dad was silent.

As Dad helped me pack the car for my move out west, I had a lump in my throat. I was pretty sure that I wasn't coming back, that I'd find my place out west. I hoped that someday my parents wouldn't see every decision of mine as a rebellion against them. That they'd come to see that I was just making my own way.

I cried a bit the first day or two on the road. I wondered if I knew what I was doing. But I also enjoyed visiting friends and acquaintances who I'd met over the years in Illinois and Minnesota. I loved hiking in Yellowstone and the Black Hills. I camped by a river in Idaho that was so loud that I barely slept. I spent my twenty-fifth birthday laughing with friends over a salmon dinner by the Puget Sound in Seattle. Then I drove south down the Pacific coast.

In San Francisco, I couch-surfed first with a friend near the row of colorful houses called The Painted Ladies, and then with friends of friends in the Castro. I was having fun – perhaps a bit too much fun – and still wasn't sure if I was staying or moving on. Then, one afternoon, I decided to go jogging. About five blocks from my couch-surf, I stumbled as I ran down a rather steep hill. I tumbled over my right ankle and seriously sprained it. With a bandage and a cane, I would not be moving on anytime soon.

I called my parents and told them what a great city San Francisco was, and about my ankle. Dad said, "Find a job!" as if the thought wouldn't have occurred to me on my own.

I got a job at Old Wives Tales Bookstore. Shortly thereafter, an acquaintance from D.C. called to tell me she had moved to Oakland. When we'd first met, Amy Oppenheimer was a newly minted lawyer living in rural Virginia and dating a friend from my soccer team. My soccer friend was a community organizer and had enlisted my help to make sandwiches for an Agent Orange conference. As I was slathering mayo on a turkey sandwich, Amy came into the apartment where we were working. I already knew from my soccer friend that Amy was a smarty pants, but I'd never seen her picture. She was adorable with a gap-toothed smile, twinkly brown eyes, and short dark hair. She bounded purposefully across the room to embrace my friend, barely noticing me.

Amy was calling me now to let me know that she'd moved to Oakland. She and my friend had broken up. She was going wind-surfing with her brother over the weekend. Would I like to join them? While the windsurfing didn't interest me, the idea of a beach where I could swim in the East Bay sounded great. San Francisco in the summer could be as cold as the winter. Amy said that this beach in Livermore would be hot. It was. So was dating Amy. I was soon smitten and we quickly became inseparable.

I'd never done a big coming out to my family, mainly because when I'd told my parents in 1979 that I was a lesbian, they had gotten upset. Mom wanted me to keep my sexuality under wraps, hoping that someday soon, I'd come to my senses, move back to Rochester, and marry a man. I respected their wishes by keeping my mouth shut.

But family members began to turn up in San Francisco. Everyone I knew wanted to visit. They came to see the Golden Gate Bridge, to drive by Victorian houses painted in pastels, to go to the beach, or hike in the hills. They came to eat Chinese, Thai, Mexican, Peruvian, or California cuisine; to visit Golden Gate Park, to go to a museum, or just to visit me. Now I brought Amy with me. Everyone liked her; eventually even my parents liked her.

Things were going well! So why did I still have a sense of inquietude? I had expected my "adult" life to feel like a water course picking up speed for rapids, slowing down for eddies, and moving in a clear direction. Sure, steering the boat would help. But the water, the inevitability that all was well, would propel me. I'd know I was on the right river. I'd know where I was going.

I felt like I was moving...but I couldn't see ahead. I didn't feel certain that I was on the right river, charting my course. I was still waiting for a message from on high to validate or clarify my purpose in life. Where was my epiphany?

CHAPTER THIRTY-ONE

Passover in Miami Beach, 1985

Amy and I weren't a couple long before she, and then I, were notified that our grandmothers were ill. I asked for time off at the bookstore to fly to Florida to visit my grandmother for Passover. She was in her eighties and several of her sisters had already died. I knew she wasn't going to live forever. I was sentimental and sad as I walked around SFO waiting to board my flight to Miami. The airport bookstore was stocked with foreign language magazines, and I noticed the German *Der Spiegel*, said *KREBS* on the cover. Krebs, the German word for cancer, was what Grandma was dying of, just like Grandpa. I wondered if my last name would be the destiny for all of us. I wondered if I changed my name, if I could change my destiny.

I had packed a small cassette tape recorder in my suitcase. I hoped Grandma would be amenable to me recording her. (I still had no idea that Aunt Lucie had done a video oral history.)

When I walked from the cab to Grandma's apartment, she met me at the door. She was smaller than the last time I saw her, perhaps by two or three inches. Still, her face was tanned and she broke out into a big smile when she saw me. I gave her a big hug and let her describe what she had planned for us.

On my second night at Grandma's, she'd had no friends over for Passover. We'd eaten early. There were lots of leftovers from the night before, when she'd had several friends join us. Sick or not, Grandma had cooked up her traditional Passover feast: veal breast, *matzashalot*, green beans, and a hazelnut torte for dessert. Grandma didn't seem tired after dinner, so I suggested that we try taping her stories.

"You know my stories. I have nothing new to tell."

"I'm sure you have a lot of stories..." I said, walking to my suitcase. I set the tape recorder on the wooden coffee table in front of the faded gold couch. I put in a new tape and turned it on. "Why don't you tell me about Berleburg?"

"You've seen it. I took you there, remember? We had a good time. You saw, I had friends, my children were young. ..." Grandma stopped mid-sentence.

I found myself panicking. Silence on the tape would not be a good thing. I jumped in to prevent a void on the tape. "Why don't you tell me about when you moved there? What did you think?"

"I moved to Berleburg after our honeymoon. I already told you about the honeymoon, didn't I?"

"Tell me again."

"We left for our honeymoon with a whole suitcase full of money. We went to an inn on the Rhine. We were supposed to stay for two weeks. But in the 1920s there was terrible inflation in Germany just like in the U.S. Prices changed every day. The inn had a blackboard in the lobby. Every morning, they posted the new rates for night. We came home after less than one week. We'd spent all the money in the suitcase. Then we moved into our house in Berleburg." Grandma smiled at me.

Another long silence. I felt panic set in. What should I ask now? It dawned on me that this was why people wrote lists of questions. Where was my list? I started lobbing out questions: Her earliest memory? Her school in Röddenau? *Kristallnacht*? How she felt when the children were in Belgium? Her immigration story? We went through all her stories within fifteen minutes.

"What about your time in New York?" I asked. "I know you took in boarders, and I know Grandpa begged you to move to Spencerport, but before that, what was it like bringing up teenagers in New York? Did you worry about them?"

"After the Nazis, what did I have to worry about? We lived a few floors above Frieda. We were always busy. The children had to work, too."

"Dad worked as a bus boy during the summer, he told me."

"And before that he delivered dry cleaning. He was always busy. We had no money."

"Were you happy in New York?"

"Of course, we were." Then Grandma reconsidered, "Well, we weren't happy when we found out what happened to our relatives." Grandma clutched her stomach.

"Are you okay?"

"I won't be around forever," she said.

"I wish you would be."

"Ha! Now turn off the tape."

"Sure," I said, not knowing if I had something good or not. I'd never taped a conversation with someone before. Or since, for that matter.

Back in the Bay Area, I listened many times to the tape that I made with Grandma. The recording quality was poor. My voice sounded tight and abrasive, and Grandma seemed far away. I transcribed the tape. Then I edited it. The conversation struck me as flat. I couldn't find Grandma and my relationship in it. There was no passion, generosity of spirit, or depth. Something was wrong that I couldn't capture the Grandma I loved. I wouldn't share this with Lucie or anyone else. Another failed attempt to wrestle some new truths from the old family stories.

Thank goodness that a decade earlier, I'd convinced Grandma to show me some of her tricks in the kitchen. Even if I couldn't capture Grandma's voice or convey the love between us on the page, I could feel her next to me in the kitchen. There, I could hear her suggestions for how to make the perfect Passover nut torte.

CHAPTER THIRTY-TWO

The Mahnmal

By the 1990s, I had segued from Old Wives Tales through a graduate degree in geography to a career administering local government environmental programs. Amy and I ticked off a decade together. We adopted two children, Talia in 1993 and Adin in 1998. Whatever qualms my parents had during the 1980s about my future vanished when Talia arrived. It turned out that grandchildren were what they'd wanted from me. So simple – how had I missed it all those years? Any questions that remained about my life's path stayed underground because I was too busy to brood for more than a few minutes.

Friends and relatives visited us regularly at our house in the Berkeley Hills. As the Bay Area is such a popular vacation destination, friends of friends and friends of relatives appeared from time to time on our social calendar. One such guest was Rikarde, Aunt Lucie's friend from Berleburg. While I hadn't visited Berleburg since my trip with Aunt Lucie and Grandma in 1979, Aunt Lucie had been going regularly, contributing to a variety of projects such as Horst Hecker's history of the Jews of Frankenberg and a monument to the Jews of Berleburg killed by the Nazis. Rikarde was one of the town employees leading the Berleburg monument project. Aunt Lucie exhorted me to entertain Rikarde and her husband. We could compare notes on local government and I should ask Rikarde about the *Mahnmal,* the German word for monument, and its progress.

Rikarde described her job as the Berleburg archivist, storing and filing historical documents. She also worked with commissions from time to time, such as the commission for the *Mahnmal.* She was optimistic that the *Mahnmal* would be built in the next year or two. The town was committed.

I smiled. Even small projects in Berkeley took years to accomplish from design, to budgeting, to revision, etc. Berkeley would have at least three commissions that would want to consider the monument from different perspectives. Sandbaggers could be counted on to appear at every turn. Would the children of former Nazis and/or Neo-Nazis really say nothing? Surely someone would be concerned about mismanagement of tax funds.

Rikarde shrugged and said she thought it would happen.

Shortly before the turn of the millennium, Aunt Lucie called to say the design and permitting for the *Mahnmal* were complete. The *Mahnmal* should be up by May and a dedication ceremony was in the works. Lucie had been invited by the mayor to speak at the dedication! Berleburg was going to pay for her to come. Rikarde had encouraged Lucie to make sure the whole family came.

I mentioned to Amy that I was considering going to the ceremony in Berleburg. I assumed she would not be interested in coming. Amy considered herself to be lefty atheist Jew. She grew up with little formal Jewish education. Amy's parents made sure her older brothers were bar mitzvah. They quit the temple shortly after her brother David became a man. Amy's mother taught her never to buy German products nor to step foot on German soil. I assumed she'd happily stay home with the kids for a week while I went to Germany.

But it turned out that if I was going to Germany, Amy was not missing the trip. She wanted to see the little town that had caused my family so much pain. She wanted to support my parents and me. And, Amy wanted to be part of the Krebs entourage attending this important ceremony.

Friends of ours agreed to stay with Talia and Adin. I called around to my cousins and aunts and found that all my cousins were going. I also learned that survivors and descendants from three other families were coming from Holland, Israel, and the U.S.

Aunt Lucie called about her speech. Should she speak in English or German? Should she kick them in the pants for the past, or praise their current efforts? What about the Sinti and Roma who were not included on the monument? Should she bring that up? As she babbled on, I couldn't tell if she wanted my input or if she was just anxious.

Lucie also expressed qualms about the monument's design. She praised the architect's initial design, an irregularly sided bronze star as seen from above. The names of those killed would be listed on the sides of the star. It would have been stark and prominent rising above the graves. But – rule by committee meant compromise – and now there would be a Bible verse and a large Jewish Star on top. Lucie was concerned that the star would attract vandals. She added, "German Jews used symbols of the Torah, or the tribes of Israel, not the star. It was Hitler who branded us with the star. Why perpetuate that?"

On the flight to Germany, I wondered how large the dedication ceremony would be, how much fuss the town would make. I also wondered how my various family members would get along, if Lucie would blow up (or what might cause her to lose her cool), and if my dad might get locked inside a hotel again. It also crossed my mind that this would be a family party of sorts, the first one in Berleburg since *Kristallnacht*.

When I saw my parents in Berleburg, they were both smiling. Dad seemed much more relaxed than on his last trip. Was it because his sisters were with him? Or had he already had a drink? Maybe it was because he and Mom had been traveling quite a bit over the past decade. He'd visited many places with fraught histories or long wars: Viet Nam, South Africa, and India. Maybe he was seeing Germany as changed since both the 1940s and the 1970s.

Bad Berleburg was a charming small town. After the second World War, and then again after German reunification, the country had made attempts at administrative simplification. Westfalen (Westphalia) was now Nordrhein-Westfalen (North Rhine-Westphalia). Bad Berleburg had undergone a name change (from Berleburg) to indicate it was a spa town. Amy and I were offered a room to stay with a local psychiatrist and his family who moved to the town in the 1980s.

The dedication ceremony was scheduled for our first full day in town. Most of my family members sat in the first few rows but I decided to stand for the ceremony. I wanted a good view of the dais, the folding chairs looked uncomfortable, and I didn't want to get drowsy. It wasn't too long into the ceremony when Lucie was invited to give her speech. Cameras snapped pictures and someone adjusted the microphone so she could be heard by everyone. She began,

> I would like to express my thanks to the city of Bad Berleburg for dedicating this handsome Mahnmal to the memory of its Jewish Mitbürger, murdered by the Nazi regime. I am deeply moved and most grateful that the city of my birth has come to face this burden of its past. Some sixty-five years have passed since those horrendous years. Assembled here are undoubtedly many people who were not yet born at that time.
>
> They may ask, why do we have to be reminded of atrocities committed before we were even born? What happened 65 years ago is now history and needs to be evaluated. We ask ourselves what do we know about it and how do we react to it? These are important questions which are answered differently according to our age, our past, and our moral orientation. We all know that one easily forgets that which one knows only vaguely.

Lucie at the dais, mayor and chorus in background, 2000

The Mahnmal urges us to be informed. May this memorial contribute to strengthen our common memory and to back it up historically with our deeply felt participation.

I no longer remember if Aunt Lucie addressed the crowd in German or English. But my mind wandered. I wondered what my life would have been like had I grown up here. Would I have fled at age seventeen to Frankfurt, Munich, or even Berlin? Would I still have wanted to travel the world? Or was my desire to flee a response to my family's flight from here? Was I destined to feel like an outsider, to feel the need to move, to invent or reinvent myself? Was this an essential Jewish experience? Or was it just me? I focused again on Lucie's speech,

At the end of the war we received the terrible news that almost all the relatives we left behind were dead. We tried to put ourselves into their place, even in our dreams, to grasp what the unfortunate ones had to endure until death became a release for them. Of some we know how and when they died, but of the others, only *für tot erklärt* (declared dead) in Auschwitz, in Bergen-Belsen, in Theresien-stadt. Nightmarish visions fill the gaps. The burden of the past weighs heavily on the minds of us survivors.

I knew that the past weighed heavily on Dad and Aunt Hilda as well, though neither of them expressed their feelings in the same way as Lucie. My cousins and I carry the weight, too. Even if I was mainly involved with work and kids, from time to time, I'd ask Dad a question, a loose thread that had unraveled from the main fabric of his story. "Was cousin Doris in Belgium with you when the Nazis invaded, or had she already gone home?" "How long were you in the Frankfurt orphanage?" "Why did Grandma and Grandpa send you to the orphanage?" I wondered if some day I'd come back to the writing project I'd begun in my twenties, if I'd sit down and try to explain my past as I'd come to understand it.

When the ceremony was over, I walked around the *Mahnmal,* trying to read the names of the dead, trying to decipher the Bible verse from Lamentations, "For these things do I weep, My eyes flow with tears. In Memory of the Jewish citizens of Berleburg. Persecuted, erred against, and murdered 1933 to 1945." Here I am.

I'm in the foreground, waiting to approach the Manmahl, 2000

CHAPTER THIRTY-THREE

Lucie's 80th

When Aunt Lucie told me that she was having a small party for her birthday, I knew "small" did not mean unimportant. Almost every year around the time of her birthday, she would mention how important birthdays are to Germans. On most other topics she did not lump herself in with Germans. I began looking into flights.

This was how on a warm sunny August morning in 2004 I sat drinking coffee with Lucie in her kitchen. The phone rang. Her friend Tsedenka was on the other line calling to ask if it was a good time to bring by the cake, her birthday present to Lucie.

"How did I get to be 80?" Lucie asked me after she hung up. Then she described the cake, which Tsedenka had been working on for days. It was to be the centerpiece of the food table, a woodsy tree limb of a cake (what we call a Yule log in English). Neither Lucie nor Tsedenka thought such a cake should be served only once a year.

Lucie suggested that we look at her garden while we waited for Tsedenka. She stopped in front of one of her Japanese maples, which I already knew grew from a sapling that she'd brought home in her suitcase from Japan many years ago. But she told me the story again, concluding with the question, "Have you been to Japan?"

"Yes, don't you remember? Amy and I visited in 1993. You were there then, too. We went to Kyoto and Nara together. We went to your favorite temple."

"Oh, yes," she said, looking down in embarrassment. When she looked up again, she smiled and said, "How could I forget?"

"What was its name?" I asked, hoping this will spur Lucie back into professor mode.

She shrugged.

"The one that looks like a phoenix taking flight. You remember."

"Oh, the Byōdō-in. Yes, of course."

I looked up into the mass of reddish leaves fluttering in the light wind. It was a lovely maple. Next to the main tree, volunteers had shot up, as if the tree needed company, or comfort.

"Let's go upstairs and get dressed. The guests will arrive soon!"

As Lucie and I came back into the house, Tsedenka arrived with the cake. Stan emerged from his study, where he'd been at work all morning. Tsedenka greeted all of us – I'd met her several times over the years – with a description of the cake. "You need to store it in the refrigerator. Keep it cool so it doesn't melt." Then she began unwrapping the cake, first peeling a perfectly ironed red checked linen tea towel. Then she removed the specially made cardboard cover that had been taped and stapled into a dome. "Ta da!" Tsedenka said, pointing out the architecture and design of log-shaped cake. Meringue mushrooms sprouted from the trunk and a side branch. Purple and yellow pansy petals were sprinkled on the ground. "The frosting is mocha," She said. "The trunk is chocolate. The side branch is vanilla. Something for everyone." And if that wasn't enough, she also brought a huge bowl of strawberries.

"You are a marvel, Tsedenka! I so wish you and Jan would come back later for the party." Lucie knew that Tsedenka's husband hated parties and the pair would not be returning later.

I helped Lucie put the cake in the refrigerator and clean up the breakfast dishes before going upstairs to change. I'd only brought a few outfits and it wouldn't take me long to get ready. I was seated in the living room reading the *New York Times* when Lucie returned downstairs.

Something was off. Lucie's shirt wasn't hanging right. I noticed a long piece of sticky tape down the front of her sweater M, M, M, M, M, M, M. I pulled the tape off.

"How could I have missed that?" Lucie asked and kissed my cheek. "It is so good to have you here! Let's go get the table ready." With that, we were back in the kitchen. I considered how odd it was that Lucie missed the tape on her sweater. She usually had an eagle eye for such things. But Stan came into the kitchen and asked whether he needed to wear a tie. Then he looked from one to the other of us and said, "It is like looking at two Lucie's. I always forget how much you two look alike."

I smiled and sighed. How many times had I heard this? Those loudmouth Bachenheimer genes. Lucie asked me to put plates on the table. Stan followed me with the cutlery. Then the front door opened, and I heard Dad call, "Yoo hoo!"

Lucie called back, "Yoo hoo!" and headed for the front door.

Stan muttered, "Forty-five minutes early. He must have left at 5:00 am."

I did the math. "Maybe 4:30. And Mom probably slept the whole way."

I only recently learned "Yoo Hoo" was popularized on a long-running radio comedy show, *The Goldbergs*. Molly Goldberg, the matriarch, played by Gertrude Berg, also a show writer and creator, greeted her neighbors with that hardy call. I imagine that Dad and his sisters probably learned some English from this show when they were, literally, just off the boat.

Dad hugged Lucie and then me. Mom followed him and squeezed my cheeks while kissing me all over my face. Stan came out of his study and asked if Dad if was ready for a Scotch. "I'll join you," I said, "but make mine small."

And even though it was still only 11:15, and the party was supposed to start at noon, the rest of the guests started to arrive. *Gantse michpocha*, as Dad would say, the whole family.

People loaded their plates with German cold cuts (freshly donated from my uncle Freddy and his son Mark, the butchers), rye bread, cheeses, cucumber salad, potato salad, and smoked fish. Cups were filled with coffee, wine, sodas, and juices...and Scotch refills.

People circulated. Jokes were made, some in English, some in German. But these were not the jokes of Mrs. Goldberg, jokes based on a malapropism or misunderstanding of something typically American but incomprehensible to a new Jewish immigrant. Those jokes were as tired as the 1940s, back when Lucie, Hilda, Dad, and their first cousins were still young immigrants.

The current crop of jokes were kicked off by Uncle Walter. "I think it's just terrible how everyone has treated Lance Armstrong, especially after winning the Tour de France while competing on drugs. When I'm on drugs, I can't even find my bike." Two cousins laughed loudly. I wondered if they enjoyed the joke or were humoring Walter. I headed off to talk to my cousin David. I told him about the sticker on his mother's sweater. He nodded thoughtfully but said nothing.

Later, someone said, "Let me get a family photo." I noted that anyone in the room who had genetic material that went back to Germany crowded around Lucie, while all spouses moved out of the frame.

Lucie stood near the living room bookcase not far from the front door of the house while people found spots for themselves. I counted heads and heights. The middle row was overflowing with people roughly Lucie's (and my) height. I took a knee and joined the row of children in the front. Dad stood behind Lucie. Hilda was to Lucie's right. In between them, a sea of cousins.

The in-laws produced a range of cameras and snapped away. The snapping seemed to go on interminably, broken up by banter about who blinked, who moved, and why yet another picture should be taken.

I noticed that Mom had wandered off. Once it would have been her with her Kodak Brownie, or Instamatic taking the picture. But she was uninterested in going digital. I imagined that she had gone to the bathroom or maybe to refill her coffee cup.

Shortly after the cameras were put away, a loud shriek came from the kitchen. It was Lucie. Stan hurried toward the kitchen.

"My cake!" Lucie shrieked loudly enough for it to reverberate through the entire house.

By the time I arrived in the kitchen along with the rest of the pack, Lucie was pointing to an empty area where someone had sliced through the middle of the tree trunk, taking a large slice of cake. "Who did this?" Lucie shouted to us guests. Her angry voice was met with deafening silence.

Finally, Dad said, "It is not a big deal. Let's not make it a big deal."

"Ros?" Lucie turned to Mom with an angry look. Mom said nothing.

Dad said, "The cake will still taste delicious! It's not a big deal. Let's not make a fuss."

But clearly there was an aggrieved party whose birthday had been ruined. Maybe this was the first ruined birthday of Lucie's life. Probably not.

Lucie's staccato tirade rose to full volume, "Have you no manners? What is wrong with you? Are you crazy? Who does something like that! I cannot believe that you have ruined my cake! My birthday! Have you no manners at all?"

I was amazed that Mom kept her composure through this dressing down, which felt like it lasted 15 minutes, maybe more. Stan and David tried to distract Lucie by arranging candles on the unscathed sections of the cake. Then Aunt Hilda started singing "Happy Birthday." As the rest of joined in, Lucie seemed to let go of her rant. She was almost smiling by the time we reached, "Happy birthday dear Lucie!..."

Most of us had experienced a Lucie rant, and I probably wasn't the only one who was relieved that Lucie had set her sights on someone else. Nor did I wonder alone what demon forced Mom's hand to cut the cake when no one else was around. Was Mom jealous of Lucie having a party? Had Mom wanted such a fuss several months ago when she turned eighty? Mom said she didn't give a fig about birthdays, Mother's Day, or Chanukkah. On the other hand,

Mom was a big fan of Freud. I'm sure the father of psychoanalysis would have had a word or two to say about Mom destroying Lucie's birthday cake before it could be admired by everyone. Or more importantly, a picture of Lucie taken with the magnificent cake in the foreground.

The next day before I drove with my parents back to Rochester, Lucie gave us a tour of her new apartment in an independent living facility. She and Stan couldn't keep the house up forever. But for the short run, the plan was to eat and sleep at the facility and to maintain the house for their work. Stan, still emeritus at Yale, had articles to write for an encyclopedia. Lucie was still working on her survey of Buddhist Art. She had missed a few deadlines. I wondered if she was going to finish. I wondered what the next decade or so would have in store for my aunt. Would she continue to travel to Japan, Germany, and elsewhere? Or would health concerns overtake her plans?

At the heart of my relationship with Lucie, she was always the art history teacher. She practically quivered with joy to impart the name of the sculptor, why a particular Buddhist deity was represented in a certain way, or how one of her favorite architects had been selected to design a museum. If Lucie didn't know the answer to an art question that I asked, she would gladly look it up. It was art that had carried her away from all her childhood problems. She had an eye for detail and beauty. She could spend hours in a museum and never get bored.

I appreciated and admired Lucie's tenacity. How else to explain her Ph.D. and a college-level teaching position? With no support from Grandma and Grandpa in New York – they insisted she get a full-time job rather than complete high school – Lucie signed up for art classes at night. After she and Stan married and moved to Tokyo, she studied art and Japanese. And finally, at age 50, she was awarded a Ph.D. by Yale. As Grandma pointed out to me, "Not just anyone can do that!"

Lucie and Grandma at Lucie's Ph.D. award ceremony, 1978

CHAPTER THIRTY-FOUR

The Stolpersteine

I read an article or two about *Stolpersteine* (stumbling blocks, or stumble stones) years before I learned of plans being made to install these memorial plaques in Berleburg. One week in early 2008, Lucie called about the Berleburg plans. She was irritated that the committee wasn't going to send her a ticket to attend the dedication.

I corresponded briefly with Gisela Weissinger, a local project coordinator of the Berleburg *Stolpersteine* project. She wrote,

> We are a small circle of inhabitants of Berleburg. And in our opinion, the memorial (in the cemetery) is not enough of a memorial to the people with the Jewish faith. For this reason, we asked the municipal council of Berleburg to let us lay, so called "stumble stones" in front of all the houses, in which the people lived, who were pursued and were deprived of their rights and a lot of them were murdered, like your great-aunt Adele. In Berleburg, in addition to the Jews, all the Roma were pursued and nearly all of them were killed.
>
> We were given the permission from the municipal council for the "stumble stones." We collected donations. On September 2, the artist who had the idea for the "stumble stones" will come lay the first 35 "stumble stones."
>
> Why September 2?

We chose this date because the commemorates the 750th anniversary of the town. Such a date is a good time to remind people of the dark and bad sides in the history of this town...

Your aunt, Lucie Weinstein, helped us by giving us information about the Jewish inhabitants of Berleburg. My family took part in the opening ceremony for the monument to the Jews and listened to her speak....[14]

I went to the *Stolpersteine* project website. I learned Gunter Demnig was the artist who conceptualized the project. Since I'd already heard Demnig was attending the ceremony in Berleburg, I wondered if he attended many such installations. Demnig cited a verse from the Talmud as inspiration, "A person is only forgotten when his or her name is forgotten." And he called the project *Stolpersteine* because,

He liked the double meaning of the German word because he wanted to provoke people into "stumbling" mentally. Contrary to what certain online sources claim, Gunter Demnig did NOT want to create a link to a certain antisemitic expression apparently used in Nazi Germany that he did not even know. When asked about the name these days, Gunter Demnig tends to cite a schoolchild who once answered a journalist's enquiry as to whether people could actually stumble on a STOLPERSTEIN and trip thus: "You don't trip on a STOLPERSTEIN, you stumble with your head and your heart."[15]

In "Monuments to the Unthinkable," the American writer Clint Smith compares how Germans and Americans respond to projects to honor those affected by the Holocaust / slavery. Smith describes a discussion with Barbara Berger of Berlin, "When I asked Berger

[14]Email of August 7, 2008

[15]https://www.stolpersteine.eu/en/faq/

what she thought of the *Stolpersteine*, she told me she feels ambivalent. On the one hand, she said, the project has brought communities together to research their history. But she finds the idea that people are stepping on the names of Jewish people deeply unsettling. "Every time, I cringe," she said. "They should be plaques on the wall. And why aren't they? Because most of the owners of buildings wouldn't accept, even to this day, a plaque saying, 'Here is where a Jewish family lived.'"[16]

I considered how best to memorialize my family's past shortly after my aunts died, Lucie in 2018 and Hilda in 2020. I had corresponded with Rikarde Riedesel, the Berleburg archivist, when each of my aunts died. I thought perhaps a local newspaper would want to publish their obituaries. Rikarde offered her condolences. Then she wrote back about a project to create an interactive internet catalog of all the *Stolpersteine* of Nordrhein-Westfalen. The project, she wrote, was looking for high-quality scans of photos to display next to each *Stolperstein*.

Had Lucie been alive, she would have called Rikarde and peppered her with questions about who was building the website and why. She would have wanted to know what sources they were using, and who was funding the effort. Lucie would have formed a strong opinion on the project. Then, she would have gone all in to help them. Or, she would have panned the effort completely. I just assumed that a town-sponsored project to remember Holocaust victims would be a good thing. I asked my cousin David for a few photo scans from Lucie's trove.

Several months later, Rikarde sent me a link to the WDR Stolpersteine NRW website.[17] I was excited to see what they'd posted.

[16]Clint Smith, MONUMENTS TO THE UNTHINKABLE, America still can't figure out how to memorialize the sins of our history. What can we learn from Germany?, The Atlantic, December 2022, https://www.theatlantic.com/magazine/archive/2022/12/holocaust-remembrance-lessons-america/671893/?utm_source=copy-link&utm_medium=social&utm_campaign=share

[17]https://stolpersteine.wdr.de/web/de/

The splash page had an English translation option, but subsequent pages were only in German. I found the page for Lucie's Stolpersteine. I pasted the text into Google translate and read:

> Lucie Weinstein grew up as Lucie Krebs in Berleburg. Her parents were secular Jews and the family was well integrated into the community. Lucie especially loved Christmas. In contrast to her non-Jewish friends, she received presents twice: first for Hanukkah and then again for Christmas, which the family celebrated together with their Christian circle of friends.
>
> When the National Socialists come to power, the atmosphere changed drastically: Lucie was repeatedly harassed in everyday school life. On Kristallnacht in November 1938, an angry mob destroyed the windows of the family home with stones. Lucie's father did everything he could to get his family out of Germany - with success: in 1941, the family traveled from Lisbon to New York on an overcrowded cruise ship.
>
> In the USA, Lucie met her husband Stanley Weinstein. She studied art history, received her doctorate from Yale and taught as a professor at Southern Connecticut State University in New Haven. Later she visited Berleburg. She was always willing to talk to children and young people about their experiences under the Nazi dictatorship. In addition, at her suggestion, a memorial for the murdered Berleburg Jews was erected.[18]

The comment about Lucie loving Christmas got under my skin. To the best of my knowledge, no one in my family ever celebrated Christmas beyond attending parties at friends' homes. I called my cousin David, who quipped, "She loved it so much that we never

---

[18]https://stolpersteine.wdr.de/web/de/stolperstein/8762, translated by me with Google Translate.

[19]Lucie Krebs Weinstein, Reminiscences of my Childhood in Berleburg, Johannes Althusius Gymnasium, date uncertain.

celebrated it."

I found the source of this comment in a text Lucie had prepared for a speech she gave to Berleburger high schoolers several years before the *Stolpersteine* project, the same speech a when she spoke of Elizabeth Bald.

> At home we celebrated Jewish holidays with visits to the synagogue, good food, and presents on the appropriate occasions. Around Christmas time, Hilda, Paul, and I considered ourselves lucky to be Jewish for a number of reasons; not least of which was our receiving presents twice: on Channukkah at home and on Christmas at the houses of friends and neighbors. We were usually invited to sing "Silent Night" and other carols at Clara and Willie Wahl's apartment upstairs in our house. I loved the fragrance of the freshly cut Christmas tree, colorfully decorated and lit with candles....[19]

I emailed the website creators. I offered to re-write the text of the first paragraph. The response I got appeared to be a form letter,

> Thank you very much for your offer to contribute to the content. But it is not possible for us to publish texts that are created from people who aren't part of the project. We do take your critique seriously and will examine the topic with the involved departments of the project....[20]

I thought about what Lucie would have done, writing them back, and then writing them back, until they buckled and changed the article to something more acceptable to me. But I decided that berating German do-gooders wasn't a battle I wanted to fight. I am not Lucie. Who am I to tell these people how best to reach German students? This generation of young children with

[20]Email from Jule Küpper May 10, 2022

no Jews in their midst. Have they met a Jew? Seen a Jew? What other topics does their curriculum cover? I don't know the answers to these questions.

Among the many points made by Clint Smith in his writings on the German and American approaches to memorializing past atrocities, is that there is no one-size-fits-all approach. I want children in the United States to learn about the enslaved and the enslavers, to dwell less on the battles, generals, and presidents. I applaud German efforts to have their young learn about the victims of Nazi persecution. In humanizing the persecuted we enable people to connect with their own complicated feelings.

I reflected that in the 1970s and 1980s, Dad and his sisters took the torch from my grandparents. Grandma and Grandpa had been the family decision makers, the primary actors. They had sent their children to Belgium on a Kindertransport, decided to escape Germany from Berlin, instead of a closer city. They saved money, borrowed money, and decided how and when to spend it.

Dad and his sisters had vivid but sometimes conflicting memories from childhood. They were still acquiring language skills and maturity. They were told different things, or remembered different things from their parents, aunts, uncles, and cousins. They were confused, angry, frightened, or saddened at different times by different things.

Now, swirling in my head, I carried the experiences of the two previous generations. Even if I couldn't speak German well, and even as my own memories were fallible or fading, I needed to take a more active role in how their history, our history, was to be written moving forward.

Stones at Ederstraße 5, Bad Berleburg courtesy of Rikarde Riedesel

CHAPTER THIRTY-FIVE

Shalhevet

We were in Rochester for my nephew Alex's bar mitzvah. My daughter Talia was in high school and thinking about college. Amy and I decided to drive around the University of Rochester with Talia during some down time, and Aunt Hilda asked if she could come with us. Amy drove and I sat up front to navigate, which meant Talia was seated next to my aunt. Our son, Adin, had opted to stay with his cousins. I listened to the conversation coming from the back seat. "What do you want to study?" asked Aunt Hilda. Talia mumbled something about physical therapy, an option she considered for a moment or two. Aunt Hilda switched topics. "Do you think you can take the winters here?" Talia said she liked snow. I wasn't sure if this was true. But she did like hats. I could see her happily wearing a different beanie every day. Today she wore a cream-colored wool hat pulled down almost over her eyes.

I couldn't find the building I was looking for, the student center that had been under construction when I was high school. Aunt Hilda began talking about antisemitism on college campuses and the importance of Hillel groups. Then Aunt Hilda began describing March of the Living, a "wonderful program, all the kids love it…" Then she reconsidered. "It's actually very challenging. You go to Auschwitz with thousands of Jewish youth groups from around the world on *Yom haShoah*. You protest that the world watched while there was a Holocaust, and that Jews will never let the Holocaust happen again. Then a few days later, you go to Israel to learn that the Holocaust was not the end of the Jews, that there is a new chapter."

"I want to do that," said Talia, emphatically.

I was surprised that Aunt Hilda had suggested Talia visit a concentration camp. I thought she shared Dad's antipathy to visiting such places. Dad had often quipped, "I already know what happened there. I don't need it in my face." He also was very clear that he didn't want to spend his money in Poland. I wondered what he'd think of Talia wanting to participate in March of the Living. I turned around to look at Talia and Aunt Hilda. Aunt Hilda was adjusting Talia's hat. She did look cute in it.

Several weeks later, as a work colleague and I chatted before a meeting, she mentioned that she'd gone on March of the Living during her senior year of high school. "Amazing," I said. "I just heard about the program, and now you're telling me about it!" The colleague was fifteen or twenty years younger than me. When I asked her if it was something I should investigate for my daughter, she took a minute to reflect.

My colleague – who is quiet, thoughtful, and understated – said, "It was very powerful. Auschwitz was huge. I hadn't pictured it so big. You could imagine it as a machine. And I felt surrounded by death...and life." Then she stopped for a minute and considered further. "I didn't know anyone else on the trip. I think now that they try to encourage kids to go with friends, so they don't feel so isolated."

Within a week, I received an email from our synagogue describing upcoming activities for teens. A group called *Shalhevet* ran a trip that sounded much like March of the Living and was inviting Bay Area teens to apply. I checked out the website and then told Talia about it. In almost the same tone she used with Aunt Hilda, Talia said, "I want to go." When Adin was the same age, he too, wanted to participate in *Shalhevet*.

For me, part of *Shalhevet* was schlepping my children from one corner of the Bay Area to another so they could befriend other teens who would be going on the trip, primarily the grandchildren and great-grandchildren of Holocaust survivors. A significant number were also the children of Israeli emigres from Silicon Valley genius types with all kinds of advanced degrees and credentials. Especially in Talia's group, several of the kids were staying in Israel after the program ended. They had grandparents, aunts, and uncles to visit.

I worked hard to connect with other parents and got little traction. I couldn't help but remember what a challenge it had been for me as a child to connect with Rochester Jewish kids. I always felt the Spencerport rube, the one on the bottom of the social pecking order. My work colleague's experience, and the brochure for *Shalhevet*, emphasized that connection was important for fighting isolation during the trip. I worried that my adopted, bi-racial Berkeley children would be shunned by the seemingly homogenous Silicon Valley group, and at the same time, I worried that I was imposing my own issues on my kids.

My other *Shalhevet*-related task was to write a letter to my children that they would be given on the day they visited Auschwitz. We parents were warned, much as my work colleague had indicated, that the experience would be stressful. A letter from home would act as a counterweight to the stress, a healing balm. We should share with our children our experiences, our links to Auschwitz, and our messages of love.

What, I wondered, should I tell my children? I didn't want my feelings or thoughts about the Holocaust to overshadow theirs. I didn't want to be a burden. But wasn't the whole topic a burden? Wasn't that perhaps the whole point of history: to clarify why we are all burdened by the past? My children couldn't escape this any more than I could. But I could work within the guardrails that the program was trying to establish. I didn't need to pass on my worries or fears. I could just be direct.

I kept a copy of the letter that I eventually wrote to Adin in 2015.

Dear Adin,

As you know, Mom and I are incredibly proud of you that you've been able to travel with Shalhevet to visit concentration camps and learn more about the Holocaust!

I can barely remember a time in my life when I didn't know that the Holocaust had happened—my grandparents spoke of Germany all the time.

Grandma with Hilda and Lucie, 1927

This picture is in Berleburg Germany. My grandma is holding Aunt Hilda. Aunt Lucie is the girl in front. Grandpa, the baby, wasn't yet born. I loved my grandmother very much. She told me a lot about her life before she came to the U.S. A lot about what she lost. Mainly relatives. Among the relatives who died, some were younger than you now. I spoke to Grandpa. He wanted you to remember these people for him. They probably all died in concentration camps, perhaps Auschwitz.

Mathilde and Hugo Lindheim and their daughter Lore. Grandpa was on a Kindertransport from Germany to Belgium after Kristallnacht. He lived with Mathilde and Hugo for two years until the Nazis invaded Belgium. Then Grandpa and his sisters returned to Germany. The Lindheims were transported to Auschwitz in 1943, where they died.

Selma Bachenheimer and her daughters Doris, Hilda, and Annaliese. Selma's husband, my grandma's brother, died after being beaten up in a concentration camp. The rest of the family was sent to Auschwitz.

Bettie Krebs—another aunt of Grandpa's (Bettie's husband Adolf escaped to England. He was my grandfather's brother & I remember him well). Bettie and Adolf's daughter, Ruth, also died in a camp.

Aaron and Johanna Neuhaus—Grandpa's uncle & aunt.

Adele Krebs, Grandpa's aunt, who lived in Berleburg and who Grandpa saw all the time.

I am trying to think what I'd want someone to say to me after visiting Auschwitz. Would I want to be held/hugged? Would I want to be left alone to cry? Would I want to listen to loud music and forget about it as quickly as possible?

I think I would want to be held—so I am trying to hug you from afar. I love you so much! Mom and I look forward to hearing about all your adventures upon your return.

CHAPTER THIRTY-SIX

German Citizenship

When Talia was in high school, she said she might someday want to work in Europe. She had been studying Spanish since kindergarten. We'd lived in Mexico for six months when she was nine years old. We'd visited Europe a few times and she'd gone with groups to Ecuador, Poland, and Israel. I patted myself on the back for raising a globally aware, internationally minded person. "Grandpa's German," she said. "Do you think I could get German citizenship?"

I'd heard about descendants of German Jews applying for German citizenship but hadn't really thought about what it might entail. I turned to Google and found a paragraph in the German constitution on the subject,

> Former German citizens who between 30 January 1933 and 8 May 1945 were deprived of their German citizenship on political, racial, or religious grounds may have their citizenship restored. This generally also applies to their descendants... A descendant born to a parent who was deprived of German citizenship and before the parent's citizenship was restored also has a claim under Article 116 II of the Basic Law. Each descendant has an individual claim, subject to eligibility. It is thus possible for grandchildren to apply, even if their parents decide not to...[21]

On the face of it, it seemed like Talia was a shoo-in. On the other hand, she was adopted. I wasn't sure how strict Germany was about a DNA connection. I thought it would be harder for them to turn down Talia if I applied, too. So I wanted to submit applications for Talia, Adin, and me at the same time. Although Germany accepted gay marriage, and might have granted Amy citizenship as my wife, she said she wasn't interested.

The critical document(s) that I needed to complete the application would come from Dad. I needed his birth certificate, or old German identification documents, such as his last passport. I wasn't sure that Dad would like this scheme. I remembered arguments from my childhood about the political evils of Europe, and those running for office. I didn't want to get into an argument about neo-Nazis or Marine Le Pen. So I played the Talia card. Dad would never say no to his granddaughter. Sure enough, Dad said on his next visit to the Bay Area, he'd bring his old German passport and would go to the German consulate in San Francisco.

I mused that if there had been an EU when I graduated from college, and Dad had helped me get citizenship then, I might have been able to move to Europe to find a job. Lucky Talia that she could have that option! Even if that was not going to be me, I could imagine extended trips to Europe in my retirement: six months in France one year, four months in Germany another year. I could take language courses or cooking or archeology in Greece. In my free time, I could galivant to other countries as a lark. I could sit in cafes drinking aperitifs. And with my new classmates, I could pick up the political conversations that I had started back in the 1970s: the merits of various European political parties, the strengths of trade unions, what to do about the new xenophobia, and the like. It would be Junior Year Abroad, Seniors Edition.

---

[21]Article 116 ii. https://uk.diplo.de/uk-en/02/citizenship/restoration-of-german-citizenship/2463592#content_2

I set up an appointment at the German Consulate in San Francisco when Dad would next be in the Bay Area. Dad brought his old German passport and U.S. naturalization papers as documentation. These clearly indicated that he'd been born in Germany.

When the day of our appointment arrived, Talia, Mom, Dad, and I drove to San Francisco. The German Consulate was in twin grand buildings built after the Great Fire of San Francisco in a

Dad's last German passport issued February 1941

Dad's naturalization papers, issued August 1, 1955, 14 years after his arrival

neighborhood of mansions. The architect was noteworthy (Walter Bliss), and the original owner was William Matson, the man whose last name is displayed on cargo containers throughout the world. The consular officers conducted the typical weapons' search before we were let into the building. Then we were told to sit in a pamphlet-lined library. Dad sat staring straight ahead while Talia and I scanned German-language study programs in various cities throughout Germany.

A consular officer soon joined us, a smiling woman who seemed to be in her thirties. What a plum assignment, I thought, remembering when I'd wanted to be a foreign service officer. I wanted to apply for citizenship for myself and my children. I showed her draft applications that I had prepared, along with the documentation called for in the application. She said everything was fine. I just needed to get it all notarized. "How long would this take?" I asked. "Is it a sure thing?"

She explained that after receiving our applications, the federal government would contact Berleburg to verify Dad's documents. She didn't know how long it would take exactly. It could be as quick as three months. But it could take longer. As Talia was still in high school and not rushing off to a job, this seemed fine.

Then I learned that a gentile co-worker whose father was born in Germany (but who had not been stripped of his citizenship) got her citizenship in less than a month. I grumbled for a while about this. Then I learned that a friend seeking French citizenship had to pass a French language proficiency exam. Amy's cousins were seeking Canadian citizenship, which they anticipated would take at least a decade. Italy offered the offspring of former immigrants a path back to citizenship, but the path seemed so torturous that none of my friends of Italian descent had taken the first step. And for immigrants to the U.S. seeking citizen status, the rules seemed to change every day.

As Amy sensibly pointed out, it was just a process. Stop the teeth gnashing and wait.

By the time our citizenship papers arrived from Germany, Talia was no longer interested in working in the EU. Whether my children, my cousins who have since become citizens, or I ever use our German passports are up for debate. But, as children and grandchildren of Holocaust survivors, it's always good to have a back-up plan. You never know.

CHAPTER THIRTY-SEVEN

Auschwitz, 2018

My mother died in 2017, the same year that Adin started college, and our synagogue announced that it would lead a Jewish heritage tour to Poland. Amy and I were intrigued by the idea of going to Poland. Amy suggested that we should invite Dad, who'd just traveled with us to Iceland. I wondered if Mom would have liked to visit Poland, too. After all, her dad, who I called Grandpa Leon, had been born in Poland. Grandpa Leon hadn't spoken to me much about his boyhood. I knew few details outside of the name of his town, that he'd left home when he'd been drafted to fight for Austria in World War I, and that any relative who hadn't made it out of Poland in the 1920s for the U.S. or Israel had been killed. Mom had met none of her grandparents.

Mom was not a sentimental person. She liked modern art on the wall rather than sepia-toned photos of old family members. She told quirky stories about recent events, not poignant anecdotes from her childhood. She never spoke of her mother who had died before I was born.

Though we visited Grandpa Leon at least annually when I was a child, Mom seemed distant, mildly amused by her father. I thought she was there out of a sense of duty. She might not have wanted to come to Eastern Europe.

My idea of Poland from movies and books was largely of flattish farmland covered in snow. Although most of the Poland that I saw was indeed flattish, not unlike western New York, we arrived during a May heat wave. I remembered laughing out loud reading Jonathan Safran Foer's book, *Everything Is Illuminated*, where family myths were comically debunked. I wondered if this trip would be similar.

Poland. I did know it wasn't just snow. I remembered watching Claude Lanzmann's movie *Shoah* from 1985, the 566-minute French documentary about the Holocaust. The film had shown a boatman on the river in spring, no ice. He had been a boy during the Holocaust. There were trees in bloom behind him. There were grasses.

In Krakow, I sat with Dad and Amy drinking liters of beer over lunch. We stared out over the town's central square, which was on top of a hill. It was bustling with bars and cafés filled with tourists. The building facades were attractively painted in varied colors. A church bell chimed. You could even rent a horse-drawn carriage. It was lovely, charming. I tried to imagine sitting in a similar café a hundred years earlier. Grandpa Leon had been born in 1895 in Ropczyce, a small town a bit east of Krakow. Had he visited this square before being drafted to fight in World War I? Had he looked out on similar horse-drawn carriages? Considered moving here when he was established? When I asked Dad what he thought, he said that he didn't know and was disinclined towards conjecture.

We'd been in Poland close to a week and I had a big decision to make for tomorrow. I could either go to Auschwitz or visit a couple of local *shtetls* (Jewish communities). Dad stated emphatically that he was not going to Auschwitz. Ellen, Dad's cousin who was also on the trip, said the same.

Amy was going to Auschwitz and thought I should go with her. "We'll probably never come back here," she said. "This is your one opportunity."

"I'm not sure," I said. Was I trying to be loyal to Dad? Was I afraid of the ghosts of the million plus people who'd been murdered there? I couldn't quite put my finger on why I was hesitant.

"Visiting Auschwitz is central to our trip, isn't it?" Amy tried a different tack. The rabbi was going. Our Israeli tour group leader Ron was going. Almost everyone else from our synagogue was going. How much more could be learned by seeing another *shtetl*?

I was still hemming and hawing the following morning. With the bus leaving for Auschwitz in fifteen minutes, I went to Ron's breakfast table with my final cup of coffee. Ron was peering into his backpack, rearranging his binders. He looked up when I sat down. We must have been about the same age. He was fit, about my height, and had sandy brown hair and brown eyes. Ron was the only son of survivors from Eastern Europe. Ron now spent much of his time in Eastern Europe taking people on tours like ours. He had visited Auschwitz dozens of times with survivors, children of survivors, and people who knew almost nothing about Auschwitz before they went. He got something out of it every time he went.

"It is up to you of course," Ron said. "Think of it this way. Auschwitz is one of the most Jewish places on earth. Ten percent of the world's Jewish population alive during the Second World War was sent here. One-point-one million people. More Jews than currently live in all of Europe."

We locked eyes. Ron always looked earnest, even when he told a joke. I thought he might tear up. Or was it me that was close to tears? Several minutes later, I got on the bus with Amy.

We left the colorful curved streets of Krakow and joined a straight modern road heading west. By the roadside, deciduous trees and grasses were coming into bloom. I thought of the hours that I'd spent watching *Shoah* in the 1980s. I remembered a witness giving testimony on the edge of a field. As he spoke, the camera would pan from a close up of his face to grasses swaying in the wind.

Ron pointed out the bus window to a wooden platform built on a house. He peered through his old army binoculars looking for a bird. Ron had come to Poland with ten days' worth of clothes (two or three outfits), ten pounds worth of binders filled with notes, and these binoculars. Ron said the platforms were for storks. He calls the stork a symbol of the Jewish people because it migrates from Poland to Israel and back. If not the Jewish people, it might be a symbol for Ron.

After about an hour, our bus turned onto a small road and parked in the bus parking area of an enormous lot. Ron went out to find our guide and buy our entrance tickets. I spotted the oft photographed *Arbeit Macht Frei* sign. My heart was pounding. I had noticed this happening at odd times over the last year. There were no Nazis here, except maybe the motorcycle group that reminded me of the Hell's Angels. I reminded myself that my kids had been here, had toured this site. They survived. I would, too.

Our group was assigned an official Auschwitz tour guide to take us through the museum. Between the crowds, her accent, and poor acoustics, I had difficulty hearing, but the lobby plaque summed up her presentation.

Auschwitz was the largest Nazi German Concentration Camp and Death Camp. In the years 1940-1945, the Nazis deported at least 1,300,000 people to Auschwitz:

1,100,000 Jews

140,000-150,000 Poles

23,000 Roma (Gypsies)

15,000 Soviet Prisoners of War

25,000 Prisoners from other ethnic groups

1,100,000 of these people died in Auschwitz, approximately 90% of the victims were Jews. The SS murdered the majority of them in gas chambers.

The numbers, while staggering, were familiar to me. The exhibits, too, seemed familiar, perhaps because I'd visited *Yad Vashem* two or three times, my first time while in the sixth grade. What eleven-year-old could forget rooms of pilfered suitcases, piles of shoes, human hair, teeth, and photos of vicious-looking guards, starved prisoners, and a child holding a teddy bear?

The last stop of our guided tour was the museum documentation room. I couldn't help but compare the Auschwitz documentation room with the one I remembered from Yad Vashem all those years ago, the time Dad had me sit for hours while he filled out forms, or so it seemed. Then, we were still counting dead. Today at Auschwitz, the names of the dead were written in books. Many, large, thick volumes. Enough volumes to give the names, birthdates, and hometown of all the people that Dad, Grandma, and others from my family told agencies about. Enough volumes to hold all the records found in European towns, deportation centers, and concentration camps. It was a stuffy, windowless room, crowded with people flipping through individual books, searching for names.

I took several photos of the Bachenheimer page. Dad has previously told me that all Bachenheimers came from the area of Frankenberg, Hesse, and that all Bachenheimers were our relatives. Zeroing in on the name Selma Bachenheimer, Dad's aunt by marriage, she was listed five times, with slightly different information. Selma Bachenheimer was missed by many. But there was no "official" version to be found in the "documentation room." I found this disturbing. Though no one could bring Selma back to life, couldn't someone at least straighten out her story? Wasn't she owed this?

Photo of book of victims taken in the Auschwitz documentation room

Ron was waiting for all of us on a bench outside the museum. Once we were assembled, he guided us down a road and away from the crowds. As we walked, we saw fewer and fewer people. I noticed that the air was filled with pollen, as if today was the day that every flower or weed in this part of the world was about to reproduce. The pollen rode the air currents in whorls. How was it that I only thought about Auschwitz as cold? People standing on cold floors shivering to go into the crematoria? This day felt like Spencerport finally coming to bloom after so many cold months. It was as magical a transformation here as any other place on earth.

At the end of the road, after visiting a former barracks, latrine, and train car, we came to a spot where the rabbi wanted us to say Kaddish. I wondered what Dad was doing. I wished he were here for this. I wondered if he'd ever said Kaddish for Selma Bachenheimer and his other relatives killed here or at another camp. I found myself crying for Dad, not just because he lost Mom last year, but because he lost most of his childhood, and so many of the people who loved him when he was a boy. Then I found myself crying for my long-over childhood and all those who I have lost. And those around the world who currently have no childhood because of wars, famines, hatred, and all the other things that we humans seem incapable of overcoming. The rabbi mentions Tikkun Olam, healing the world. How I wish we could.

CHAPTER THIRTY-EIGHT

Berlin

The day after the Jewish heritage tour ended, Dad, Ellen, Amy, and I took the train to Berlin. We followed our rabbi's advice and hired an Israeli ex-pat to give us a guided tour of Jewish Berlin. Yoav's website oversold him, at least after Ron. The broody hung-over thirty-something (or was he forty?) arrived with only some random notes on his iPhone. In fact, he wanted to start our tour at a coffee place with our group buying him a coffee and croissant. Our first stop was a cluster of *Stolpersteine*. "You can see these all-around Berlin," Yoav said dully.

"What are they?" asked Dad.

"They've got them in Berleburg, too," I chimed in, trying to be helpful.

Dad looked confused. "What are they?"

In the same drone, Yoav said, "Each *Stolperstein* commemorates a victim of the Holocaust at that person's last known address. The brass plaque includes the victim's name, date of birth, deportation date, and death date, if known."

"They did this in Berleburg." I added. "I'm sure you heard about it. I got a whole packet of pictures. I'm sure you did, too." Dad looked blank. I wasn't sure if he didn't hear me or didn't believe me.

Yoav sighed and returned to his script, "We will see many more *Stolpersteine* today."

We walked another few blocks and Yoav pointed out the Empty Library, a memorial to the largest book burning held by the Nazis. As Amy, Dad, Ellen, and I looked down through a plexiglass slab to a room below ground lined with empty bookshelves, Yoav read monotonously from his phone, "The shelves were built to accommodate the 20,000 volumes burned in this spot in 1933, one of the first acts of the Nazis to degrade and erase Jewish culture. They burned not only Jewish prayer books, but literary and scientific works by Jews and other undesirables." Dad leaned on his cane, looking off into the distance. Ellen translated the inscription near the room, written by the German-Jewish writer Heinrich Heine, whose books were burned on this spot, "That was just a prelude; where you burn books, you also burn people in the end."

I remembered a Sunday morning many years ago, when I first learned about the Nazi book burnings while watching a news program at Grandma and Grandpa's. Watching the flames on the black and white television somehow electrified me in terror. Or maybe Grandma and Grandpa's terrified memories were what most frightened me.

Our last stop with Yoav was at Otto Weidt's brush workshop. Otto Weidt, we learned from the man who sold us tickets, hired Jewish, blind, or disabled employees to make brushes. These were people who the Nazis would have deported had Weidt not needed them. Weidt sold his brushes to the Wehrmacht. Meanwhile he was active in pacifist and anarchist groups and had contacts who made false work papers and identity cards for his Jewish staff. The factory was raided more than once and had a hidden room in which his workers hid. Most of his employees were eventually deported, but he did save several. And after the war, Weidt established an orphanage for concentration camp survivors. Yad Vashem named him one of the righteous for his actions.

Later in the day, Dad, Amy, Ellen, and I discussed the new-to-us information about Jews who had hidden in Berlin. New to us, not because Yoav presented unknown material, but because we'd all recently seen the movie, *The Invisibles*, which told the tale of four Jewish Berliners who went into hiding in Berlin. These four survived. Probably many had not. We wondered how large the number of Jews who tried to hide in plain sight was. Some have estimated it was in the thousands.

I was reminded of a visit with a cousin of Dad's who was an Invisible. I'd met him at Grandma's behest shortly after moving to San Francisco. When I described this visit to Dad, he was sure that the cousin, Alex Katten, had tried to pull one over on me. He called Alex a "bullshit artist" and me "incredibly gullible" for believing his story. I hadn't visited with Alex since that first visit even though we both lived in the Bay Area.

I considered bringing Alex Katten up with Dad again on this day in Berlin. But neither the time nor the place seemed right. I let it go. On the plane ride home, I wondered if Alex Katten was still alive, or if he had recorded his testimony for Fortunoff or one of the other Holocaust oral history projects. I wondered if I might be able to hear his story again, and what I would make of it now, in light of *The Invisibles* and Otto Weidt. Perhaps I had been too swayed by Dad's thinking. I decided that when I got back to Berkeley, I'd look Alex up on the internet.

CHAPTER THIRTY-NINE
The Kattens

Before I drove out west from Spencerport in 1982, Grandma gave me a piece of paper with the name and phone number for Alex Katten. Grandma's mother had been a Katten. Alex was from this side of the family. Grandma had not been able to meet him when she visited San Francisco a decade earlier. Alex had been out of town. She wanted me to call him and send him her best wishes. She also thought he might be helpful, should I decide to live in San Francisco, in finding a house or a job.

I called Alex Katten sometime between when I'd hurt my ankle and started work at Old Wives Tales. Alex suggested that we meet at the Cliff House, a spot I knew, all the way out at Ocean Beach. He told me he'd be wearing a cowboy hat. I mentioned my cane. Opening the door, I saw only one man in a cowboy hat. I raised my eyebrows in greeting and headed over to Alex. He had a table with a first-class view of the sea lions diving and cavorting in the Pacific.

Alex extended his hand to shake mine. I studied him quickly. He wore a light blue cowboy shirt with horn buttons and white piping. He appeared to be about five foot ten, which I once heard someone describe as the Jewish six foot. He was kind of greying, kind of balding, and had thin lips and a prominent nose. Sure, I thought, he could be family. After I sent greetings from my grandmother, I asked how he came to San Francisco. He began with his sixth birthday...in Berlin.

Luckily the waiter showed up right about then. Alex ordered a glass of wine, and I ordered an Irish coffee. It was a cold day and I had had to hobble into the restaurant. I could tell this was going to be a long story. We both looked out the window, watching the sea lions, as Alex returned to his what-seemed-likely-to-be a long and winding story of how he got to San Francisco.

"I got a gold star to pin on my coat on my sixth birthday. It was the first birthday present that I remember. That was when the Nazis started making you wear a star, when you were six."

"Where did you live?"

"Berlin," Alex said. "We had a large apartment then, at least in my memory. The address was 27 Luitpoldstrasse. It was a very nice neighborhood."

"What year did you turn six?"

"I was born in 1935. This would have been September 1941."

I paused, realizing that in September 1941, Dad was starting junior high in New York. Alex should have been starting kindergarten had the Jews of Germany still been allowed to attend school. I wondered, but did not ask, when the Nazis began deporting Jews from Berlin. I would have thought it might have already begun.

The waiter returned with our drinks. Alex continued telling his story. "Once I wore the gold star, I could only play in certain areas of the park and sit down on one bench. They had these signs, '*Juden Verboten*,' everywhere. You know kids can be very cruel." Alex cleared his throat, "I wore the star for a year and half until we went underground."

I made a mental note. The Nazis let them live in Berlin till 1943. Then they went underground. Underground? Like Anne Frank? I took a sip of my drink and nodded at Alex.

"Actually, my earliest memory is from when I was going on four. *Kristallnacht,* we now call it. I remember the day after the rioting, my father walking me to nursery school. I saw the streets were a big mess. There was glass everywhere. I asked my father what happened. He said 'There was a big storm last night. Didn't you hear it?' I said no, I didn't. Later on, my father told me that when I'd asked him about it, there had been police standing around. He didn't want to get their attention, so he'd lied to me."

As Alex went on with his story, I got confused. Alex said his dad had worked for the Berlin police. One of his dad's police friends told Alex's dad that the Gestapo was going to raid his apartment and that they should get out. So Alex's family fled in the middle of the afternoon with a few belongings and went underground.

Grandma's cousin, a policeman? She had never mentioned that, not that she had mentioned what his line of work was. Later, when I began to tell Dad the story, this is when he started crying bullshit. "Berlin police? There were no Jewish police officers in Berlin in 1943! Are you crazy believing this guy?..."

I could see Dad's point. I said, "I don't think Alex said he was in the police in 1943. But before that...."

While I may have left the Cliff House imagining follow up visits with Alex, after that ugly conversation with Dad, I procrastinated. So much so that now, in 2018, I was staring at Alex's obituary on my computer screen.

Alexander Carl Katten Obituary

Alex died at the Jewish Home in San Francisco on August 23, 2013, at age 77. He was born in Berlin on September 18, 1935. He and his parents survived WWII living in Berlin and he came to the US in 1953. He served in the US Army as a registered nurse and enjoyed his retirement in San Francisco. Alex is survived by his cousins Bert 'Robert' Wolfgang Katten and Roma Katten of London.[22]

I also found that Alex had been interviewed twice by the USC Shoah Center.[23] I watched both interviews over the coming weeks.

---

[22]https://www.legacy.com/us/obituaries/sfgate/name/alexander-katten-obituary?id=16104983

In Alex's interview from 1990, he was seated in front of a china cabinet in his home. He wore a white button-down shirt with a spectacular bolo of a large silver owl, perhaps three inches wide and four long. The cord was black woven leather with silver tips. Alex's hair was gray and wavy and thinner on top than I remembered. His interviewer asked Alex for his early memories of Berlin. He shared the same story about *Kristallnacht* that he had shared with me years earlier. His account was so close to my memory of what he's said that it seemed almost like he was reciting from a script. Then the interviewer asked, "How did you feel?"

"You couldn't tell a child what had happened." Alex's remark struck me as something his father might have told him after the fact, rather than his own feelings.

Alex described his family's flight from their Berlin apartment. He told how just months later they moved again to a new apartment in the Friedrichshain neighborhood. There, with fake passports and fake working papers, his parents left him alone every day and went off to work. Alex reported he did and didn't go to school, could and couldn't go to the playground. Mainly he was stuck in the one-room apartment alone. I studied his face. Like Dad, he wore a lonely look. He really did look like family.

The interviewer tried to interrupt Alex "for clarification" several times. But he struggled when asked to go off script. I couldn't tell if he had memorized a script from his parents (he would have been younger than ten when the war ended). Or if his own memories had calcified over years of telling the same story. Or if his memory was failing him altogether at the time of the interview.

Alex's memories of the Soviets marching into Berlin were interesting to me but didn't entirely make sense. Or perhaps my brief trip

[23]ALEXANDER KATTEN Holocaust Oral History Project Dates May 18, 1998 and January 28, 1990. Portions of the 1990 interview are on YouTube: https://www.youtube.com/watch?v=vC_OF5fwa7o

to Berlin hadn't equipped me to see the scene in focus. Alex said he and his father escaped their apartment building through the sewer, his father with a fake bandage on his foot. They turned themselves in to the Russians. (It was unclear where his mother was.)

The post-war period, another topic that put off my father in 1982, was similarly confusing in Alex's interview with USC. Alex told the interviewer that his father went back to work for the German police. Did he mean the Stasi?

I searched on Google, this time looking up Fritz Katten, Grandma's first cousin, Alex's father. I found an article from 1956 about Fritz's release from an East German prison,

> Fritz Katten, who was vice president of the Berlin Jewish Community and president of the Berlin Mizrachi Organization when the Communists arrested him seven years ago on trumped up political charges, was released from an East German prison today. He immediately rejoined his wife, the manager of a Jewish old age home in Dusseldorf, West Germany.
>
> Katten, a 58-year-old Orthodox Jew, was born in a small town in Hesse, where his grandfather was president of the local Jewish community. He settled in Berlin as a young man and was unable to emigrate when the Nazis came to power. During the war he was drafted for forced labor. When the deportations to death camps in the East began, he managed to go into hiding with his wife and son. As one of about 2,000 Jews who lived underground in Berlin, he survived until the Red Army marched into the city in 1945.
>
> He immediately helped set up the Jewish community organization, whose vice president he became. His labors on behalf of Nazi victims came to the attention of the authorities who prevailed upon him to become vice president of the Berlin police. Confident he was helping to fashion a better Germany, Katten accepted the post and joined the Social Democratic Party.

By coincidence, he was a resident of what became the Soviet sector of the city. In 1948, the Soviets arrested him, in large measure because of charges that he had used the authority of his office with the police department to facilitate Joint Distribution Committee relief shipments to Jewish communities. When he was released, shortly thereafter, friends urged him to move to West Berlin. He refused, insisting that he wanted to clear his name first. Then, in April 1949, he was re-arrested and sentenced to 25 years on trumped up charges of "espionage."[24]

This article bolstered Alex's claim that his father was in the East German police force after the Second World War. It also listed him as leader of the East German post-war Jewish community. That struck me as very interesting. I turned to the Horst Hecker book on the Jews of Frankenberg. Hecker calls Fritz Katten, "one of the more interesting Jews of the Twentieth Century from Frankenberg." Hecker includes a photo of Fritz Katten as a soldier in the First World War. The inscription on the missile says, "I didn't want the war, May 17, 1917."[25]

Soldier Fritz Katten, 1917, courtesy of Frankenberg Stadtarchiv

[24]https://www.jta.org/1956/07/09/archive/leader-of-berlin-jewish-community-released-from-communist-prison

[25]Hecker p. 77: "Die wohl interessanteste Erscheinung unter den Frankenberger Juden im 20. Jahrhundert ist Fritz Katten (1898-1964). Photo from p. 78

Hecker's biography of Fritz Katten emphasizes Katten's ideal-
ism, his desire to help fashion a better Germany after the Second
World War. He neither wanted to leave Germany nor move to a
Western sector of Berlin.

Fritz's passions and dedication to rebuilding Jewish Berlin
might not have left much time for Alex. I pictured Alex with the
lonely far away look I saw in the video. I tried to imagine Alex listening intently at a Shabbat dinner with other war survivors. How
many of the changes that he already endured made sense?

Did Alex consider himself traumatized? Had he sought a rabbi's
counsel or professional help after leaving Germany to heal from
his trauma? Had his parents? When I met Alex, I wouldn't have
asked a question like that.

But Alex did want to talk to me and the interviewer for his
oral history. He wanted to tell his story. He didn't want his past
erased over time. I'm glad I got to know Alex, even if it was just
for a moment.

CHAPTER FORTY

Two Great Aunts

I have a very clear memory of an early conversation with my grandparents about concentration camps. I was certainly less than ten years old, maybe only seven or eight. My sister and I had spent the night at Grandma and Grandpa's. We were watching television together on Sunday morning waiting for my parents to pick us up. There were slim pickings for television programs on Sunday mornings in the early 1960s in Rochester. We selected a news program on Joseph Goebbels. After the terrifying scenes of book burnings and Hitler standing in front of huge crowds, they showed starving people in striped uniforms in concentration camps. I assumed this was footage from the end of the war.

We selected a program that showed starving people with shaved heads in striped pajamas. Why couldn't they escape? Amy and I couldn't understand the answer. On the farm, cows seemed to get out all the time. People should have been able to get out too, no? Grandpa lifted his arm over his head, indicating that the fences were very high. Then we went back and forth about who might have tried to escape and who wouldn't have. Finally, Grandma offered that she had a sister who survived a camp. Her sister Martha, Martha's husband Menna, and their sons Alex and Walter. "Some people survived," she said. "But most did not."

"How come I've never met Martha?"

"She lives in New York." Grandma said.

"I don't remember her," I said. "I only remember Aunt Frieda."

"That's not true. You've met Paula. You've met Otto. I'm sure you met Martha." The litany of Bachenheimer siblings. All I could remember was Aunt Frieda.

"Was Martha skinny like the people on television?"

"Of course, yes. She was barely fed." Grandma was frowning at me.

Grandpa suggested that I go get the checkers. He was ready for a game. I could never tell if they didn't want to upset me, or if my raising the topic brought back bad memories for them.

In 1985, when Ronald Reagan decided to visit Germany's Bitburg Cemetery, a burial site for some Nazi generals, I had been living in San Francisco for several years. Planning a trip to back to New York, I called Grandma to give her my dates and itinerary. Martha, she told me, had been calling her twice a week, afraid of what Nazi muck might be stirred up in Europe by what might be seen as Reagan's tribute to the Nazis. Grandma said she and Martha used to speak once a month. But now, with her nightmares, Martha called several times a week. Grandma couldn't "come over it." She had never heard Martha speak about Bergen-Belsen. But now Grandma was hearing about it so much that she, too, was having insomnia.

When I mentioned that I planned to spend a few nights in New York City before coming to Spencerport, Grandma said I should visit Martha. Grandma would let her know my dates. All I needed to do was call her when I got to New York. Aunt Martha? I had no memory of meeting her. Had I? Grandma said it didn't matter. I should pay her a visit. She was looking forward to hearing from me.

I arrived at Aunt Martha's Upper East Side apartment on a muggy July day. I left for the visit in my mid-1980s attire – baggy beige pleated pants and an oversized pink cotton blouse – but between the subway ride, the walk from the subway, the pollution, and the humidity, I felt less than fresh. And here was Aunt Martha looking immaculate in a well-tailored navy suit with a crisp white blouse. She looked like a smaller, more sophisticated version of Grandma. Her pearls were probably real. Her makeup was expertly applied. Her hair looked like she'd been to the beauty parlor earlier that day. She gestured me into her apartment, saying, "Ah yes, you do look like Lucie." I smiled.

Aunt Martha ushered me through to a nicely set table in her breakfast alcove. She was serving what Grandma would serve on a hot day in July: a selection of breads, salads, cold cuts, and fruit. She motioned for me to sit down.

"One moment." I excused myself to wash up. In the bathroom, I ran cold water through my hands and splashed my face, trying to get off some of the city's grit. Aunt Martha's house seemed so meticulous. I felt out of place.

"I hear you are interested in history and politics," Martha said once I'd joined her at the table. "I hear you want to know about my experiences during the war."

"Yes," I said softly.

"We had some experiences. I can tell you that!"

"I'm sure you did."

Martha's story, as I already had heard, was similar to the story of Anne Frank's family. In the mid-thirties, Menna, Martha's husband, lost his banking job in Frankfurt. The family moved to Berlin for a few years, and then to Amsterdam. I noticed how Martha seemed to select each word carefully. She spoke slowly, evenly, and precisely. She stopped speaking every so often and turned to her food to take a bite or two, chew, and sip her tea.

She hadn't minded moving, she told me. She enjoyed Frankfurt, Berlin, and Amsterdam. Menna had good jobs. They had fun together. They lived well, went on vacations. They had two boys less than a year apart. The boys, Alex and Walter, went to good schools, had friends. She was happy.

Each move, of course, was due to the antisemitic Nazi laws. Most of Menna's colleagues believed it was rubbish, but their hands were tied. They had to fire anyone Jewish. Unfortunately, the Nazis invaded Holland before they knew it. When they started arresting Jews, Aunt Martha heard about people who were going into hiding, like Anne Frank's family. Someone at Menna's office offered to take the boys. But she thought the family should stay together.

I kept eating as Martha continued her story. I felt self-aware, sure that I was eating too much or too quickly. I did not want to offend by seeming sloppy, clumsy, or inconsiderate. Martha ate only a little.

"They always came in the middle of the night, the Nazis. You'd hear sirens, banging on doors, sometimes gunshots or people crying out. I hate to say that we got used to it. But it happened all the time. The Nazis went block by block through the city arresting all the Jews. We knew it was only a matter of time before they visited us so we each kept a bag packed under our beds."

Martha looked over at my plate. "Have you had enough? I have cookies for dessert, if you'd like."

"I'd love a cookie," I said. Martha stood and began clearing the table. I had wanted to help her clear and bring the cookies, but she gestured for me to stay seated. I watched her take the cookies from a pink bakery box – butter cookies, Linzer cookies, and Florentines. She returned carrying clean small plates and a huge platter of cookies. Then, when she was seated again in her chair, she took the smallest plainest butter cookie and put it on her plate.

"In September 1943 we were arrested. But we'd been arrested before and simply walked away. This time, though, that was not possible. They put all four of us on a truck and drove us to Westerbork. Westerbork was a couple of hours northeast of Amsterdam in the middle of nowhere, but very close to the Dutch border with Germany." A website states,

Camp Westerbork was a transit camp in Drenthe

province, northeastern Netherlands, during World War 2. Established by the Dutch government in the summer of 1939, Camp Westerbork was meant to serve as a refugee camp for Jews from Germany who had illegally entered the Netherlands. Camp Westerbork was utilized as a staging ground for the deportation of Jews. Only one-half square kilometer (119 acres) in area, the camp was not built for the purpose of industrial murder as were the Nazi extermination camps in Poland.[26]

"We were worried that they would send us to Theresienstadt. That was the only camp name we knew. We knew they would send us somewhere, that they wouldn't let us stay in Holland.

Martha didn't look at me directly. Rather she looked a bit over my shoulder. I wondered if she was seeing a more vivid scene across time and space. She started speaking again in a low tone. I sat up straight so she'd know I was listening carefully.

She said, "They kept us at Westerbork till January 1944. It wasn't terrible, at least compared to what came next. There was a court-yard. They let the children play. I think they even had classes from time to time. But we slept in dormitories. We started to adjust downward. You have to. If you must sleep in a dormitory, you do. If you must eat turnip soup with just a small piece of gristle instead of beef soup with carrot and potato, you do. If your rations are cut from three meals to two, you finish your plate. If they are cut to one, you eat what you are served. If you must beg or barter for food, you do. You do what you need to do to survive."

Aunt Martha put her fork down. She looked me squarely in the face. "It was a terrible time. But given what came next, Westerbork was nothing. We were just being taken down a small manageable step." I could see Martha was holding back emotion, though I

[26]https://www.normandy1944.info/holocaust/concentrationcamps/westerbork

wasn't sure it if was anger or sadness. I thought about prying into something just below the surface. But what? She hadn't spoken for so many years. Perhaps she was afraid no one would believe even this introduction to her story.

I had many questions but didn't want to interrupt. I tried to picture Westerbork. Had I seen pictures of it? How did Martha feel being incarcerated? Did she witness violence and brutality there? Or did that come later?

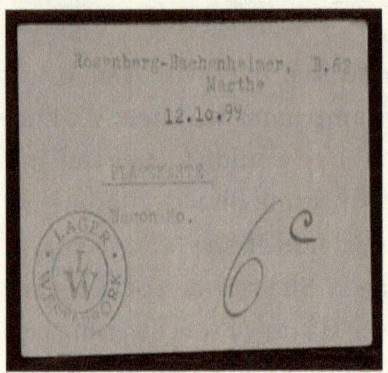

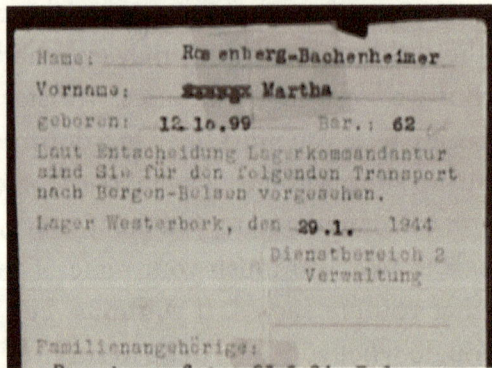

Screenshots from Walter's Holocaust Testimony. The full paragraph says, "According to the decision of the camp headquarters, you are intended for the following transport to Bergen-Belsen."

Martha continued with her account. "There was always gossip. And every Tuesday the trains came in. There would be a list of who'd be on the next train to the east. We didn't want to be on that list. But eventually that day came."

Martha's younger son, Walter, kept her car assignment card for the train from Westerbork to Bergen-Belsen.

According to the U.S. Holocaust Museum website,

> The first deportation transport left Westerbork on July 15, 1942, for Auschwitz-Birkenau. This first transport was followed by more than 90 subsequent transports to Auschwitz-Birkenau, Sobibor, Theresienstadt, and Bergen-Belsen. Most of those people deported to Auschwitz-Birkenau and Sobibor were killed upon arrival.
>
> From July 15, 1942, until September 13, 1944, the Germans deported approximately 100,000 Jews from the Netherlands via Westerbork.
> • More than 55,000 Jews and 245 Roma were deported to Auschwitz-Birkenau;
> • 34,313 Jews were deported to the Sobibor killing center;
> • 4,000–5,000 Jews were deported to Theresienstadt;
> • More than 3,500 Jews were deported to Bergen-Belsen concentration camp.
> There were also several small deportation transports to the Ravensbrück and Buchenwald concentration camps.[27]

I would later listen to Martha's sons' oral histories archived at USC.[28] Each of her sons remembered different experiences of their transports to Belsen. One son remembered a normal train. The other son remembered a cattle car. Records I've seen indicate that the Nazis used both types of conveyance. Most Jews sent to Belsen, including my family, were assigned to the *Sternlager*, the sub-camp for Jews. There were several other camps for prisoners that the Nazis hoped to use for POW exchanges.

Aunt Martha told me that she was assigned to work in the infir-

---

[27]https://encyclopedia.ushmm.org/content/en/article/westerbork

[28]USC Shoah Foundation Institute testimony of Walter Rosley, VHA Interview Code: 41916. Oral history interview with Alexander Rosenberg Accession Number: 1999.A.0137.12 I RG Number: RG-50.549.05.0012. Alex was also interviewed for a book, This is Home Now, Kentucky's Holocaust Survivors Speak, by Arwen Donahue (2009).

mary, though she quipped, "I was never a nurse. I had no training." She was proud, though, of being able to offer comfort and hope. She told people to wash when they could, to eat when they could, to try to keep their spirits up. She looked at me sharply. "Every Jewish person who died was a victory for the Nazis. I told people 'Don't give the Nazis the satisfaction of your death!'"

Then she looked towards her plate, considered drinking her tea. Finally, she said, "I was NOT going to die in that place. I told myself—and I told my husband and children—that we were going to die in our own homes, in our own beds, under our own clean white sheets. I was NOT going to let any of them die there!"

Aunt Martha's Bergen-Belsen Identity Card

Searching the internet for more information about Bergen-Belsen, I found a webpage entitled, *The Rosenberg-Bachenheimer Saga.*[29] Edward Victor, a philatelist, posted a number of Aunt Martha's documents. (I have no idea who he was or how he got these documents.) This is apparently Martha's identity card from Bergen-Belsen, showing her to be a *Heimflegerin* or caregiver.

[29]http://www.edwardvictor.com/Holocaust/Rosenberg_saga.htm. Per the website, Edward Victor's research was gifted to the Los Angeles Museum of the Holocaust in 2011. (LA Museum website: http://www.lamoth.info/?p=collections/ findingaid&id=32&q=&rootcontentid=8004) I was able to download this image from that website, too.

Most of the photos currently available of Bergen-Belsen were taken by British photographers when the British liberated the camp in April 1945. I have never visited the camp, though one of Martha's sons described his visit there in the 1990s, making it sound like he was visiting a campground, most of the buildings purposefully destroyed by the British.[30]

It is also noteworthy that Bergen-Belsen was not far south of Hamburg. It was fully within Germany proper. While the major killing centers, like Auschwitz, were in Poland, Germany was dotted with smaller facilities where people were imprisoned, forced to do slave labor, and killed regularly. The *Sternlager*, the subcamp for Jews, to which Martha and family were assigned at Bergen-Belsen, was along a wide road through the camp. Her sons reported often doing physical labor outside the camp. Surely, Germans walking near the camp would have spotted starving Jewish prisoners in striped uniforms working. Sometimes, they must have witnessed people dropping dead from exhaustion.

When the British came to liberate, Martha and her family were not in camp. They had been forced to march out of the camp several days before liberation. They believed they would be exchanged for someone. In fact, they were put on a "Train to Nowhere" or "Lost Transit." Edward Victor wrote,

> In the beginning of April 1945, it was clear to the Germans that (Bergen-Belsen) would soon be liberated. They decided to transport the remaining Sternlager prisoners to Theresienstadt. Three trains were used for this purpose. The Rosenbergs, along with about 2,500 other prisoners, were on the third train which departed on April 9, 1945. For two weeks, these prisoners were confined to the train as it attempted to move east. As can be imagined, the conditions were beyond description. The trip came to an end on April 23, 1945, at the village of Tröbitz in eastern Germany, where

---

[30]https://encyclopedia.ushmm.org/content/end/map/bergen-belsen-concentration-camp-1944

the train was liberated by the Russians. There were fewer than 2,000 survivors of this trip.[31]

In his testimony, Martha's older son Alex reported passing through Berlin. He saw, "total destruction. We were delighted!" Alex also said that once the Russians captured them, they didn't know what to do with them. Walter remembered that their presence was made known to Britain, France, and the U.S. after some French women left the group and walked west until they met other allies. Eventually, those on the Lost Transport were taken by the Americans to a Displaced Persons (DP) camp near Leipzig. Alex reported that his first time on a scale he weighed 78 pounds. He was 18 years old. He also had typhus and lice, as did his brother and parents.

But the main question that I had after watching the tapes, was how this family managed to survive Bergen-Belsen intact as a family. The number of families who survived over a year in a concentration camp must not be in triple digits. While neither Walter nor Alex's interviewers ask specifically this question, both "boys" point to their mother's determination to keep them going. Martha told them that she didn't want the Nazis to have the satisfaction of her death, and that they, too, needed to keep going, that they needed to stay alive as a way of thwarting the Nazis. Perhaps Alex and Walter, having survived, felt they needed to obey all future directives from Martha, including not to discuss the camp after liberation, and to die in their own beds under clean sheets.

Another lingering question: How did sitting in an infirmary with dying people (and no training, or supplies, or doctor as backup) affect her? Did Aunt Martha keep count of the number of hands she held as people took their last breath? Did she remember the names of some of those people? How did she maintain that "I'm gonna

---

[31] http://edwardvictor.com/Holocaust/Rosenberg_saga.htm

survive!" mantra day after day after day of watching (helping, comforting, crying with) dying people? I didn't specifically ask Martha this question all those years ago. Neither did her sons discuss this.

While I was still in college, before I ever met Martha, Dad's cousin Nancy invited me to dinner to meet Aunt Anni, another of Grandma's sisters. She'd moved from New York City to Memphis before I was born. When I told Grandma of the invitation, she said I had met Anni, that she'd visited the farm. Maybe I was too young to remember.

The journey from Georgetown to suburban Maryland where Nancy lived took about 90 minutes by bus. I left after class with a big bookbag, planning on getting some homework done on the bus, which ended up being hot and crowded. By the time I arrived at Nancy's, I looked unkempt: possibly without a bra, certainly without makeup, and likely in a shirt wrinkled by a combination of the bookbag and my sweat.

Nancy did not give me the once over, but Aunt Anni certainly did. She was dressed formally in a tailored skirt suit with jewelry and makeup; she looked pulled together in the same way Martha would when I saw her several years later. Anni seemed frosty to me all evening. I was relieved when Nancy offered to drive me back to campus. Nancy said Aunt Anni was a bit full of herself, but she'd been through a lot.

What had Anni been through? She'd immigrated years before Grandma and Dad. I assumed she was just an uptight rich woman from the South. She fit the profile that I'd always heard about Aunt Martha: bossy, judgmental, and opinionated. Luckily, Nancy dropped me off before I embarrassed myself by saying this.

I reported almost nothing to Grandma about this dinner. But I was candid with Lucie when she and I spoke about that evening. Before I could even complete my story, Lucie cut me off, "What do you expect?"

In 2002, Lucie donated "Correspondence, writings, clippings, and photographs documenting (her) efforts to establish a memorial to Jewish victims from Bad Berleburg who died in the Holo-caust, and efforts by family members to assist and trace relatives in Europe during and after World War II."[32] Lucie sent me a CD of some of these things, which were temporarily on display in one of Yale's libraries. Among the contents were photos of Aunt Anni and also Aunt Mathilde, the aunt who Dad, Hilda, and Lucie lived with in Belgium. I had never seen a photo of Aunt Mathilde before. I didn't know any existed. The Anni I saw was a young woman, laughing. She barely resembled the grumpy 70-something I met in the 1970s. There was nothing in these documents about Aunt Martha. But there was correspondence between Julius Frank (An-ni's husband), and various American departments (Labor, State) working in Europe during the 1930s and 1940s. Julius was trying to get Aunt Mathilde and her family to the U.S. He was checking on their immigration status. Then he was trying to find out what happened to them.

As I read over Julius Frank's efforts, and the lack of response from the U.S. government agencies, I thought of Martha, and how she let the family know of her whereabouts from the DP camp near Leipzig. I remembered myself in Martha's breakfast nook, while she said, "The DP camp was clean. They gave us clean clothes. They fed us real food. I felt like I was returning to the world.

"I met an American soldier from Memphis. He worked in the camp kitchen. The service was segregated in those years. All the kitchen staff was black. When I found this young man was from Memphis, I asked for his help. No one in our family had heard from us for years. Maybe someone in his family could contact Anni. That was how everyone found out we were not dead."

I could no longer remember the rest. Had the soldier arranged for a phone call? Or had he called? Or sent a letter? Then had Anni

---

[32]https://archives.yale.edu/repositories/12/resources/3542

or Julius contacted Grandma and Grandpa and the rest of the family in New York? I also wondered how long it had been. When was Martha's last letter sent from Amsterdam? Could she send letters to the U.S. after 1941? 1942? I can't imagine that Martha was able to pen a letter from Westerbork (fall 1942). No one would have known that she was arrested, or when, or where she went. It must have felt like a miracle when Martha got word to Anni in Memphis. Martha was alive. Menna was alive. The "boys" were alive. They all survived!

But was it *dayenu*? *Genug*? Enough?

I think Grandma kept worrying. Where was Mathilde? When had she last been heard from? Might she be somewhere in Eastern Europe? Might she turn up? Selma, Doris, Anneliese, and little Hilda: What about them? Bettie and Ruth? Might there still be good news? What about the Katten cousins? What about the other cousins whose names I never learned? Good news? Somewhere?

I heard Grandma asking these questions. If she didn't directly ask me, she glanced upwards and asked rhetorically in my presence. What happened? She stood on a tightrope with happiness on the left and disaster on the right. "Walk," she said. She sent me to Martha. She wanted me to know. She wanted me to bear witness. She told me I should learn the horrors that Martha had experienced and then buried for so many years. I should bear witness to Martha's exhumation, her picking the carcass of the Holocaust clean. I should listen and carry the stories with me until such time as I could tell them to the next person.

A document that Lucie donated to Yale suggests that Grandma didn't worry alone. Her brother-in-law Julius Frank wrote to his rabbi,

Dear Jimmie,

Here are the names of our relatives who were killed in concentration camps, and whose names we will appreciate your putting on the memorial book.... As we don't know the exact date on which they lost their lives, Anni and I will leave it up to you to designate a date. Please be good enough to advise us so that we can inform the other relatives accordingly.

Thank you and with best wishes and kindest regards,

Sincerely yours,

Julius Frank

March 11, 1949

If anyone in my family had a memorial or annual Jahrzeit for those killed, no one told me about it.

CHAPTER FORTY-ONE

Aunt Mathilde's Jahrzeit

After reading Julius Frank's letter, I decided to turn to the internet to see if Yad Vashem, or another organization, had more information on the Lindheims as to what happened to Grandma's sister Mathilde, her husband Hugo, and their daughter Lore. When she died, Grandma had likely still been wondering what happened to them. When had they been rounded up? Where had they had been sent? How had they died? But for me, now, maybe there were answers. All those lists and directories published by Yad Vashem or the U.S. Holocaust Museum. Some concentration camps had lists as did an office of the German government. Surely there was information somewhere.

I found a website about *Stolpersteine* in Frankfurt. As of mid-2022, at least 1,800 *Stolpersteine* had been installed around the city. A group of *Putzpatinen/Putzpatininnen* cleans the blocks every Yom HaShoah. The Lindheim *Stolpersteine* had their own web-page.[33] It gave a brief history of the Lindheims before they arrived in Frankfurt, noted that Lore was born there, and then delved into Hugo's business. The page showed photos of the Lindheims and their *Stolpersteine*.

[33]https://frankfurt.de/frankfurt-entdecken-und-erleben/stadtportrait/stadtgeschichte/stolpersteine/stolpersteine-im-ostend/familien/lindheim-hugo-laura-lore-und-Mathilde

Courtesy of Initiative Stolpersteine Frankfurt am Main & Belgian
Algemeen Rijksarchief - Archives générales du Royaume

The Lindheims last lived at *Gagernstraße* 17. I looked on Google Street View, but a parked car blocked the view of the *Stolpersteine*. Number 17 looked like a large house hidden behind a large tree. A park is a few blocks to the east, and the Frankfurt Zoo a mile to the west. I'm sure it was a lovely place to raise a child.

Bernd Wältz researched the Lindheims for the *Stolpersteine* project webpage. He had little to say about Mathilde or Lore, but much to say about Hugo and his business, Lindheim & Co., a furniture making factory that employed over one hundred people when Hugo ran it.

When the Nazis came to power, Hugo was forced to sell. In 1937, Karl Kübel agreed to purchase the company (probably with very favorable terms). Kübel later grumbled that the workers refused to work full time, implying that under a Jew of course the staff would take advantage. But Kubel, an Aryan, expected compliance with his workplace rules.

Despite Kübel's less than diligent workforce, he made enough money over the decades to retire in the 1970s and fund a charitable foundation.[34] The Karl Kübel Foundation funds educational and family support programs in Germany and India. While the foundation's website highlights Kübel's roots as a master carpenter and a man informed by his strong Catholic faith, it makes no mention of Lindheim & Co.

The family of Hugo's brother, Berthold, who emigrated to the United States in 1940, donated their papers to the U.S. Holocaust Museum.[35] These papers include Fred Lindheim's Memoir, *The Life and Times of Fred Lindheim*. Dad and his sisters briefly overlapped with Fred (then Horst) when they first arrived in Mechelen to live with the Lindheims. Fred, an only child, had come on an earlier *Kindertransport*. His memoir states,

> I arrived in Brussels to find my aunt Mathilde and uncle Hugo waiting for me at the railroad station. After having lunch, we drove to their home in Malines (Mechelen in the Flemish part of Belgium). I unpacked what little clothing I was allowed to bring with me.
>
> Also in the home was their daughter Lore, who was my only first cousin...
>
> Within a couple of days, the rest of the motley crew arrived, all of them followed by my grandfather. Fortunately, by early summer, my parents got out of Germany and arrived to pick me up for the next leg of our adventure— Great Britain.

[34]Kübel was interviewed by Benno Höhne in July 1997. These interviews formed the basis of book put out by the Karl Kübel Foundation for Children and Families, Womit kann ich dienen? Der Unternehmer und Stifter Karl Kübel, S. 106 Translation by Google Translate from the Wikipedia page of Hugo Lindheim, https://www.wikiwand.com/de/Hugo_Lindheim#

[35]https://collections.ushmm.org/search/catalog/irn86156#?rsc=196715&cv=0&c=0&m=0& s=0&xywh=-1521%2C-286%2C7092%2C5705. I was granted permission to download the collection.

"Motley crew?" Obviously, Aunt Mathilde was not the only one who saw Dad and his sisters as poor refugees. If the Lindheims had once been cattle dealers in Rennerethausen, another small village along the Hesse—Westfalen border, by the 1920s, Hugo and his brother Berthold had risen above. Bert had a Ph.D. in chemistry and worked at chemical company in Frankfurt before immigrating to the U.S.

Another funny coincidence: Dad and Fred both attended Brooklyn Tech High School in New York. Dad remembered running into Fred, but not staying in touch.

The Kazerne Dossin Museum located in Mechelen, Belgium, is the most significant Holocaust Museum in that country. It is situated on the former military barracks that the Nazis used as a detention/transit camp, the Belgian equivalent of Westerbork in the Netherlands.

When a Belgian acquaintance mentioned that Mechelen was a charming city that people enjoyed visiting, I showed Dad the Google Street view of Auwegumstraat. "Yes, it looks the same," he said. This house doesn't look as tony to me as the Lindheim home in Frankfurt. Then again, I don't think Dad had any memories of being at Mathilde's house in Frankfurt. (Maybe he wasn't invited.)

From Dad's stories, it sounded like Belgian Nazis working in the police department routinely harassed Hugo. Per Dad, Hugo had been arrested a bit before May 10, 1940, and was sent to Gurs, France, where the Nazis had a concentration camp, while the rest of the family tried to escape to France. Eventually Hugo returned home. The family stayed on Auwegumstraat after Dad returned to Germany. Lore received this identity card on February 7, 1942.

Lore Lindheim's identity card
courtesy of Belgian Algemeen Rijksarchief - Archives générales du Royaume

The Nazi genocidal machinery came to Belgium in July 1942. Perhaps, as Alex Rosenberg reported about his experience in Amsterdam, the Lindheims were arrested and managed to extricate themselves. But sometime in late 1942 or January 1943, probably in the middle of the night, there would have been a banging on the door to their home signaling a round up. Mathilde, Hugo, and Lore would have dressed quickly, grabbed their suitcases which had been stored fully packed under their beds, and followed the SS down to a truck parked somewhere on Auwegumstraat. That would have been the end of their lives as they knew them.

The truck would have taken them to the site of the Kazerne Dossin Museum, which was then called *SS-Sammellager Mecheln*. Here is a photo from the Museum's webpage showing the *Sammellager* after prisoners had arrived. The photo is zoomed out enough that one can't read faces, just people, their belongings, and trucks.[36] Nor can one tell if the camp's top brass was onsite.

---

[36]https://kazernedossin.eu/en/what-we-do/historiek/

The photo is undated. I don't know if this was the day that the Lindheims arrived.

Kazerne Dossin Courtyard courtesy of Kazerne Dossin - Fonds Kummer

Phillip Schmitt and Rudolph Steckmann oversaw the camp. They employed a mix of German and Flemish Nazis. A dog named Lump, Steckmann's shepherd, was sic'd on people just to instill fear and keep them in line.

Max Boden was the man in charge of lists at the camp. As anyone who's seen *Schindler's List* knows, the Nazis kept lists. People in. People out. Boden had a staff of multi-lingual translators who elicited information from prisoners when they arrived at camp.

Boden's list, of course, became the transport list. In the case of the Lindheims, they were entered on a list for Transport XVIII. Here is a page from the list that shows the Lindheims as Transportees 689, 690, and 691. I picture the Lindheims standing in line behind 54-year-old Fritz Kahn of Liedolsheim, which Google places in the Ruhr Valley. He might have been by himself. Perhaps Hugo, just three years younger, took comfort in Fritz Kahn's company. Or maybe Hugo spent his time in line sizing up his chances compared to Fritz Kahn.[37]

Transport List Mecheln-Auschwitz, transport XVIII, p. 50 (AOS-AVG-TL XVIII, p. 50)
courtesy of Archives Service for War Victims Brussels

Behind Lore in the queue was Moise Levy Bochner, a salesman from Chrzanow, a city in Poland just north of Oswiecim, or Auschwitz. Moise was over sixty. I am guessing Lore didn't speak to him. They were probably instructed to be silent in line.

The Kazerne Dossin reports, "Between 1942 and 1944, 25,484 Jews and 352 Roma and Sinti were deported from the Dossin Barracks. Barely five percent returned alive from Auschwitz-Birkenau."[38]

The Lindheim's train, Transport XVIII, departed for Auschwitz on January 15, 1943. If the Lindheims had been rounded up just a bit later, in February or March 1943, and were assigned to Transport XX, they might have survived. Transport XX was stopped by resistance fighters Youra Livchitz, Jean Franklemon, and Robert

---

[37]Apparently, most of the notations on the transport list were made after the war when the Belgian Ministry of Reconstruction and Repatriation was trying to determine the fate of the deportees. "V", "X", or "•" indicate that then name has been checked.

[38]https://www.kazernedossin.eu/NL/Museumsite/Museum/Inleiding

Maistriau after it left the station in Mechelen (bound for Auschwitz). Per Maistriau, the trio stopped the train, fired off several shots, and cut a few wires to a train car. Some prisoners escaped there, others slipped away further down the tracks. While the Nazis shot or rearrested some of the escapees, 131 Jews survived.[39]

But the Lindheims' train was unexceptional. After three days of travel, my relatives arrived in Auschwitz. Deboarding the train car on January 18, 1943, the Lindheims were inspected and forced into the left line for the crematoria, or the right line for forced labor. Or was it the other way around? Was Dr. Mengele there on the 18th? Did he give Lore the once over? Perhaps sending her away from her parents to work until she dropped dead from hunger and exhaustion. Or from typhus. Or cold.

Perhaps on January 18, 1943, Julius Frank was still writing letters to the American Counsel in Brussels on behalf of the Lindheims.

Perhaps Grandma sat down that day to write a letter to Mathilde, hoping she was still on Auwegemstraat. Or hoping her letter would be forwarded to wherever Mathilde was.

Maybe eighteen-year-old Aunt Lucie thought of her aunt that day, probably nothing positive, but maybe she saw a dress that reminded her of Mathilde, or another woman who was looking down their nose at her, making her feel like a poor refugee, a member of the motley crew.

Maybe my dad, then fourteen years old, read a newspaper and learned that a report would be coming out shortly entitled, *The Mass Extermination of Jews in German Occupied Poland*. Or maybe he read an article that Jan Karski was in the United States doing front work for the report. Did I ever tell Dad about the lecture I heard Karski give when I was a college student at Georgetown? Karski

[39]Book Review of Silent Rebels: The true story of the raid on the 20th train to Auschwitz by Marion Schreiber in The Guardian, June 19, 2003 https://www.theguardian.com/ g2/story/0,3604,980276,00.html and https://www.thebulletin.be/brussels-honour-three-resistance-fighters-who-saved-jews-during-war

could get no one to believe that the Jews were being slaughtered city by city, village by village, and that Poland, if things continued at the current rate, would be forever altered, a major ethnic cleansing (though that word was not used in the 1970s).

I am sure Dad read something in the paper on January 20, 1943. Dad followed all the moves of those untrustworthy bloodthirsty German SOBs. And Dad was already a worrier-insomniac. Quite possibly at midnight on January 20, 1943, he wondered what was going on with his cousin Lore in Belgium. Was she dead? Was she doing slave labor?

And Grandma? January 20 was two days before her 41st birthday. Perhaps she felt sad that her sister Mathilde, the one who had taken in her children in Grandma's hour of need, would not be there to celebrate with her. Perhaps she cried, thinking about a birthday party long ago in Röddenau when Mathilde was the one who made a cake for Grandma. A time when Grandma still sat on her big sister's lap and got tickled.

What date did Julius Frank's rabbi assign as the Jahrzeit for the Lindheims? Was it January 20? Or perhaps sometime in the summer? Surely, the Lindheims' memories were not forgotten. They became a part of my story through Grandma, Dad, and my aunts.

The Lindheims were lurking behind my fear of my parents' death, that I would be sent to Aunt Hilda's until I was independent. Not that Aunt Hilda had ever shown me unkindness, but I was terrified. The Lindheims lurked somewhere behind my homesickness when I went off to summer camp and then college. I might never see my parents again. And ghosts of the Lindheims appeared in my dreams, the ones where I was on an overcrowded train bound to a terrible destination, the train I wanted to stop before it arrived at its final station.

CHAPTER FORTY-TWO

Cousin Doris

The last family story that seemed incomplete to me was of Dad's cousin Doris. Doris had spent two years in Belgium with Dad and his sisters. Hilda had spoken to me of Doris. She said she looked at Doris' framed photograph every day and still couldn't believe that the poor girl hadn't made it to New York.

Grandma said Doris's family was unlucky. Luck seemed such a trivial word, a throw off. How could Doris just be unlucky? She was a girl. Maybe considering Doris unlucky helped Grandma with her survivors' guilt.

I looked at documents from Yad Vashem, the Theresienstadt database of former prisoners,[40] the Horst Hecker book, and many trails to see if I could find something more than bad luck to explain what happened to Cousin Doris that she never made it to New York. I looked at a photo of Doris's parents that I'd never seen in the Horst Hecker book. The source of the photo was Lucie. I couldn't understand why I'd never seen it before.

Hecker also had a photo of Doris's youngers sisters Anneliese (born 1927) and Hilda (born 1937). The photo was from 1940, when Doris was in Mechelen with Dad and his sisters.

---

[40] https://www.pamatnik-terezin.cz/database

Jennifer Krebs

*Selma und Julius
Bachenheimer, um 1925
(Privatfoto Lucie Krebs
Weinstein, Hamden, CT)*

*Family photo, reproduced in Jüdisches Leben in Frankenberg, Horst Hecker
Caption says that the photo was from 1925, when the couple already had two children*

Anneliese and Hilda Bachenheimer, 1940

Hecker wrote that Anneliese was supposed to go to Mechelen with Doris on the Kindertransport. Perhaps Selma, the girls' mother, couldn't bear to part with two daughters. Selma would have been making the decision on her own because her husband Julius had been arrested on *Kristallnacht*.

Dad told me that Doris returned to Germany with him and Aunt Hilda in the fall of 1940. But Doris was two months older than Lucie. If Lucie wasn't allowed to get papers to enter Germany because she was over sixteen, Doris would have had the same problem. So when did Doris return to Germany?

The Theresienstadt database shows Doris, Anneliese, Hilda, and Selma on Train X/1 from Dortmund to Theresienstadt on July 30, 1942. Train X/1 may have transported the last remaining Jews from this part of Westfalen. The passenger list for Train X/1 contains many familiar names from Berleburg, including Grandpa's sister Adele Krebs. Adele was two years older than Selma Bachenheimer, neé Elsoff. They attended the Berleburg *Volkschule* together. They would have seen each other in synagogue and were likely at Grandma and Grandpa's wedding and Dad's bris. They must have known each other, if not well, then at least casually.

I like to think that Selma asked her oldest two daughters to help Adele board Train X/1. I like to think that these four travelers sat together and comforted each other on the four-hundred-mile trip from Dortmund to Theresienstadt. Perhaps little Hilda, who was only five years old, babbled to Adele. Or perhaps Adele shared a story from her childhood with the girls. Or perhaps someone rubbed someone else's back when they cried or had a panic attack.

Perhaps Selma, Adele, and the girls chatted about the girls' father, Grandma's brother Julius Bachenheimer. Maybe the girls gave their separate accounts of what happened to their father who was rounded up on Kristallnacht, taken to Buchenwald, and severely beaten. After several months, he arrived home and shortly died of cancer. At least, this is what Horst Hecker wrote.

Dad had a story about Julius' burial. "The poor man; no one

would bury him. They wouldn't touch a Jew. Grandpa had to go to the Jewish Cemetary in Frankenberg, dig the grave, and bury him." Grandpa must have told Dad this story because Dad was in Mechelen in July 1940 when Julius died.

Something about that story of Julius' burial haunted Dad. Perhaps Grandpa said some things that Dad wouldn't repeat. Dad was insistent. He and Mom, neither of whom believed in God, should be buried in accordance with Jewish law: rabbi, pine casket, pallbearers, and all. An unveiling should take place the following year. Dad purchased a plot for his burial shortly after joining Temple Brith Kodesh in Rochester in 1966. Mom and Dad's plot is just down the road from Grandma and Grandpa's, in Mount Hope Cemetery.

The Theresienstadt database lists the date of Adele's death as April 25, 1943, roughly eight months before her father died in New York.[41] In February 1943, Tante Adele sent someone in New York a letter containing a poem she wrote. I first saw the poem when I was a teen. In my twenties, I translated it with Aunt Lucie's help.

Theresienstadt was the concentration camp that the Nazis held up as proof that the final solution was not killing machinery. The U.S. Holocaust Museum says,

> In Nazi propaganda, Theresienstadt was cynically described as a "spa town" where elderly German Jews could "retire" in safety. The deportations to Theresienstadt were, however, part of the Nazi strategy of deception. The ghetto was in reality a collection center for deportations to ghettos and killing centers in Nazi-occupied eastern Europe.[42]

While Aunt Adele and the others wasted away, it might have been possible for Hilda to learn to read. At least some of the time, there

---

[41]https://www.holocaust.cz/en/dateabase-of-victims/victims/19695-adele-krebs
[42]https://encylopedia.ushmm.org/content/en/article/theresienstadt

was a school on the premises. Perhaps Anneliese made a friend. Perhaps Doris fell in love. Perhaps Selma and Adele made a potato cake to celebrate a birthday. They would have wanted to survive, to live.

Perhaps they looked up through the heart-shaped leaves of a Tilia tree that grew inside the walls of the camp. Perhaps they collected its white flowers and brewed them into tea that they ate with a potato cake. Perhaps they did this on Rosh Hashana to celebrate the New Year. Or perhaps by September 1942 they all had given up on God.

Was Adele sick on January 29, 1943, the day that Selma and the girls were forced to board another train, this one to Auschwitz? Or did they say goodbye to one another? Might Adele have given each girl a small memento: a hanky, a shiny stone from the ground, or a feather?

Premonitions of Death
by Adele Krebs

The storm rages, the wind whistles
In Theresienstadt we are prisoners
Shabby, impoverished
Misery each day more grotesque.

My cheeks pale, my limbs weaken
How long can I resist this disgrace?
My heart bleeds, my hair grays
In this life-consuming suffering.

When you close my eyes
Grant me at last eternal peace.
I fought, lived, aspired to be
But everything that was my life betrayed me.

My loved ones you will find in far away places
Send them my greetings, press their hands solemnly

My yearning, my hope
Is for the reunion in our family home.

Send greetings to my hometown
My hopes also return there
To the mountain, forests, and hills
The sights I'm forbidden to see.

When you look to the stars
See a comet at the heavenly gate
Imagine me sitting by the everlasting throne
Living with the Heavenly Father.

There I shall be
Resting in everlasting peace
When the Messiah comes, again we'll meet
The time is soon, he will come, he will come.

Translated by Lucie Weinstein and Jennifer Krebs
published in The Tribe of Dina, 1986

CHAPTER FORTY-THREE

Murmur

Mom had been dead for almost three years when I went to the hospital to have my mitral valve repaired. Mitral valve problems, it turns out, run in my family. Grandma's father died of a heart attack. Aunt Hilda had a mitral valve repair, as did another cousin. When the surgery was described to me, it sounded significantly more serious than any other medical procedure I'd endured. They were literally taking my heart offline, making adjustments, and then starting me up again. But if I didn't have the surgery, I would likely have a heart attack. It was just a question of when. I remembered this when they spoke to me for the last time before the anesthesia.

Seven hours later, I was swimming in a river with Mom, or so I felt when I came out of the anesthesia. She said the same thing to me that the doctor had said before he put me under. "Breathe deep, don't panic." This was because I was intubated. "Try to pretend the tube isn't there." And so, I swam the river, navigating boulders and whirlpools.

"You can do it," Mom told me. Then I felt the presence of others swimming with me, others who were still alive: a cousin, a teacher, a friend. The river was cold. Was I cold? I heard rushing in my ears. I opened my eyes just a little. "You can do it," Mom said again.

Someone was at the foot of the bed, a nurse, PA, or a doctor. The person smiled at me and asked me a question. I no longer remember what they asked. If it wasn't the first question, it was the second or the third, "Are you in pain?"

When I was no longer swimming, I realized I was completely pinned to the bed. I could not move a limb. Because of the intubation tube, I couldn't open my mouth. I tried to nod yes.

The person at the foot of my bed explained that the surgery had gone on longer than expected, that they'd need to leave the tube in longer, because they wanted my heart rate to hit certain metrics that it had not yet reached before they removed the tube. I'd need to be patient.

I tried to summon Mom again but could only picture the last time I saw her, alive but dying. This did not console me. I tried to breathe gently. I tried to relax. But the semi-conscious state had passed. I couldn't will myself back to the river.

I tried to remember if Mom had been with me at Dr. Grainer's when he first told me I had a heart murmur. Perhaps it was my last appointment with him. He was retiring as I was going off to college. He told me he heard a small sound between some of my heart beats. Instead of Lub-Dub, every few beats, he heard Lub-lu-lu-Dub. "It might never turn into something. Or it might. Be sure to let your next doctor know."

Until two months before the surgery, not a single doctor I'd visited had ever expressed any concern. I never even looked up the definition of heart murmur, "a recurring sound heard in the heart through a stethoscope that is usually a sign of disease or damage." While I was never a great athlete, I enjoyed walking, swimming, hiking, even run-walking half marathons. My heart had never been an issue.

But then it was. I first noticed it beating as if I was run-walking a half marathon one night in bed. In bed? I was supposed to be relaxing, falling asleep. Instead, all night long, I felt like I was running a marathon. I found a cardiologist. That was 15 weeks before the surgery. At least the surgery was over. I was awake. I was alone, and in pain. I began to cry.

Finally, someone came in to remove the breathing tube. She explained the procedure, a procedure that was explained more often than the actual heart surgery's procedure. A large percentage of people tense up when they're supposed to relax in order to let the medical staff remove the intubation tube. I managed to survive what felt like having my throat ripped out. But that pain was countered by other pains: a stabbing sensation in my right rib cage, the catheter in my urethra, God knew what else.

With the tube out, they let Amy in. She smiled, as best I could tell beyond all the apparatus. She listed everyone she'd called to let them know I was out of surgery and into the ICU. I don't think she told me that I looked good. I think she was worried because she already knew what they told me later, that the surgery took longer because the cuff that they had attempted to put around my mitral valve was improperly sized. They had to take it off and replace it with a different one. She had probably been worried for a good long time.

One of the projects that I had begun sometime between my first visit to the cardiologist and the day of my surgery, was to begin a long piece of writing. I had signed up for a class, Novel (or Memoir) in a Year. I had completed an outline of a book about my years as an environmental planner, which was to be a self-deprecating and irreverent look at why so many great ideas to clean up or improve the environment enjoy modest success. In fact, I was going to pair some of the book chapters with various health issues that I encountered, as well as bad parenting moments. I was thinking of something in between David Sedaris and *H Is for Hawk*.

As I lay there, all my health issues over the years came back to me. I was no stranger to pain. My childhood was one ear infection after another. Beginning in my twenties, I suffered from backaches. In my thirties, it was TMJ of my jaw. I'd broken bones, sprained joints, and had a variety of illnesses.

Shortly before this heart surgery, when I was still drafting chapter outlines for the environmental memoir, I heard a cow bell. I knew it couldn't be a real one, as there are none in Berkeley. I closed my eyes and was back in Berleburg watching Grandpa call the cows, "Come Bass! Come Bass!" And the fat cows on skinny legs followed him down the hill to the barn so they could be milked.

I realized that I had not finished what I set out to do in my twenties, writing the family story. That story of fear, argument, grief, and loss had been just out of reach to me then. Though I blamed some of the reasons that I never finished on Aunt Lucie, her screed about everything I had done wrong, the truth probably was that I wasn't ready then. But now, how much time did I have? Lub-dub. Lub-dub. I watched the cows graze in Grandpa's fields, the fields he'd never returned to, the ones he lost in 1935 or so. He was a busy man with a smile on his face. His hair was still black, and he didn't need suspenders to hold his pants up.

I wondered if this was his first day back on the farm since he'd gotten home from the Great War. If he was healing from his years around the shelling, and the dying, and the terrible orders from the generals. Were his brothers coming to meet him? Were they planning the farm's future? Or was he thinking of his impending wedding to Grandma and how the business would have to shape shift to accommodate the next generation? The children. Surely there would be children.

But even before those children were grown, another cataclysm, one that Grandpa couldn't have imagined. Or didn't imagine. The family would be broken up, to different parts of Germany. Some people would not survive. Those people that I'd heard about years ago, the ones who had been haunting me. Some of them had names, like Tante Adele. Others, like the young children in the orphanage with Dad and Aunt Hilda in Frankfurt, the children Dad knew were "doomed," did not.

I still didn't know if I could write about these people, if my heart was strong enough. And would the writing stop me from being haunted?

As I listened to the loud beeping in the room, as my heart sought to accommodate the repaired mitral valve, I had to try. If not now, when? Lub-dub. Lub-dub.

I visualized the Frida Kahlo's painting, *The Two Fridas*. I'd sit with each of the relatives who'd been telling me stories all these years. We'd hold hands, and I'd let the blood flow between us. I would listen, cry, ask questions, and pray for all of us to heal from this – I hate to use this overused word – trauma.

Maybe this was the work that Grandma wanted me to do all along, that "duty" I felt she asked of me. I should help with the healing. I should help bring us all to a peaceful place, like the farm in Berleburg. Lub-dub. Lub-dub. Lub-dub. I should heal myself.

CHAPTER 44

Mach's Gut

I didn't quite make it back to Rochester in time for Dad's death last March. Three days before he died, I received a call from one of the social workers at the Rochester Jewish Home. Dad had been living there for roughly six months. The social worker said, "Your father has adult failure to thrive."

"What does that mean?" I asked, confused.

"He's been losing weight, and he isn't socializing."

"Are you saying I should book a flight to Rochester?"

"No, not yet."

Dad had been very happy at The Summit, an independent living facility. It was kind of like being on a cruise or at an all-inclusive resort. He walked on the treadmill, played bridge, tasted wine, went to movies, and attended concerts. He had many friends.

The Summit seemed extremely well run. I was not surprised when they shut down at the onset of the COVID outbreak. But sadly, this meant that Dad and the other residents could no longer participate in all the great activities. In spite of spending so many days alone in his apartment, Dad eventually caught COVID pneumonia and landed in the hospital. Six months later, it happened again. As I observed with Mom, Dad grew frailer after each hospitalization.

In June 2023, Dad's medical team recommended that he move

from The Summit to the Jewish Home. I knew he'd be upset. The Jewish Home was no country club. Dad was to stay on one floor, which served Kosher food. Dad was not a big fan of Kosher, which to him, meant tasteless. He couldn't find a foursome for bridge. None of his Summit friends came by to visit. Some were already on other floors of the Jewish Home. Some had died. Dad spent most of the day in his room watching the news.

I asked the social worker again if I should get on a plane. I reminded him that I lived in California.

"It could be another week or two. I'll keep you posted."

The following day he called back and told me to buy a ticket.

At San Francisco International, I remembered Mom's death. I had been with her, holding her hand, when she took her last breath. There seemed some symmetry with my birth. It was just the two of us. The nurse had told me that hearing is the last sense to go, that even if Mom seemed not to be listening, she might be. I should say whatever I needed to be said. I told Mom that I loved her. That she had been a good mother. That she had done her best. I said it was okay to go.

Amy called me just after I landed in New York City, where I was switching planes for Rochester. She was sobbing. After a minute, she said "Jen, he's gone." I was sad and disappointed that I hadn't been there for Dad. But Amy had surely made him comfortable. I started to run through some of the details that would fill my next few days in Rochester: speaking to the funeral home, the rabbi, relatives, and friends. Looking through the last of Dad's belongings. Writing a eulogy. Saying kaddish.

Grandma always said *"Mach's gut"* before hanging up the phone. Recently, Dad and I had begun to say that to each other. When he heard me speak German, he'd giggle. Then I'd giggle because he was giggling.

Mach's gut, Dad. I love you.

CHAPTER 45
Saying Goodbye

Dear Grandma, Next week is my birthday. I know that if you were still dropping letters in the mail, you'd send me a birthday card with flowers on the front, probably blue ones because you loved hydrangeas, pansies, lilacs, Grandpa's eyes, and all things blue. You would have written edge to edge in your tight precise handwriting. You'd tell me about the weather, what's going on at the farm and with my dad, and what you've heard from, or about, my cousins. Then, somewhere, in a margin, you'd write, "Twenty-five dollars enclosed. Happy Birthday!"

I'd write back, "Thanks so much for the generous birthday present. I deposited the money in the bank." Of course, I spent the money on something ephemeral: going to the theater or a concert, buying expensive ingredients to cook a nice dinner for friends, going back to that little gallery I liked for a pricey pottery coffee mug. You knew this.

You would have disapproved if the letter I sent you wasn't filled with a full page of information, so I would have added an anecdote about my birthday, maybe about how I took a day off from work and rode my bike out to Mount Vernon, which is what I did on my twenty-second birthday. I have a photo in my album to prove it. Did I ask a stranger to take a picture of me with my blue Peugeot ten-speed bike, permed hair, and lime green Bad Berleburg t-shirt?

Or did my friend take the picture a bit later in the day when she came to take me out for dinner and then a night on the town at an Irish pub?

The t-shirt is the key to the year the picture was taken. I bought it when you, Aunt Lucie, and I visited Bad Berleburg three months before my twenty-second birthday. If it had been my twenty-third birthday, the t-shirt would have been a faded mess, and perms were out of fashion, at least for me. Not that I would have put a description of either the t-shirt or the perm in the letter to you. Nor would I have mentioned the Irish pub, the number of Guinnesses I drank, or who I slept with that night. Nope, I would have moved on to something else. Maybe something about the job (which obviously I did not enjoy; otherwise, I would have worked that day). It was a beautiful day: wisps of clouds in the sky, and a t-shirt was just the right amount of cover for an entire day out.

You would love that phone calls, emails, and texting are now free, not that it would be easy to explain to you what a text message is. You'd say something like, "I can't come over it! How wonderful that it is so inexpensive to stay in touch with your family!" On the other hand, you would never have purchased a $1,000 telephone with a $100/month plan so that you could text me for free. (INSERT EMOJI.)

What did I write in my last letter to you? It would have been October 1985. We both knew that you didn't have much more time. Did I write about how I just moved from San Francisco to Berkeley, how I was busy working at the bookstore, and that my upcoming visit to see you would have to be short? I probably left out, or downplayed, that I was in love, and that we were moving in together. My mom and dad had told me that they would not answer questions or defend my sexual orientation. I should keep them, the family, and their friends out of it. Surely, it was a phase.

Dad must have rented a hospital bed. You were sleeping downstairs. You were too weak to sit in the chair for my visit, so I pulled one of the dining room chairs to your side. You extended your frail hand to me, and I held it in mine. For years now, I have remembered the pattern of veins that popped prominently above the narrow bones in your hand. I remember the ganglion on your right pointer finger knuckle. Your cheeks were so hollow. You hadn't put in your "miserable" false teeth. You smiled at me and pulled me toward you for a kiss and a hug.

Perhaps we discussed Dad's report that a calf had been born earlier that day. Or that a piece of machinery had broken down again. Maybe we reminisced about the old farm hand, Don. We would have laughed that neither of us could understand a word he said, as he always mumbled and looked down at his feet.

Maybe we would have talked about Passover six months earlier when I flew out to visit you in Florida, how you prepared your favorite treats: roasted veal breast with matza stuffing, *matzashalot* with lemon sauce, spring green beans, and hazelnut torte with lots of whipped cream. Or how much you missed your sister Frieda, who lived next door to you there for so many winters. Did we discuss the audio recording I made after Passover dinner? Did I blather on offering excuses for why I hadn't done anything with it? The poor recording quality of my little Sony cassette recorder? Its placement on your coffee table? Or was I honest? That I couldn't stand to hear myself speak on tape. That I sounded ridiculous, especially as I cut you off far too often to avoid dead space on the tape.

After the oral history, did we circle back to our trip together to Berleburg? The small town at the bottom of a valley, where the *Fürst* von Wittgenstein has a castle. The town with the saying, "Look all around you: Everything you see belongs to the *Fürst!*" Did you ask me if I remembered? Probably. We were both babbling on, afraid of the protracted silence that would come to be far too soon.

I never mastered the elevator speech. When you or anyone else asked me about my work, or what else I spent my time on, I'd babble, hoping for once to sound like I knew what I was doing, or where I was going, or even what I wanted to do fairly soon/what I was preparing to do. I was not yet thirty and Aunt Lucie was still hoping I'd apply to graduate school in History, where she was sure that I would find myself. I was afraid I'd lose myself.

But now, I am no longer lost. Life is not perfect. I never expected it to be. I have added new names to the family tree, my children's. I have spoken to them of you, and your loved ones whom I never met. I have spent hours researching, listening to testimonies, and imagining how things might have gone down, as they say today.

I don't "know" everything. Perhaps I "know" no more than when you were alive. But I have performed alchemy, turned pieces of stories, gaps, questions, and pleas to God into something whole and beautiful. I hope I have honored your legacy.

For all those parts of the story, still incomplete, I'll try to plug the holes with *Apfelkuchen*. It worked for you. There is always a fruit available in California that can be turned into a *Kuchen*. And guess what? Yeast cake doughs are coming back. I think of you, serving me a large slice, along with a steaming cup of coffee, whenever my cake is ready. It tastes the best, still warm, when a bit of fruit juice slides off onto the plate. I picture you with your little teaspoon, scooping it up, eating it and smiling, as I watch the smiles of my family or friends, the generations of the present and future. We are smiling with you.

All my love,
Jennifer

A Prayer for the Dead

The Mourner's Kaddish was written in an endangered Semitic language, Aramaic. The word Kaddish means "holy," and the Kaddish prayer has been recited by Jews for one or two millennium, depending upon the source.

I have often felt confused about what holiness is and embarrassed to pray. But reciting the Kaddish has always brought me comfort, and seems an appropriate way to end this book. A translation is:

> Magnified and sanctified is the great name of God throughout the world, which was created according to Divine will. May the rule of peace be established speedily in our time, unto us and unto the entire household of Israel. And let us say: Amen.
>
> May God's great name be praised throughout all eternity. Glorified and celebrated, lauded and praised, acclaimed and honored, extolled and exalted ever be the name of thy Holy One, far beyond all song and psalm, beyond all hymns of glory which mortals can offer. And let us say: Amen.
>
> May there be abundant peace from heaven, with life's goodness for us and for all thy people Israel. And let us say:

Amen.

May the One who brings peace to the universe bring peace to us and to all the people Israel. And let us say: Amen.[43]

Acknowledgements

I would like to express my deepest gratitude to my family for putting up with my relentless questions, trips to the library and computer archives, and discussions to try to gain an understanding of the material in this book. Most especially Amy who read draft after draft, each of which she said was DONE.

Special thanks to my writing teachers and comrades these past few years from the Sonoma County Writers Camp. To friends who subscribed to my Substack, Stumbling Blocks, who submitted insightful comments and edged me to the finish line. Kind, generous, and thoughtful readers included Ellen Sussman, Aline Soules, Lisa Yost, Tom Skovolt, Ann Spivack, Malkah Geller, Patty Mayeux, and Saeri Geller. Lisa Yost contributed a beautiful watercolor which was transformed into cover art by the Legacy Book Press LLC team.

I couldn't have completed this project without librarians and archivists, especially those at Fortunoff-Yale, USC-Shoah and Yeshiva University; Rachel Pistol of Kings College, England; and Rikarde Riedesel of Berleburg. Or the many people who've offered varied perspectives on how to heal from the intergenerational trauma of the Holocaust, including rabbis and therapists, history teachers, and other children of Holocaust survivors, especially those in my family.

www.ingramcontent.com/pod-product-compliance
Lightning Source LLC
Chambersburg PA
CBHW021222130626
46554CB00004B/1321